An Apple a Day

A division of Book Sales, Inc.
276 Fifth Avenue Suite 206
New York, New York 10001

EDITOR Catherine Nichols
CONTRIBUTING EDITOR Helen Martineau
DESIGNER AND PHOTO RESEARCHER Tim Palin Creative
PROOFREADER Tracy Sway Hofstatter

ISBN-13: 978-1-937994-11-2

Printed in China

2 4 6 8 10 9 7 5 3 1

www.racepointpub.com

An Apple a Day

Recipes by Karen Berman & Melissa Petitto

With additional contributions from:
Scott Anderson
Mark Fischer
Yvette Garfield
Michael Gilligan
Mary Hulse
Ian Kittichai
Dave Martin
Catherine McCord
Eva Pesantez
Linton Romero
Ryan Shelton
Deborah Shum

Race Point
PUBLISHING

Contents

Conversions

Liquids, Herbs, and Spices

1 teaspoon = 5 mL

1 tablespoon or ½ fluid ounce = 15 mL

1 fluid ounce or ⅛ cup = 30 mL

¼ cup or 2 fluid ounces = 60 mL

⅓ cup = 80 mL

½ cup or 4 fluid ounces = 125 mL

⅔ cup = 150 mL

¾ cup or 6 fluid ounces = 175 mL

1 cup or 8 fluid ounces or ½ pint = 250 mL

1 ½ cups or 12 fluid ounces = 350 mL

2 cups or 1 pint or 16 fluid ounces = 500 mL

3 cups or 1 ½ pints = 700 mL

4 cups or 2 pints or 1 quart = 1 L

4 quarts or 1 gallon = 4 L

Weight*

*Note: these conversions do not apply to fluid ounces

1 ounce = 28 g

4 ounces or ¼ pound = 113 g

⅓ pound = 150 g

8 ounces or ½ pound = 230 g

⅔ pound = 300 g

12 ounces or ¾ pound = 340 g

16 ounces or 1 pound = 450 g

2 pounds = 900 g

Weights of Common Ingredients

All-purpose flour • 1 cup = 120 g

Granulated cane sugar • 1 cup = 200 g

Confectioners' sugar • 1 cup = 100 g

Brown sugar (packed) • 1 cup = 180 g

Cornmeal • 1 cup = 160 g

Cornstarch • 1 cup = 120 g

Rice (uncooked) • 1 cup = 190 g

Macaroni (uncooked) • 1 cup = 140 g

Couscous (uncooked) • 1 cup = 180 g

Oats (uncooked, quick) • 1 cup = 90 g

Table salt • 1 cup = 300 g

Butter • 1 cup = 240 g

Vegetable shortening • 1 cup = 190 g

Fruits and vegetables (chopped) • 1 cup = 150 g

Nuts (chopped) • 1 cup = 150 g

Nuts (ground) • 1 cup = 120 g

Bread crumbs (fresh, packed) • 1 cup = 60 g

Bread crumbs (dry) • 1 cup = 150 g

Parmesan cheese (grated) • 1 cup = 90 g

Length

⅛ inch = 3 mm

¼ inch = 6 mm

½ inch = 13 mm

¾ inch = 19 mm

1 inch = 2.5 cm

Temperature

C = (F-32) x 5/9

F = (C x 9/5) + 32

Is there anything more delicious than biting into a fresh, crisp apple? No matter what its origin, the apple has developed a uniquely American identity. This versatile fruit is often the star in desserts we know well: baked apples, apple crisp, apple pan dowdy, apple brown betty, and, of course, the pinnacle of fall: apple pie.

Each year it seems the apple undergoes a renewal, as supermarkets carry new varieties and local orchards push out a diverse array of bounty—some grown for centuries by the same farms, others newly cultivated based on flavors, growing conditions, and the previous harvest.

The fruit's hidden gift is something we all know but don't often discuss—apples are good for you. Full of fiber (about 4 grams per apple!) and antioxidants, they are refreshing and filling at the same time. While they may or may not "keep the doctor away," apples certainly contribute to your health by lowering cholesterol, reducing the risk of obesity, and even assisting in the fight against certain types of cancer.

These health benefits might be complex, but bringing the apple to your table doesn't have to be. Whether you crave the pick-your-own apple experience or prefer to hit up the local farmer's market or supermarket, this hardy fruit is available year-round. So after you have polished off your share of crunchy fresh apples and baked the pies, what's next?

Bringing together a wealth of knowledge and love of flavors, the recipes in this book will inspire you to tie on your apron and start cooking. Along with many of your old favorites, you'll find plenty of new and exciting apple recipes. Liven up your table with Apple Mushroom Risotto. Impress your backyard guests by topping Turkey Burgers with Apple Chipotle Sauce. Combine great fall traditions in one bowl with Pumpkin-Apple Soup. Brighten your evening with an Apple Cosmopolitan. Imagine no limits.

All in all, your taste buds and your company will appreciate the savory and sweet flavors these apple-based dishes will bring to the table, and your health will thank you for the natural sweetness and fiber they add to your diet.

An apple a day is always worth your while. So be sure to become familiar with local growers and learn from what they stock—you never know how you may be inspired.

Christopher Headen
Chairman of the Board
National Farmers Market Association (NFMA)

Apple Rum Crepes with Apple Cinnamon Filling

Start the year off right. Whip up a batch of these mouth-watering crepes for a celebratory brunch.

Makes about 24 crepes

Batter

3 large eggs

¼ cup granulated sugar, plus 3 tablespoons for sprinkling

1 teaspoon lemon zest

1 teaspoon pure vanilla extract

1 cup all-purpose flour

1½ cups milk

¼ cup unsalted butter, melted and cooled

Filling

¼ cup apple-flavored rum

2 cups ½-inch-diced apple, such as Fuji or other firm semi-sweet apple

3 tablespoons granulated sugar

½ teaspoon ground cinnamon

4 tablespoons unsalted butter

Nonstick vegetable oil spray

To make the batter, combine the eggs, ¼ cup sugar, lemon zest, vanilla, flour, milk, melted butter, and rum in a blender. Blend 1 minute. Place the blender, lid on, in the refrigerator and chill for 2 hours.

To make the filling, toss the diced apples, sugar, and cinnamon in a small bowl. Set aside.

In an 8-inch sauté pan, melt 4 tablespoons butter over medium-low heat. Add the apples and any juices in the bowl. Sauté gently until soft and juicy, 5 to 7 minutes.

To make the crepes, spray a crepe pan or a 6-inch nonstick sauté pan and set over medium heat. Pour about ¼ cup batter into the preheated pan. Tilt the pan in a circular motion, allowing the batter to evenly coat the bottom.

Cook the crepe for 1 minute or until the underside is light brown. Loosen the edges with a spatula and turn over. Cook the second side to a light brown, about 1 minute longer. Transfer the crepe to a plate and sprinkle with a little of the reserved granulated sugar.

Continue making the crepes with the remaining batter, sprinkling them with sugar and stacking them on top of each other. Place one crepe on a plate, spoon about 1 tablespoon filling on top, off-center, then fold into quarters. Repeat with the remaining crepes and filling.

Arugula with Apples and Parmesan

Just a few simple ingredients make a sublime salad. Buy the best quality Parmesan you can and use it as liberally as you like.

Makes 4 servings

2 bunches arugula, trimmed, washed well, and patted dry

Chunk of Parmesan cheese

1 recipe Apple Cider Vinaigrette (see page 11)

1 large apple of your choice

Put the arugula into a large bowl. Use a cheese slicer or vegetable peeler to shave the cheese into large pieces and set aside.

Make the vinaigrette in a small bowl, according to the directions on the next page. Core the apple and cut it into ⅛-inch wedges. Place each piece immediately into the vinaigrette and turn to coat as you work to prevent it from browning.

Transfer all the apple wedges into the arugula and pour the remaining vinaigrette over the salad. Toss gently to distribute the vinaigrette. Add the shaved cheese, toss gently, and divide the salad among 4 salad plates. Serve immediately.

Apple Cider Vinaigrette

This tangy, apple-infused vinaigrette can work with any green salad.
Apple cider vinegar is strong, so use with care.

Makes about ½ cup

1 tablespoon apple cider vinegar
3 tablespoons apple juice
3 tablespoons extra virgin olive oil
½ teaspoon Dijon mustard
Pinch salt

Whisk the vinegar, juice, oil, mustard, and salt in a small bowl until thoroughly combined. Taste and adjust the salt if necessary.

Core Fact

What's the difference between apple juice and apple cider?

Apple cider, unlike apple juice, isn't processed and needs to be refrigerated.

Apple and Carrot Juice

Up the nutrition content of your morning quaff by mixing these two very different juices.
The result is an energizing treat.

Makes 2 servings

1 cup apple juice
1 cup carrot juice

Pour the juices into a pitcher and mix until thoroughly combined.

Apple Dumplings with Apple Caramel Sauce and Apple Gelato

Apple dumplings, an old-fashioned homey treat, get a fruity update with Apple Caramel Sauce and Apple Gelato. Make the caramel sauce before you start the dumplings because you'll need a bit for the filling.

Makes 4 dumplings

Pate Brisee (Flaky Pastry Dough)

2½ cups all-purpose flour

¾ teaspoon salt

2 teaspoons to 2 tablespoons granulated sugar (optional)

1 cup cold unsalted butter, cut into small dice

¼ to ½ cup ice-cold water

Filling

¼ cup raisins

2 tablespoons apple juice, Calvados, rum, or bourbon

¼ cup finely chopped, toasted pecans

4 teaspoons Apple Caramel Sauce, plus more for serving (see page 15)

4 (3½- to 4-ounce) apples of your choice

1 or 2 lemon slices

1 egg white

1 tablespoon cream

Granulated sugar, for sprinkling

Apple Gelato (see page 15) or vanilla ice cream, for serving

Whipped cream, for serving

To make the dough, pour the flour, salt, and, if desired, sugar into a food processor and pulse several times. Add the butter and pulse 10 to 15 times. Turn the mixture onto a work surface and use your hands to sprinkle evenly with ¼ cup water. Toss the mixture until it just holds together. Add more water by tablespoons to form the dough. Shape the dough into two disks, wrap well in plastic and refrigerate for 30 minutes or up to two days.

When you are ready to bake, preheat the oven to 425° F. To make the filling, soak the raisins in the apple juice, Calvados, rum, or bourbon until plump. Drain. Add the toasted pecans and Apple Caramel Sauce.

Peel the apples and cut a thin slice off the bottoms. Core the apples, removing the stem and seeds, but not going all the way through the bottom. Rub the apples with a slice of lemon to prevent browning.

Roll the dough into a 14-inch square about ⅛ inch thick. Cut it into 4 (7-inch) squares. Fill each apple with 1 to 2 tablespoons of the raisin mixture. Place an apple in the center of a pastry square. Bring the corners together at the top of the apple. Pinch the four seams closed. Repeat to form the remaining dumplings.

Place the dumplings on a baking sheet lined with parchment paper. To make egg wash, combine egg white and cream. Brush the dumplings with egg wash and sprinkle with sugar. Bake for about 8 minutes; then reduce the heat to 375° F and bake for 10 more minutes. Cool slightly. Serve with Apple Gelato, Apple Caramel

January 6

Apple Gelato

This refreshing, fruity gelato is delicious on its own or alongside any dish in need of a sweet, frosty accent. An ice cream maker is required.

Makes about 1 quart, depending on your ice cream maker

8 ounces defrosted, but not diluted, apple juice or apple cider concentrate
¼ cup plus 2 tablespoons granulated sugar
¾ cup whole milk
1½ cups heavy cream
4 egg yolks

Bring the juice or cider concentrate, 2 tablespoons sugar, milk, and ½ cup cream to a simmer in a saucepan set over medium-high heat. Remove from the heat. Beat the yolks and ¼ cup sugar in a bowl and slowly pour in the hot cream mixture, whisking constantly.

Return the mixture to the pan and cook over medium heat, stirring, for 2 to 3 minutes, or until the mixture thickens. Do not let it simmer or boil. Remove the pan from the heat and add the remaining 1 cup heavy cream. Strain the mixture over another bowl. Prepare an ice bath (a bowl of ice water just big enough to hold the bowl containing the gelato mixture without letting any water touch the gelato). Refrigerate for several hours or overnight. Add to your ice cream maker and churn according to the machine's instructions.

January 7

Apple Caramel Sauce

Calvados, the French apple liqueur, gives this caramel dessert sauce an extra zing. Use it over ice cream or gelato, in cheesecake or frosting, or any dessert that needs a caramel kick.

Makes about 1¼ cups

1 cup granulated sugar
½ teaspoon fresh lemon juice
½ cup water

½ cup plus 2 tablespoons heavy cream, at room temperature
2 tablespoons Calvados or apple cider

In a heavy-bottomed saucepan set over medium heat, combine the sugar, lemon juice, and water and stir until the sugar is dissolved. If there are any sugar crystals on the sides of the pan, wipe them down with a pastry brush dipped in cold water.

Bring mixture to a boil. Cover the pan for 1 minute to let the steam wash down any remaining sugar crystals. When the syrup begins to boil, watch it carefully and swirl the pan to promote even coloring. Cook the syrup to a medium amber caramel, 328° F to 335° F on a candy thermometer.

Remove the pan from the heat and hold it carefully at arm's length because the cream will boil up vigorously when added. Immediately stir in the heavy cream, return the pan to the heat, and bring the caramel sauce to a boil, stirring, for 30 to 60 seconds.

Remove the pan from the heat and pour the sauce into a stainless steel or other heat-proof bowl to cool. Stir in the Calvados or the cider. Let the sauce cool to room temperature, stirring it occasionally to prevent separation.

Crustless Apple Quiche

This quick, easy, and light dish also makes a delectable appetizer for a party when thinly sliced.

Makes 1 (9½- to 10-inch) quiche

Nonstick vegetable oil spray

4 large eggs

½ teaspoon salt

1 cup crème frâiche or sour cream

1 Gala or Fuji apple, cored and cut into ½-inch chunks

8 ounces Gruyere cheese, grated

1 teaspoon finely chopped fresh sage (optional)

Preheat the oven to 350° F. Place the oven rack in the center position. Spray a 9½- to 10-inch pie pan with vegetable oil spray.

Beat the eggs in a medium bowl. Add the salt and crème frâiche or sour cream and mix until thoroughly combined and light yellow in color. Set aside.

Place the apple chunks into the bottom of the pan. Sprinkle the cheese and sage, if using, over the apples. Pour in the egg mixture, smoothing it over the surface with a wooden spoon. Bake for about 25 minutes, or until the top is golden in color and a toothpick inserted into the center comes out clean.

January 10

Applesauce

Use less or more sugar, depending on your taste and the sweetness of the apples. The lemon juice brightens the flavor and balances the sweetness.

Makes about 2 cups

4 pounds peeled, cored and quartered cooking apples, such as Braeburn, Cortland, Honeycrisp, Jonagold, McIntosh, or Winesap

Juice of 1 lemon

1 cinnamon stick

¼ cup dark brown sugar, packed

2 tablespoons granulated sugar

1 cup water

½ teaspoon salt

Put all the ingredients into a 5-quart pot. Cover and bring to a boil, lower the heat, and simmer for 20 minutes, or until the apples start to fall apart. Remove the sauce from the heat and discard the cinnamon stick.

If you have a handheld immersion blender, process the cooked apples until smooth. If you don't, transfer the sauce in batches to a blender and puree until smooth. You may also use a food mill, or, for a coarser consistency, a potato masher.

Serve either warm or refrigerated. This recipe freezes easily and lasts up to one year frozen. Be sure to cool to room temperature before freezing.

January 9

Baked Apple Chips

These satisfying chips encourage healthful snacking. Bet you can't eat just one!

Makes about 1 cup

1 large apple, such as Honeycrisp, Granny Smith, or Fuji

2 tablespoon granulated sugar

1 teaspoon ground cinnamon

Preheat the oven to 250° F. Thinly slice the apple crosswise about ⅛ to ¼ inch thick. Line a baking sheet with parchment paper and arrange the apple slices in a single layer on it.

In a small bowl, combine the sugar and cinnamon and sprinkle the mixture over the slices on both sides.

Bake in the bottom third of the oven until the apples are dry and crisp, about 2 hours. After 1 hour in the oven, turn them over so they bake evenly. The chips will keep for up to 3 days in a sealed container.

Crispy Pork Belly Salad with Apple and Thai Herbs

This mouth-watering recipe is from **Chef Ian Kittichai**, who pairs apples with traditional Thai salad ingredients.

Makes 4 servings

Crispy Pork Belly

2 pounds pork belly

1 teaspoon freshly ground black pepper

1 teaspoon Chinese five-spice powder

½ tablespoon sea salt

½ tablespoon white vinegar

Chili Dressing

1 cup grapeseed oil

¼ cup fresh lime juice

¼ cup soy sauce

4 to 5 pieces finely chopped long red chili pepper or jalapeno, seeds removed

4 to 5 cilantro roots (available in Asian markets), rinsed

5 cloves garlic, peeled

Apple Salad

2 cups matchstick-sized strips of apple, tossed in lemon juice

½ cup julienned green mango

½ cup seeded, julienned green papaya

4 kaffir lime leaves, deveined and thinly sliced

4 stalks lemongrass, rough outer leaves discarded and soft parts thinly sliced

15 mint leaves, cut into large pieces

15 Thai basil leaves, cut into large pieces

1 cup (¼-inch) cucumber chunks, seeds removed

½ red onion, thinly sliced

½ cup thinly sliced scallion

1 cup chopped cilantro leaves

2 long red chili peppers, thinly sliced

3 tablespoons crispy shallots (available in Asian markets)

2 tablespoons crispy garlic (available in Asian markets)

Begin by scoring the pork belly. With a sharp knife, slice into the fat, making cross marks, but do not cut through. Poke the bottom and sides with a fork.

Mix the pepper and five-spice powder in a bowl. Place the pork in a large sealable plastic bag and pour in the spice mixture. Seal and begin massaging the pork, so that it is covered with the spices and the mixture is rubbed into the meat well. Refrigerate overnight.

When you are ready to cook the pork, line a large baking pan with foil and place a baking rack into it. Preheat the oven to 425° F.

Remove the pork from the bag and place fat side up on the prepared baking sheet. With paper towels, completely dry the top fat, removing any moisture. Sprinkle with the salt and brush the vinegar on top of the fat. Bake for 30 minutes, during which the pork will begin to brown and crisp. Reduce the heat to 350° and cook for 1 more hour. Remove from the oven and let cool.

Meanwhile, make the dressing. Put the oil, lime juice, soy sauce, chili pepper, cilantro root, and garlic into a food processor or blender and blend for 1 to 2 minutes, or until smooth. (This dressing will keep in an airtight container in the refrigerator for up to 1 week).

To make the salad, toss the apple in a medium bowl with the mango, papaya, kaffir lime leaves, lemon grass, mint leaves, basil, cucumber, red onion, scallion, cilantro leaves, and chili peppers and some of the dressing.

When the pork belly is cooled, cut it into bite-size pieces, place it in a separate bowl and dress with the dressing. Place some of the pork belly on a large serving platter, top with the apple salad, and arrange the rest of the pork belly around the salad. Scatter the crispy shallot and garlic over the top and serve immediately.

Chef Ian Kittichai

CURRENTLY OWNER/CHEF AT: Issaya Siamese Club, Hyde & Seek Gastrobar, and Smith Restaurant & Bar in Bangkok; Koh by Ian Kittichai in Mumbai; Ember Room, Spot Dessert Bar, and Jum Mum in New York City

MENTOR: His mother, who owned a food cart and grocery in Thailand

NOTABLE FOR: The first Thai national in the world to become Executive Chef of a five-star hotel property

Whole-Wheat Apple Ginger Muffins

Two forms of ginger, fresh and ground, give these apple muffins a wonderful
flavor that is an excellent addition to the apple.

Makes 12 muffins

⅞ cup (1 cup minus 1 tablespoon)
    all-purpose flour

⅔ cup whole-wheat flour

⅞ cup brown sugar, lightly packed

⅛ teaspoon salt

½ teaspoon ground ginger

5 tablespoons unsalted butter, plus
    more for greasing, softened
    slightly

1 teaspoon baking powder

⅓ teaspoon baking soda

2 large eggs

½ cup buttermilk

1 tablespoon finely grated ginger

1 large Golden Delicious Apple,
    peeled, cored, and cut into
    ¼-inch dice

Preheat the oven to 400° F. Place the oven rack in the center
position. Line a 12-cup muffin tin with paper liners or grease
well with butter.

Sift the flours, brown sugar, salt, and ground ginger into a large
bowl. Add the butter and use your fingertips to mix it into the
dry ingredients until the mixture is crumbly. All the butter
should be well coated. Measure ½ cup of the mixture into a
small container and reserve for topping.

Whisk the baking powder and baking soda into the remaining
flour and butter mixture.

In a separate bowl, whisk the eggs, buttermilk, and grated
ginger. Add the wet ingredients to the dry and stir just to
combine. Stir in the apple.

Scoop the batter into the muffin tin, filling each cup almost to
the top. Sprinkle the tops with the reserved flour-sugar mixture.
Bake for 15 to 18 minutes, or until a toothpick inserted into
the center of a muffin comes out clean.

Apple Tip:

Large and sweet tasting, Golden Delicious is
an ideal choice for applesauce, apple butters,
and salads. Handle Golden Delicious apples
with care, as they tend to bruise.

Apple Granola Bars

Chewy, fruity, and loaded with good food, these bars make a healthy and delicious snack.

Makes 15 bars

Bars

1⅓ cups old-fashioned rolled oats

½ cup unsweetened shredded coconut

1½ cups puffed rice cereal

3 tablespoons honey or pure maple syrup

6 tablespoons unsalted butter, melted

1 cup dried apples, finely chopped (see Dried Apples, page 323, or use store-bought)

¼ cup raisins or dried cranberries

Syrup

½ cup unsalted butter, melted

3 tablespoons honey

½ cup brown sugar

Preheat the oven to 375° F. Line a baking sheet and an 8-inch square baking pan with parchment paper.

To make the granola, combine the oats, coconut, rice cereal, honey or syrup, and butter in a large bowl and toss. Spread the mixture onto the prepared baking sheet and bake, stirring frequently, for 25 to 30 minutes, or until lightly browned. Transfer to a large bowl and let cool slightly, but do not cool completely. Stir in the apples and raisins or dried cranberries.

Meanwhile, make the syrup. Combine the butter, honey, and brown sugar and mix to blend very well. Pour the syrup over the granola and mix well to coat. Press the mixture firmly into the prepared 8-inch square pan. Refrigerate until firm. Turn out onto a work surface and cut into 15 bars.

Alpermagronen

Alpermagronen is a specialty of the Swiss Alps that dates back to the introduction of pasta to the region. The noodles were combined with local staples to create this hearty dish, which included apples or applesauce.

Makes 6 servings

1 pound elbow noodles

2 potatoes

2 tablespoons vegetable oil

2 tablespoons butter

2 medium onions, roughly chopped

1 clove garlic, finely chopped

1 cup half and half

½ teaspoon salt, plus more to taste if needed

Freshly ground black pepper to taste

½ cup grated Gruyere cheese

2 thick (about ⅛-inch) slices ham, cut into bite-size pieces

6 large apples of your choice

Preheat the oven to 350° F. Cook the noodles according to the package instructions. Drain and keep warm. Meanwhile, boil the potatoes, skin on, for 15 to 20 minutes or until slightly softened. Drain and keep warm.

Heat 1 tablespoon each of the oil and butter in an ovenproof skillet set over medium-high heat until the butter is melted. Add the onion and cook, stirring, until softened, translucent, and lightly golden brown. Add the garlic and cook for about 30 seconds until softened.

Peel and cut the potatoes crosswise into ⅛-inch slices and add to the skillet. Add the drained noodles and half and half and stir to combine. Season with salt and pepper, taste and adjust the seasoning if necessary. Sprinkle with the cheese and scatter the ham over the top. Bake for 20 to 25 minutes or until the potatoes can be easily pierced with the tip of a sharp knife and the cheese is melted and lightly browned.

Meanwhile, core the apples and cut them into ⅛-inch wedges. Melt the remaining butter and oil in a frying pan set over medium heat. Add the apple wedges and cook, stirring occasionally, until soft and golden brown. When the Alpermagronen is done, transfer to a serving dish, surround with apples, and serve.

January 15

Beet, Apple, and Goat Cheese Tart

This sweet-savory tart tastes best at room temperature. A mandoline makes this meal a snap to prepare.

Serves 4

½ recipe Quick Puff Pastry (see Apple Apricot Bistro Tarts, page 26) or 1 sheet frozen puff pastry, thawed

Nonstick olive oil spray

1 teaspoon extra virgin olive oil

1 Honeycrisp apple, cored and thinly sliced on a mandoline

4 baby beets, candy striped, red, or golden, peeled and thinly sliced on a mandoline

½ cup crumbled goat cheese

½ teaspoon chopped fresh thyme leaves

2 teaspoons honey

½ teaspoon sea salt

½ teaspoon freshly ground black pepper

If you are making the puff pastry from scratch, prepare and chill it according to the directions on page 26. When you are ready to bake the tart, preheat the oven to 400° F. Spray a baking sheet with olive oil spray.

Roll out the pastry to a 12- by 9-inch rectangle about ⅛ inch thick. (If you are using frozen pastry, open the thawed sheet.) Lay the rolled out pastry on the baking sheet and drizzle with olive oil.

Arrange the apple and beet slices on the puff pastry in any pattern you wish. Top with the crumbled goat cheese and thyme. Drizzle with honey and season with salt and pepper.

Transfer the baking sheet to the bottom rack of the oven and bake until the pastry is crispy, golden brown, and slightly puffed, about 25 minutes.

Cut into 4 pieces and serve warm or at room temperature.

January 16

Apple Compote

This compote is delicious over French toast, waffles, pancakes, or as a topping for ice cream or pound cake.

Makes about 6 cups

2 cups apple cider

¼ cup light brown sugar

1 tablespoon apple brandy

1 teaspoon pumpkin pie spice

⅛ teaspoon salt

8 large Golden Delicious apples, peeled, cored, and cut into 1-inch chunks

Combine all the ingredients in a 3-quart saucepan. Bring to a boil over high heat and cook for about 5 minutes, stirring constantly.

When the mixture has thickened slightly, lower the heat and simmer, stirring occasionally, until the apples are very tender, about 30 minutes.

Remove from the heat and let cool to room temperature before serving.

January 17

Grilled Cheese with Ham, Apples, and Tarragon

Grilled cheese gets gussied up in these tasty sandwiches, which are nice for a special lunch, but can also be cut in quarters and served as hors d'oeuvres.

Makes 4 sandwiches

½ cup shredded Cheddar cheese

1 large apple, peeled, cored, and finely diced

4 slices ham, diced

1 teaspoon minced fresh tarragon

8 slices sandwich bread, crusts removed

3 tablespoons unsalted butter, softened, as needed

Nonstick vegetable oil spray

Mix the cheese, apple, ham, and tarragon in a small bowl.

Place all 8 slices of bread on a work surface and spread one side of each with butter, coating the entire surface. Reserve any leftover butter. Turn 4 slices over so the butter faces down.

Divide the cheese mixture evenly between the 4 unbuttered sides of the bread. Cover with the remaining slices of bread, buttered side up.

Put any remaining butter into a large frying pan and spray the pan well with nonstick vegetable oil. Set the pan over medium heat to melt the butter. Carefully place the sandwiches into the pan in a single layer, working in batches if needed. Cook, occasionally pressing down on the sandwiches with a spatula, for 1 to 2 minutes, or until the cheese has begun to melt and the bread is golden. Be careful that it does not burn.

When the cheese adheres to the bread, turn and cook, pressing with a spatula, for 1 to 2 minutes, or until the bread is golden and the cheese has melted. Remove from the pan, slice, and serve.

Apple Apricot Bistro Tarts

The simplified puff pastry in these elegant tarts can be mixed by hand, but a food processor produces better results.

Makes 12 (6- by 3-inch) tarts

Quick puff pastry dough

2¼ cups all-purpose flour, plus more for kneading

1 teaspoon salt

1¼ cups cold unsalted butter, cut into ½-inch dice

¼ cup plus 3 tablespoons ice-cold water

Filling

⅔ cup apricot jam

½ lemon

6 medium Granny Smith apples

2 to 4 teaspoons granulated sugar

To make the dough, combine the flour and salt in a food processor fitted with a metal blade and pulse 2 or 3 times. Cut in ¼ cup of the butter pieces by pulsing 12 to 14 times, until it is thoroughly blended into the dry ingredients and no longer visible as separate bits. Add the remaining 1 cup butter and pulse 3 or 4 times. This time the butter should stay visible. Add the ice water and pulse 3 more times. The mixture should begin to hold together, but remain rough and shaggy looking. Add a few more drops of ice water and pulse 1 or 2 times if needed to bring the dough together; it should be in clumps, not a ball, and the butter should be visible.

Turn the dough out onto a well-floured work surface. Press it into a square. If the dough is very soft, you can chill it for 30 to 40 minutes for easier handling. (Avoid working with warm dough or the butter will melt, the dough will stick, and the layers will not puff properly. Keeping the dough floured helps prevent sticking; rolling it between pieces of parchment or plastic can help.)

Roll the dough out to a 14-inch square. Fold it in thirds, like a letter, to form a rectangle about 14 by 4⅔ inches. Chill the dough, well wrapped, for at least 30 minutes, until firm.

On a floured surface, roll the dough from 14 to 16 inches long, just to get it pliable enough to fold. Fold the dough from each long end into the middle. Fold again as if closing a book. You will have a rectangle about 4⅔ by 4 inches.

Roll the dough out to a 6- by 15-inch rectangle. Fold in thirds as above to form a 6- by 5-inch rectangle. Chill the dough, well wrapped, while you prepare the apples and preheat the oven.

Melt the jam in a small saucepan over very low heat, stirring frequently. Set aside to cool. Strain it if you wish. Preheat the oven to 400° F. Place the oven rack in the center. Line 2 baking sheets with parchment. Prepare a bowl of cold water and squeeze the juice of the half lemon into it. Peel, halve lengthwise, and core the apples. Drop them into the water. When you are ready to assemble the tarts, pat the apple halves dry.

Roll half the dough out on a lightly floured work surface to a 12- by 9-inch rectangle about ⅛ inch thick. Cut the rectangle in half to form two 6- by 9-inch rectangles and then cut each in thirds to form six 6- by 3-inch rectangles. Repeat with the remaining dough for a total of 12 rectangles.

Place the rectangles of dough on the parchment-lined sheets. Prick the dough with a fork down the center. Brush cooled apricot jam down the center of each rectangle, using about 2 teaspoons each, leaving the edges uncoated. Reserve the remaining jam.

Slice each apple half thinly, no more than ⅛ inch thick, and arrange the slices on top of the jam in overlapping rows, using half an apple per tart. Leave a border about ¼ inch. Sprinkle with the sugar. Bake immediately for 13 to 15 minutes, until the dough is crisp, puffed, and golden and the apples have softened. Brush the hot tarts with the remaining apricot jam. Remove the tarts to a cooling rack for 2 to 3 minutes. Serve warm.

January 19

Salmon with Sauce Beurre Pommes

This sauce is a variation on beurre blanc sauce, using apple brandy instead of wine and apple cider vinegar instead of wine vinegar. It's a tart, lively sauce that is delicious on fish. The recipe calls for broiling the salmon, but you can grill it or microwave it if you like.

Makes 4 servings

Broiled Salmon

4 (6-ounce) salmon fillets

4 teaspoons olive oil

Salt and freshly ground
 black pepper to taste

Sauce

¼ cup apple brandy

2 tablespoons apple cider
 vinegar

2 tablespoons apple cider

1 clove garlic, minced

½ cup vegetable broth

2 tablespoons butter

¼ teaspoon salt, plus
 more to taste if needed

Freshly ground pepper,
 to taste

Place the salmon on a broiling pan and drizzle the oil over it. Season with salt and pepper.

Pour the brandy, vinegar, and cider into a saucepan and add the garlic. Set over medium heat and cook until most of the liquid has evaporated and the pan is almost dry. Add the broth and butter and stir to melt. Reduce the heat if necessary. Strain the sauce and discard the garlic. Taste and season with salt and pepper. Set aside.

Broil the salmon for 3 to 5 minutes per side, or until it is cooked through. The timing will depend on the thickness of the fish.

Place the fillets on four serving plates. If you need to reheat the sauce, microwave it on medium power for about 1 minute. Drizzle the sauce over the fillets and serve.

Apple-Cinnamon Granola

While this recipe makes a lot of granola, it can easily be halved. Eat a bowlful in the morning with milk or sprinkle a handful over yogurt for a filling snack.

Makes about 16 cups

3 Granny Smith apples, cored and cut into large chunks

1 cup pure maple syrup

¼ cup vegetable oil

1 tablespoon ground cinnamon

½ teaspoon grated nutmeg

½ teaspoon kosher salt

10 cups old-fashioned rolled oats

¾ cup wheat germ

½ cup sesame seeds

½ cup sunflower seeds

2 cups raw sliced almonds

2 cups chopped walnuts

Preheat the oven to 250° F. Combine the apples, maple syrup, vegetable oil, cinnamon, nutmeg, and salt in a blender. If your blender isn't able to puree this, add enough water to make a paste. Process until the apples are pureed.

In a large bowl, combine the rest of the ingredients and mix well. Pour the apple mixture into the bowl and stir until everything is coated.

Line a large roasting pan or 2 jelly-roll pans with parchment paper. Spread the granola mixture in an even layer on the pan. Transfer the pan to the middle rack of the oven and bake for approximately 90 minutes, stirring every 15 minutes. Turn the oven off, but leave the granola in until it completely cools, another hour or two. The granola will harden more as it cools.

Break the granola up into bite-size chunks if necessary. Store in a covered container for up to 3 weeks or freeze for 6 months.

Skewered Apple Slices

Use some of the delicious granola you just made to make this fun snack for all ages.

Makes 2 servings

1 large apple of your choice, cored and cut into 8 wedges

8 (4-inch) wooden skewers

½ cup smooth peanut butter

1 tablespoon honey

1 cup Apple-Cinnamon Granola (at left)

Spear each apple slice onto a skewer.

In a small bowl, combine the peanut butter and honey. Stir until smooth. Spread the peanut-butter mixture on the cut sides of each apple slice, using a tablespoon per slice.

Spread the granola on wax paper. Roll the sticky apples in the granola and serve.

Sweet Potato Hash with Apples and Walnuts

This deliciously different side dish offers an amalgam of flavors. The creamy sweetness of the potatoes marries well with the savory tang of garlic, the nutty flavor of walnuts, the salty smokiness of bacon, and the sweet crunch of apples.

Makes about 6 servings

2 large sweet potatoes

2 strips bacon

1½ tablespoons vegetable oil

2 cloves garlic, finely minced

2 large apples of your choice

½ cup coarsely chopped walnuts

2 to 4 sprigs fresh thyme

¼ teaspoon salt

Preheat the oven to 350º F. Place the potatoes, skin on, in a pot with enough water to cover them by 1 inch. Bring to a boil and cook 15 to 20 minutes. Drain and let cool.

Meanwhile, cook the bacon in a large (12-inch) ovenproof skillet set over medium-high heat until crispy and cooked through. Drain the bacon on paper towels. Pour all but 1 tablespoon of the bacon grease out of the skillet.

Add the oil to the skillet and return it to the heat. Add the garlic, and cook, stirring often, for 30 to 45 seconds, or until softened. Remove the pan from the heat.

Peel the potatoes and cut them into ½-inch chunks. Crumble the bacon into tiny pieces. Peel and core the apples and cut them into ½-inch chunks. Return the pan to the heat, add the potato, bacon, apples, and walnuts and stir to coat with the fat. Pull the leaves off the thyme sprigs and scatter over the pan, discarding the stems. Season with the salt and stir to combine. Cover with foil and bake for 30 to 40 minutes or until the potatoes are thoroughly cooked through and can be pierced with the tip of a knife and the apples are soft. Stir the mixture once or twice during the baking.

Apple Cider— Honey Vinaigrette

Amazing all year round, this vinaigrette is especially tasty with bitter winter greens such as escarole and curly endive.

Makes 1½ cups

¼ cup apple cider vinegar, unfiltered if possible

½ cup good quality honey

2 tablespoons Dijon mustard

½ cup fresh lemon juice

1 shallot, minced

1 clove garlic, minced

½ teaspoon sea salt

½ teaspoon freshly ground pepper

¾ cup extra virgin olive oil

In a small bowl, whisk together all the ingredients except for the olive oil. Slowly drizzle in the olive oil, whisking to form an emulsion.

Refrigerate in an airtight container for up to 1 month.

Spiced Hard Apple Cider

Curl up before a roaring fire with a cup of this comforting winter drink spiked with brandy.

Makes 6 drinks

1 tablespoon allspice, tied in cheesecloth

1 cinnamon stick

3 cups hard apple cider

1 cup fresh orange juice

½ lemon, sliced

1 teaspoon honey

¼ cup Calvados

Combine all the ingredients except for the Calvados in a 3-quart medium saucepan. Bring to a boil, reduce heat, and simmer, covered, for 10 minutes. Remove from the heat and discard the spice bag. Stir in the brandy and serve.

Roasted Butternut Squash and Apple Soup

Roasting the squash and apples caramelizes their natural sugars, giving this easy-to-prepare soup depth of flavor. It freezes well, so cook up a double batch.

Makes 6 servings

3 cups peeled and roughly chopped butternut squash

2 tablespoons olive oil

1 cup cored and chopped Honeycrisp apple

½ teaspoon herbes de Provence

¾ teaspoon sea salt

Freshly ground black pepper, to taste

1 medium onion, diced

2 cloves garlic, minced

1½ teaspoons dried thyme

4 cups chicken or vegetable stock

1 cup vanilla-flavored almond milk

¼ cup crème fraîche

2 tablespoons roasted, salted pumpkin seeds

Preheat the oven to 400° F.

In a large bowl, combine the chopped butternut squash and apple and toss to coat with 1 tablespoon of the olive oil, the herbes de Provence, ½ teaspoon of the sea salt, and freshly ground black pepper to taste.

Arrange the seasoned squash and apple on a foil-lined baking sheet. Bake in the bottom third of the oven for 30 minutes, or until golden brown and tender.

In a 4- or 6-quart Dutch oven or 5-quart pot, heat the remaining tablespoon of olive oil over medium high heat. Add the diced onion and sauté, stirring occasionally, until translucent, about 5 minutes.

Add the garlic and thyme and stir until fragrant, about 30 seconds. Add the cooked squash and apple.

Add the chicken or vegetable broth and bring to a boil. Lower heat and simmer, uncovered, for 15 minutes, or until the squash and apple begin to fall apart.

If you have a handheld immersion blender, puree until soup is smooth. If you don't, transfer the soup in batches to a blender or food processor and puree until smooth. Return the soup back to the Dutch oven or saucepan. Add the almond milk and season with the remaining salt and pepper to taste.

To serve, ladle into individual bowls and garnish with crème fraîche and the pumpkin seeds.

Baked French Toast

This tasty brunch dish can be prepared the night before or in the morning.
Allow at least an hour for the bread to soak up the batter.

Makes 4 servings

2 large apples of your choice
Nonstick vegetable oil spray
1 tablespoon unsalted butter, plus more for greasing
8 large eggs

¾ cup milk
6 tablespoons pure maple syrup, plus more for serving
1 teaspoon ground cinnamon, plus more for sprinkling
8 slices bread

Peel and core the apples and cut into thin wedges. Coat a frying pan with vegetable oil spray, add the butter, and set over medium heat. Add the apple wedges and cook, stirring gently until the apples are just softened and lightly golden. Remove from the heat and let cool.

Butter a casserole dish. Combine the eggs, milk, maple syrup, and cinnamon in a large bowl and mix well. Place 1 or 2 slices of bread into the egg mixture and pierce with a fork a few times to allow the egg to soak into the bread. Transfer to the baking dish and repeat until you have 4 slices in the bottom of the

baking dish. Cut the slices to make the bread fit into the bottom of the dish in a single layer. Arrange half of the apples over the top. Repeat with the remaining bread and apples to make 2 layers. Pour any remaining batter over the top and sprinkle with a little cinnamon. Refrigerate for 1 hour or overnight.

When you are ready to bake, preheat the oven to 350° F. Bake for 40 to 50 minutes, or until a toothpick inserted into the center of the casserole comes out clean and the French toast is cooked through. Serve with maple syrup, if desired.

January 27

Penne with Shrimp, Spinach, and Apple-Brandy Cream Sauce

Serve this sophisticated dish on a special occasion, or any day you want a dash of elegance.

Makes 8 servings

1 pound penne pasta

1½ tablespoons olive oil

1 shallot, minced

⅓ cup apple brandy, such as Calvados

1 cup heavy cream

2 (9-ounce) packages fresh baby shrimp

½ teaspoon sea salt

Freshly ground black pepper

½ cup apple juice

1 teaspoon chopped fresh thyme

2 garlic cloves, minced

2 (9-ounce) packages fresh baby spinach

Cook the pasta in boiling salted water according to package directions.

While the pasta is cooking, heat ½ tablespoon of the olive oil in a large nonstick sauté pan set over medium-high heat. Add the minced shallot and saute until softened, about 1 minute.

Combine the apple brandy and the heavy cream and add to the pan. Cook for 2 minutes. Transfer this sauce to a bowl. Set aside.

In the same large nonstick sauté pan, heat ½ tablespoon of the olive oil over medium-high heat. Add half of the shrimp and season with half of the sea salt and pepper. Sauté until just pink. Transfer the cooked shrimp to a bowl and cover to keep warm. Repeat with the remaining oil, shrimp, salt, and pepper. Transfer the shrimp to bowl.

Do not clean the sauté pan. Add the apple juice, fresh thyme, and garlic to the pan, scraping up any loose brown bits, and boil 1 minute. Add the spinach in two batches and cook until the leaves begin to wilt. Return the cream sauce base to the pan, bring to a boil, and then remove from heat. Add the cooked shrimp to the pan and stir to coat with the sauce. Spoon the mixture over the penne and serve.

Apple Scones

If you like a uniform size and shape, roll the dough and cut it with a cutter as explained below. You can also use a tablespoon and spoon the dough onto the baking sheet. Either way, the results will be delicious.

Makes 20 scones

2 cups all-purpose flour

1 tablespoon baking powder

½ teaspoon salt

½ cup granulated sugar

5 tablespoons cold unsalted butter

1 large apple of your choice

¾ cup milk, plus more if needed

1 egg, beaten

Preheat the oven to 400° F. Lightly grease a baking sheet.

Sift the flour, baking powder, salt, and sugar into a large bowl. Cut the butter into the mixture and blend it in with your hands to form coarse crumbs.

Peel and core the apple and chop it into small pieces.

Add the milk, egg, and apple and mix to form the dough. If the batter is too crumbly to hold together, add a bit more milk. Knead gently, mold the dough into a ball, and then roll out to a thickness of about ½ inch. Use a round cutter to cut out the scones and place them onto the prepared baking sheet. Re-roll the scraps and make more scones until all the dough is used.

Bake for 10 to 12 minutes, or until the scones are just golden brown on top and a toothpick inserted into the center comes out clean.

Decorate with Apples

Many popular home crafts, such as wreaths and garlands, start with baked apple slices. Begin with a firm, unblemished apple. Cut it into ¼-inch thick slices. Soak the slices for 20 minutes in a mixture of lemon juice and salt. Dab the slices dry with a paper towel. Bake the slices on a wire rack set atop a cookie sheet for 6 hours at 150° F, turning them every 2 hours. (Don't overlap the slices.) Once cooled, evenly coat the slices with clear acrylic spray to preserve them.

Red Cabbage and Apple Slaw with Ginger Dressing

Use a food processor with a shredding attachment, if you have one. You'll have this salad prepped in no time.

Makes 12 servings

Slaw

- 1 head red cabbage, shredded
- 2 large apples, such as Gala or Golden Delicious, cored and sliced
- 2 carrots, peeled and shredded
- 3 celery stalks, chopped

Dressing

- ¼ cup apple cider vinegar
- Juice of 1 lemon
- 2 tablespoons grated fresh ginger
- 2 tablespoons honey
- 1 tablespoon celery seed
- 1½ teaspoons sea salt
- Freshly ground black pepper
- 6 tablespoons extra virgin olive oil

Combine all the ingredients for the slaw in a large bowl and toss to mix. Set aside.

To make the dressing, whisk together all the ingredients except for the oil. Slowly drizzle in the olive oil to form an emulsion.

Pour the dressing over the slaw and toss to coat. Transfer to a leak-proof container and refrigerate 1 hour to overnight. The longer this slaw sits the more flavorful it becomes. Turn the container every now and then for best results.

Apple-Orange Smoothie

Start your morning with this energizing drink and feel good all day.

Makes about 3 servings

1 apple of your choice

2 navel oranges

1 carrot, peeled and grated

½ cup orange juice

¼ teaspoon ground ginger (optional)

1 cup ice cubes

1 tablespoon flax seeds (optional)

Peel and core the apple and cut into chunks. Peel and chop the oranges. Place the apple and orange pieces with the carrot in a food processor. Add the juice, and, if you wish, the ginger and/or flax seeds. Process until smooth. Add the ice and process until the ice is crushed and the mixture is smooth and frothy.

Baked Brie with Golden Raisins and Apples

Baked Brie in pastry, a reliable do-ahead for party-givers, gets an update with dried apples and apple jelly.

Makes about 24 servings

½ recipe Quick Puff Pastry (see Apple Apricot Bistro Tarts, page 26) or 1 sheet frozen puff pastry, thawed

⅓ cup chopped dried apples (see Baked Apple Chips, page 17, or use store-bought)

⅓ to ½ cup bottled apple jelly

1 (5-inch) wheel Brie cheese

1 egg beaten with 1 tablespoon water

If you are making the puff pastry from scratch, prepare and chill it according to the directions on page 26. When you are ready to bake the Brie, preheat the oven to 400° F.

Roll out the pastry to a 12- by 9-inch rectangle about ⅛ inch thick. (If you are using frozen pastry, open the thawed sheet and roll it into a square.) Spread the pastry with the jelly. Arrange the apples in the center of the pastry and place the wheel of cheese over them. Moisten the edges of the pastry sheet a bit and fold them up and over the cheese to seal the cheese and apples in a pastry package. The cheese should not be visible. Brush the pastry with the egg wash, coating the entire package lightly.

Place on a baking sheet. Bake for 20 minutes, or until the pastry is golden and flaky and the cheese is softened.

Apple and Leek Soup

A rich and savory soup is just the thing for a cold winter night. This recipe calls for only the white parts of the leek. You can use the tender green parts of the leeks if you like; the soup will take on a greenish color. This is one of those soups that's even better the next day, when the flavors have had time to marry.

Makes about 4 servings

3 leeks, washed well, with white parts only

1 cup water

2 cups chicken broth

2 large apples of your choice

¼ teaspoon salt, plus more to taste if needed

Pinch white pepper, plus more to taste if needed

½ cup half and half

Roughly chop the leeks, making sure that all sand is washed away. If necessary, wash again in a strainer under running water.

Pour the water and broth into a large pot set over medium heat. Add the leeks and bring to a simmer. Peel and core the apples and chop roughly. Add the pieces to the pot as you go, so they don't brown. Simmer for about 20 minutes, or until the leeks and apples are softened.

Remove from the heat and purée in the pot with an immersion blender. Season with salt and pepper, add the half and half, and stir to blend. Taste and adjust the salt and pepper if needed. If you are serving right away, you can return the soup to the heat for a few minutes to heat through, but do not let it boil. If you are serving the next day, cover and refrigerate and reheat before serving.

Peanut Butter and Apple Sandwich

Try a tasty twist on traditional peanut butter and jelly, with added nutrition as a bonus. Peanut butter and jelly sandwiches are a matter of personal taste, so the proportions given in this recipe are flexible.

Makes 2 sandwiches

4 slices good-quality whole grain bread

2 to 3 tablespoons peanut butter, or to taste

2 to 4 tablespoons chopped dried apples (see Dried Apples, page 323, or use store-bought)

2 tablespoons bottled apple jelly, or to taste

Spread 2 of the slices of bread with peanut butter. Divide the apples evenly between them, pressing lightly so the apple chunks stick to the peanut butter.

Spread the other 2 slices of bread with the jelly and place them on top of the apples, jelly side in. Slice in half and serve.

Apple Cosmopolitan

Apple slices, apple brandy, and apple juice play nicely with vodka and other juices to make a sophisticated cocktail.

Makes 2 cocktails

2 ounces white cranberry juice

2 ounces apple juice

1 ounce fresh lime juice

4 ounces vodka

1 ounce Calvados or other apple brandy

Apple slices dipped in apple juice, for garnish

Mix the cranberry, apple, lime juices, vodka, and Calvados in a shaker with ice.

Pour into 2 martini glasses and garnish with the apple slices.

Spiced Apple and Fig Chutney

This expertly-spiced chutney is from **Chef Deborah Shum**, who suggests serving the condiment warm with roasted pork chops, wilted Swiss chard, and sweet potato puree. Extra chutney can be refrigerated for up to 2 weeks.

Makes about 3 cups

Spices

1 cinnamon stick
3 cardamom pods
1 star anise
6 cloves
6 allspice berries
15 black peppercorns
1 bay leaf

1 shallot, minced
1 sprig of thyme, leaves removed and stem discarded

1 teaspoon salt
1 tablespoon olive oil
3 tart apples, such as Granny Smith, peeled, cored, and finely diced
½ cup finely diced dried mission figs
½ cup golden raisins
¼ cup minced fresh ginger
2 cloves garlic, finely grated
Zest of 1 orange
½ cup light brown sugar, packed
½ cup champagne or apple cider vinegar
½ cup port
3 tablespoons fresh lemon juice

Tie the spices together in cheesecloth.

In a heavy saucepan set over medium heat, sauté the shallot and thyme with salt in olive oil. Stir until the shallots begin to brown.

Add the remaining ingredients. Simmer until the apples are tender and juices are reduced, about 10 to 15 minutes.

If the mixture seems runny, strain the fruit and set aside. Reduce the liquid until it is almost syrupy.

Return the fruit to the pan and discard the spice sachet.

Adjust seasoning to taste. The chutney should be a nice balance of sweet, sour, and spicy.

Chef Deborah Shum

SPECIAL EVENTS CHEF AT: Hotel Tabard Inn, Washington, D.C.

NOTABLE FOR: Graduated with honors from L'Academie de Cuisine

SPECIALTY: Boutique catering, New American cuisine

February 5
Apple and Potato Pierogies

Light and savory, these pierogies are a great way to use up leftover mashed potatoes.

Makes 24 large pierogies or 36 mini pierogies

Dough

2 cups all-purpose flour
1 teaspoon salt
1 large egg, lightly beaten
½ cup warm water
2 tablespoons olive oil

Filling

1 tablespoon olive oil
1 medium sweet onion, diced
2 garlic cloves, minced
½ cup prepared mashed potatoes or 1 Yukon Gold potato, peeled and diced
½ cup chicken or vegetable stock
2 tart apples, such as Granny Smith, shredded
½ teaspoon salt
½ teaspoon freshly ground black pepper

Finishings and Toppings

¼ cup butter or extra virgin oil (optional)
Salt, to taste
Freshly ground black pepper, to taste
Applesauce (see page 17, or use store-bought)
Sour cream
Chopped parsley

To make the dough, mix the dry ingredients in a large bowl. In a small bowl, mix the wet ingredients until just combined. Add wet ingredients into dry and mix with a fork until the dough just comes together. Knead dough in bowl until smooth, about 30 turns. Cover and let rest 30 minutes. While the dough rests, bring a 5-quart pot filled with water to a rolling boil.

To make the filling, heat 1 tablespoon olive oil in a large nonstick sauté pan set over medium heat. Add the onion and garlic and sauté 5 minutes.

If not using prepared mashed potatoes, add the diced Yukon Gold potato and broth to the onions. Cook over medium heat 10 minutes, or until the potatoes are tender and the broth has evaporated. Mash with the back of a spoon and set aside. If using the prepared mashed potatoes, add them to the onions and mix together. In a medium bowl, combine the potato-onion mixture, shredded apples, salt, and pepper.

Once the dough has rested, roll it out on a lightly floured surface to ⅛-inch thickness. Using a 6-inch biscuit cutter for large pierogies, 4-inch biscuit cutter for mini pierogies, or a floured glass, cut circles out of dough. Reroll one time but not more, as the dough will toughen.

Place 1 tablespoon of filling on each large dough circle (or 1 teaspoon on each small circle) off-center and fold the circle in half over the filling. Pinch to seal the pierogies.

Boil the pierogies for 5 minutes, or until they begin to float.

You may serve the pierogies boiled, or, for a bit of crunchy crust, you can pan-fry them after boiling: Heat a large nonstick sauté pan over high heat with the butter or olive oil, salt, and pepper. Add the boiled pierogies and sauté 3 minutes, or until lightly browned and crispy. Serve with applesauce, sour cream, and chopped parsley.

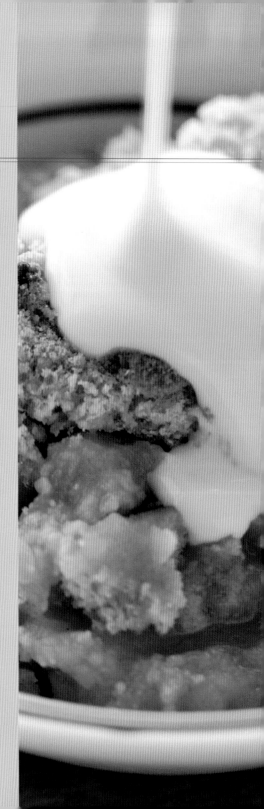

February 6

Apple Crisp with Apple Crème Anglaise

This homey, satisfying dessert is easy to prepare.
Crème anglaise is a lovely finishing touch,
but the crisp is also delicious on its own.

Makes 4 servings

¼ cup cold unsalted butter, plus more for greasing

¾ cup all-purpose flour

¾ cup plus 2 tablespoons granulated sugar

½ teaspoon ground cinnamon

¼ teaspoon salt

3 or 4 large sweet-tart apples such as Gala or Fuji

1 teaspoon cornstarch

1 recipe Apple Crème Anglaise (see page 47, optional)

Preheat the oven to 375° F. Butter a baking dish or 4 ramekins.

Mix the flour, ¾ cup sugar, the cinnamon, and salt in a bowl. Cut in the chilled ¼ cup butter and mix with your fingertips until coarse crumbs form.

Core and peel the apples and cut into ½-inch chunks. In a separate bowl, mix them with the remaining 2 tablespoons sugar and the cornstarch. Pour the apples into the prepared baking dish or ramekins and even out the surface with a spatula. Top with the crumbs.

Bake for 50 to 55 minutes, or until the crumbs have baked into a golden brown crust.

Meanwhile, make the crème anglaise as directed on the next page. When the crisp is done, drizzle with crème anglaise and serve warm.

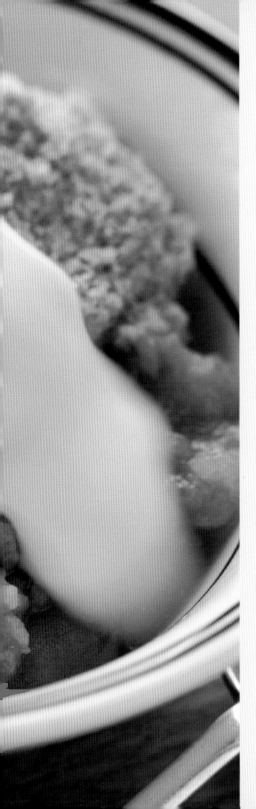

Apple Crème Anglaise

Apple juice and Calvados give an apple-y twist to this classic French dessert sauce. Crème anglaise is delicious on apple crisps, pies or tarts, poached or stewed fruits, and a host of other desserts.

Makes about ½ quart

2 to 3 ounces defrosted, but not diluted, apple juice concentrate

3 tablespoons granulated sugar

6 tablespoons whole milk

¾ cup heavy cream

2 egg yolks

1 tablespoon Calvados

Bring the juice concentrate, 1 tablespoon sugar, the milk, and ¼ cup cream to a simmer in a saucepan set over medium-high heat. Remove from the heat. Beat the yolks and 2 tablespoons sugar in a bowl, then slowly whisk in ½ cup or so of the hot cream mixture.

Pour the yolk-milk mixture slowly back into the pot, whisking to combine. Cook over medium heat, stirring, for 2 to 3 minutes, or until the mixture thickens. Do not let it simmer or boil. Remove the pan from the heat and add ½ cup heavy cream. Stir in the Calvados. Strain the mixture over another bowl.

Prepare an ice bath (a bowl of ice water just big enough to hold the bowl containing the mixture without letting any water touch the sauce). Chill the mixture in the ice bath. Serve, or cover and refrigerate until serving. The sauce will keep in the fridge for 4 days or in the freezer for up to 2 weeks.

Apple and Dried Fruit Chutney

Spice up a roast pork or turkey dinner with this cinnamon-and-coriander-infused chutney.

Makes about 3 cups

1½ cups dry red wine

⅓ cup granulated sugar

1 tablespoon fresh lemon juice

1 cinnamon stick

1½ teaspoons coriander seeds

1½ teaspoons black peppercorns

½ cup dried cherries

⅓ cup coarsely chopped dried pears

⅓ cup coarsely chopped dried figs

¼ cup golden raisins

1½ tablespoons minced crystallized ginger

2 small apples, such as Fuji or Pink Lady, cored and cut into ½-inch dice

1 Navel orange, peeled, white pith removed, and segmented

Combine the first six ingredients in a 4-quart non-reactive saucepan set over high heat. Bring to a boil. Reduce the heat and simmer, covered, for 15 minutes. Strain mixture, discarding solids.

Return the liquid to the saucepan. Add the dried cherries, pears, figs, raisins, and ginger. Cover and simmer until the fruits are plump and tender, about 10 minutes. Add the apples and simmer until apples are tender, about 15 minutes.

Cool until lukewarm. Stir in the orange segments. Cover and refrigerate until ready to serve.

Enjoy a Moment!

Enjoy a cup of Hot Buttered Apple Rum by candlelight. Set a votive candle on the top of an apple, tracing the candle's circular outline. Use a sharp knife to cut a circle slightly larger than the candle's rim, but the same depth. Carve out the apple flesh. Dab lemon juice in the hole to keep the apple's interior from browning. Set the candle inside the apple's hole. Place the apple votive on a flame-resistant dish.

February 9

Hot Buttered Apple Rum

Just the thing to warm your bones on a nippy night!

Makes 2 cocktails

⅔ cup boiling water
1 teaspoon granulated sugar, or to taste
4 ounces apple-flavored rum
1 tablespoon unsalted butter, or to taste

Divide the water equally between 2 mugs. Add half the sugar to each and stir to dissolve.

Pour half the rum into each and top each with half the butter. Let the butter melt a bit, then serve.

Glazed Carrots and Apples

The combined sweetness of carrots and apples make this a natural side dish for roasted poultry or pork.

Makes 4 servings

1½ tablespoons butter
2½ cups (⅛ inch thick) carrot rounds (5 or 6 carrots)
½ teaspoon granulated sugar
2 large apples

Melt the butter in a frying pan set over medium heat. Add the carrots, sugar, and enough water to cover. Stir to dissolve the sugar a bit. Simmer, covered, for about 10 minutes.

Meanwhile, peel and core the apples and cut into ⅛-inch wedges. When the carrots have cooked for about 10 minutes and are beginning to soften, add the apples and mix just to incorporate and coat with the buttery water.

Cook, uncovered, for another 10 to 15 minutes, or until the liquid has evaporated and the apples and carrots are soft and coated in a butter-sugar glaze.

Stacked Heart Fruit Salad

Surprise your loved ones with this eye-catching fruit salad. Have a few extra apples and oranges on hand to practice on until you get the hang of cutting the heart shape. The good news is that if you make a mistake, you can eat it up!

Makes 2 stacked fruit salads

2 blood oranges
2 oranges
2 large apples

Peel the oranges. At the orange's widest point near the center, slice horizontally to make 2 or 3 (¼-inch-thick) slices and set them aside. Squeeze the juice from the remaining orange pieces into a bowl.

Slice the apples lengthwise at the center (from the stem down), and submerge in the orange juice to prevent browning. (They make a natural heart shape.) Reserve the 2 or 3 largest slices and eat the rest or reserve for another use.

Remove the apple slices from the juice and reserve the juice. With a sharp knife, cut around 1 apple slice to refine the heart shape. Submerge the cut heart in the juice once more; then remove from the juice and pat dry with paper towels. Place the apple on parchment paper, lightly trace it with pencil and cut it out. Use this as a guide for cutting the rest of the fruit.

Place orange slices on a work surface. Using the parchment as a guide, cut the oranges into heart shapes with kitchen shears, trimming neatly and making sure that none of the bitter pith remains.

Use the parchment guide to cut the remaining apples.

Stack the heart shapes on a salad or dessert plate, using a very flat piece on the bottom (you might have to shave it a bit with a knife) and alternating the apple, orange and blood orange heart shapes.

Chocolate Fondue with Apples

A decadent Valentine's treat. Calvados gives this
chocolate fondue an apple-y, but grown-up flavor.

Makes 4 servings

¼ to ½ cup orange juice

2 large apples or a
  combination of apples
  and other fruits or
  pound cake

2 tablespoons unsalted
  butter

½ cup heavy cream

1 to 2 tablespoons
  Calvados (optional)

6 ounces good-quality
  bittersweet chocolate,
  chopped

Pour the orange juice into a small bowl. Core the apples and cut into bite-sized
chunks and place them into the juice as you work to prevent browning. Toss to
coat and let them soak for about 30 seconds. Remove and drain. If you are using
pound cake or any other fruit, cut it into bite-sized pieces. (If you are using
bananas, they must be dipped into the orange juice as well.)

Combine the butter, cream, and Calvados, if using, in a saucepan set over
medium heat and bring to a simmer. Add the chocolate and continue
simmering, stirring, until the chocolate is melted and the mixture is thoroughly
combined. Reduce the heat if necessary and watch carefully to prevent burning.

Remove from the heat and transfer to a warm serving bowl or a fondue pot if
you have one. Serve with chunks of apple, other fruit, and pound cake.

Apple Brownies

After one bite of these moist, dense apple brownies, you won't miss the chocolate.

Makes 36 brownies

Nonstick vegetable oil spray

1 cup unsalted butter, room temperature

2 cups granulated sugar

2 large eggs, room temperature

½ cup 2 percent milk

1 teaspoon pure vanilla extract

2 cups all-purpose flour

1 teaspoon baking powder

½ teaspoon salt

2 teaspoons ground cinnamon

4 small apples, such as Fuji or Honeycrisp, peeled and diced (about 3 cups)

Preheat the oven to 350° F. Spray a 9- x 13-inch cake pan with nonstick vegetable oil spray.

Cream the butter and sugar with a handheld mixer until fluffy, about 2 minutes. Add the eggs, one at a time, incorporating into the batter after each one. Add the milk and vanilla and stir into the batter.

In a medium bowl, combine the flour, baking powder, salt, and cinnamon. Add dry ingredients to wet and stir to combine. Add the diced apples and mix well.

Spread the thick batter into the pan. Bake for 45 minutes, or until a toothpick comes out clean. Cut into 36 brownies.

Baked Apples with Chocolate and Marshmallows

Baked apples are an easy and nutritious winter dessert. In this recipe,
the apples are filled with chocolate and gooey marshmallows for an extra treat on Valentine's Day.

Makes 4 servings

2 medium apples, such as
   Gala or Honeycrisp, halved
   lengthwise

Ground cinnamon, to taste

8 mini marshmallows

2 ounces semisweet or
   bittersweet chocolate chips,
   coarsely chopped

4 tablespoons unsalted butter

2 tablespoons apple cider

4 large marshmallows

Preheat the oven to 400° F.

Scoop out the seeds of each apple half with a melon baller, creating a hole. Sprinkle the surface with the cinnamon. Fill each apple cavity with 2 mini marshmallows and ¼ of the chocolate. Dice 2 tablespoons of butter and evenly place over the chocolate.

Combine the apple cider and remaining 2 tablespoons butter in a 9- x 13-inch baking dish. Add the 4 apple halves to the dish. Bake for 30 minutes, or until a paring knife inserted into the apples comes out with no resistance.

Remove the apples from the oven and set the oven to broil. Top each cooked apple half with 1 large marshmallow. Broil about 30 seconds, or until golden brown.

Apple and Passion Fruit Smoothie

This tasty, healthful smoothie will chase away winter doldrums.

Makes about 2 servings

1 apple
½ cup passion fruit juice or passion
   fruit juice blend
1½ cups vanilla ice cream
1 cup ice cubes
Granulated sugar to taste, if needed

Peel and core the apple and cut it into chunks. Place them into a food processor, add the juice, and process until smooth. Add the ice cream and ice. Process until the ice is crushed and the mixture is smooth and frothy. Taste and, if necessary, add sugar, 1 tablespoon at a time. Pulse the processor a few times to combine thoroughly.

Curried Chicken Salad with Apples, Grapes, and Almonds

This salad is a delicious way to use up leftover roasted chicken.

Makes 8 servings

¾ cup nonfat plain Greek yogurt

¼ cup low-sodium soy sauce

2 teaspoons curry powder

½ teaspoon sea salt

½ teaspoon freshly ground black pepper

4 boneless, skinless roasted chicken breast halves, diced

1 stalk celery, diced

1 small apple, such as Fuji or Honeycrisp, cored and diced

⅓ cup golden raisins

½ cup seedless red grapes, halved

½ cup toasted sliced almonds

In a large bowl, whisk together the yogurt, soy sauce, curry powder, salt, and pepper. Add the diced chicken, celery, apple, raisins, grapes, and almonds. Toss to coat the salad with the dressing.

Serve room temperature or chilled.

Thai-Style Chicken Curry with Apples

Apples may not be a traditional ingredient in Thai cookery, but that nation's taste for sweet, salty, sour, and spicy-hot flavors all in one dish make them a natural match.

Makes 4 to 6 servings

1 cup uncooked jasmine rice or other long-grain rice

3 tablespoons vegetable oil or more if needed

2 large onions, peeled and cut into bite-sized wedges

4 large shallots, peeled and roughly diced

2 sweet-tart apples such as Fuji or Gala, cored and cut into ½-inch chunks

2 red bell peppers, seeded, pith removed, and cut in thin slices

½ pound long beans or green beans, trimmed and cut into 1-inch pieces

4 skinless, boneless chicken breast halves, cut into bite-sized pieces

3 (14-ounce) cans light or regular coconut milk

1 to 2 tablespoons red curry paste (available in Asian markets and some supermarkets)

1 tablespoon curry powder

3 medium-sized all-purpose potatoes, peeled and cut into bite-sized chunks

2 to 3 tablespoons palm sugar (available in Asian markets) or brown sugar, plus more to taste if needed

6 to 10 fresh basil leaves, thinly sliced

½ tablespoon Asian fish sauce

Prepare the rice according to the package directions. Keep warm. (Remember to rinse and drain it before cooking.)

Meanwhile, heat 1½ tablespoons oil in a wok or skillet set over medium-high heat. Add the onions and shallots and cook for about 5 minutes, stirring, until translucent and soft, but not browned. Transfer to large saucepan or stockpot and set aside.

Add ½ tablespoon oil (or a little more if needed) to the wok, heat for a few seconds, and add the apples, red peppers, and beans. Cook, stirring, for 3 to 5 minutes or until just softened. Transfer to the saucepan with the onions and shallots and set aside.

Add the remaining 1 tablespoon oil to the wok if necessary and then add the chicken. Cook over medium-high heat, stirring, for 3 to 5 minutes, or until the chicken is golden brown. Transfer to the saucepan with the rest of the vegetables.

Reduce the heat to medium and return the wok to the heat. Pour in about 1 cup coconut milk. Add the curry paste and curry powder and slowly bring to a boil, stirring and mashing the paste so that it dissolves and the liquid becomes a rusty golden color. Simmer until droplets of oil appear on the surface. Gradually add 3 cups coconut milk, a cup at a time, and bring it to a boil again. Pour into the chicken mixture and add the potatoes and the remaining coconut milk.

Cook over medium heat for about 30 minutes, or until the potatoes are cooked through and can be pierced easily with the tip of a sharp knife. Stir in the sugar and basil and simmer for about 1 minute. Add the fish sauce and stir once. (More stirring makes fish sauce taste "fishy.") Taste and add more sugar if necessary. Spoon over the rice and serve hot.

Green Papaya and Apple Salad

If you enjoy traditional papaya salads at Thai restaurants, try this version with tart apples.

Makes 4 servings

¼ cup seasoned rice vinegar (available in Asian markets and some supermarkets)

2 teaspoons honey

1 teaspoon Sriracha (available in Asian markets and some supermarkets)

1½ tablespoons fish sauce (available in Asian markets and some supermarkets)

2 tablespoons fresh lime juice

2 cups peeled, seeded, and shredded green papaya

1 tart apple, such as Granny Smith, cored and shredded

1 cup shredded carrots

¼ cup thinly sliced green onions, green and white parts

¼ cup roughly chopped, roasted, salted cashews

In a large bowl, mix the rice vinegar, honey, Sriracha, fish sauce, and lime juice. Add the papaya, apple, carrots, and green onions. Toss to coat salad.

To serve, plate and sprinkle with cashews.

Third Rail, the Remix

The Third Rail, a classic cocktail named for its potency, calls for apple brandy, rum, and absinthe. This version emphasizes the apple theme, with apple rum instead of plain. Who knew an apple could be so electrifying?

Makes 2 cocktails

4 ounces apple-flavored rum
3 ounces Calvados or other apple brandy
¼ ounce absinthe or Pernod

Mix the rum, brandy, and absinthe or Pernod in a shaker with ice.

Strain into 2 short cocktail glasses.

Kasha with Apples

Buckwheat groats, otherwise known as kasha, are a powerhouse of nutrition. Their rich, nutty flavor makes them an excellent foil for apples.

Makes 4 to 6 servings

1½ tablespoons vegetable oil
1 medium onion, chopped
1 large apple
1 cup kasha
2 to 2½ cups vegetable broth
Freshly ground black pepper
¼ teaspoon salt, plus more to taste if needed
2 tablespoons chopped parsley

Heat the oil in a saucepan set over medium-high heat. Add onion and cook, stirring occasionally, for 3 to 4 minutes, or until the onion is soft and translucent but not brown.

Meanwhile, peel and core the apple and chop it into ½-inch chunks. Add to the onions and cook for about 3 minutes or until softened and the tip of a knife pierces the apple without resistance.

Add the kasha and stir gently until it is coated with the oil. Add 2¼ cups of the broth, stir, and bring to a boil. Reduce the heat to medium and simmer for 17 to 20 minutes, or until the liquid is absorbed and the kasha is soft, creamy and cooked through. If all the broth is absorbed and the kasha is not cooked, add a little more broth and continue cooking until softened.

Season with black pepper. Taste and season with salt if necessary. Sprinkle with parsley and serve hot.

President's Day Apple Cherry Buns

Can't tell a lie—the apples and dried cherries make these buns unique, and very tasty.

Makes 15 buns

2¼ teaspoons instant yeast

½ teaspoon honey

¾ cup warm water
(100° F on an
instant-read or candy
thermometer)

1 cup warm whole
milk (100° F on an
instant-read or candy
thermometer)

½ cup unsalted butter, cut
into pieces

½ cup plus 2 tablespoons
granulated sugar

3 large eggs

1 teaspoon kosher salt

1½ teaspoons pure vanilla
extract

5 to 5½ cups unbleached,
all-purpose flour

1 cup dried cherries

2 tablespoons Kirsch (clear
cherry brandy)

1 large apple, such as
Golden Delicious or
McIntosh

Confectioners' sugar, for
dusting

Proof the yeast by dissolving it in a small bowl with the water and honey. Let it sit for 10 minutes or until it bubbles.

Pour the warm milk into a large bowl and let the butter melt in it. Add ½ cup sugar, the eggs, salt, and vanilla and whisk well. Stir in 3 cups flour. With a mixer set at medium speed, beat well for 1 minute. Add 2 to 2½ cups more flour and knead it in to form a soft dough. Knead 4 to 5 minutes with a mixer or 8 minutes by hand, until the dough is smooth and springs back when pressed lightly.

Place the dough in a covered container or a bowl covered tightly with plastic wrap and let rise at room temperature (68° to 70° F) for about 2 hours or until doubled in volume.

Meanwhile, soak the cherries in the Kirsch until they are softened. Drain. Cut the apple into fine dice.

When the dough has risen, press it down and turn it out onto the counter. Flatten it slightly. Sprinkle it with the cherries, apple chunks, and remaining sugar. Press the fruit into the dough and then form the dough into a ball. Cover with greased plastic wrap. Let rest for 20 minutes.

Roll or press the dough into a 15- by 12-inch rectangle. Roll it up into a 15-inch log. Slice the log at 1-inch intervals to make 15 buns.

Place the buns onto parchment-lined baking sheets. Leave 1½ inches between the buns. Cover them loosely with greased plastic wrap. Let rise at room temperature for about 45 minutes, or until doubled in volume.

When you are ready to bake, preheat the oven to 375° F. Position the oven rack in the bottom third of the oven. Bake for 15 to 20 minutes, until well risen and golden. Cool on a rack. Dust with confectioners' sugar.

Apple 'n Prune-Filled Cookies

Crumbly on the outside, gooey on the inside and just plain good all over.

Makes 24 cookies

Dough

2⅓ cup unbleached, all-purpose flour

⅔ cup light brown sugar

⅛ teaspoon kosher salt

1 teaspoon baking powder

¾ cup cold unsalted butter, cut into 1-teaspoon pieces

1 egg

1 teaspoon pure vanilla extract

Filling

¾ cup dried apple, finely chopped

½ cup pitted prunes, finely chopped

2 tablespoons apple juice or water

Icing

1 cup confectioners' sugar

2½ tablespoons milk

To make the dough, combine the flour, brown sugar, salt, and baking powder in a food processor fitted with a metal blade and pulse 4 to 5 times. Add the butter and pulse 10 to 12 times.

Whisk the egg and vanilla in a small bowl. Drizzle the egg mixture over the flour mixture and pulse 6 to 10 times, until the dough just begins to come together. It should not form a ball, but just start to clump. Place the dough onto a large piece of plastic wrap, press it together, and flatten it into a disk. Wrap in the plastic and refrigerate it for 1 hour, up to 1 day, until well chilled.

Preheat the oven to 350° F.

To make the filling, mix the dried apple, prunes, and apple juice or water in a small microwaveable bowl. Microwave on high power for 20 to 30 seconds, until the fruit is soft. Let cool and purée in a small food processor or blender to form a paste that is slightly rough. The mixture should not be completely smooth.

Divide the dough in half. Place half on a piece of parchment paper and roll it out to form a 13- by 4-inch rectangle. Starting ½ inch from the edge and working down the length of the rectangle, spoon 12 small mounds of filling onto the dough at even intervals, using about 1½ teaspoons per mound and leaving about ½ inch of dough on each end. Repeat with the remaining dough and filling.

Fold the dough over the filling lengthwise to form a long strip with the filling encased. Use the parchment to help lift the dough if necessary. Press the edges together to seal. Smooth the edges. Press between the lumps of filling to seal the dough there, too.

You can use the same parchment to line the baking pan. Lift the 2 strips of paper and place the whole thing on a rimmed baking sheet. Bake for 10 to 12 minutes, until lightly golden. Cut the strips between the lumps of filling to separate the individual cookies. Cool completely.

While the cookies are baking, make the icing by mixing the confectioners' sugar and milk until thickened. Drizzle the cooled cookies with the icing.

Apple and Peanut Butter Rice Cake

Whip up this easy and filling snack any time you'd like a crunchy, healthy treat.

Makes 1 serving

¼ cup raisins
2 tablespoons water
½ teaspoon honey
Drop of pure vanilla extract
Pinch of ground cinnamon
¼ apple of your choice, thinly sliced
1 tablespoon crunchy peanut butter
1 rice cake

Combine the raisins, water, honey, vanilla extract, cinnamon, and apple slices in a bowl and microwave 1 minute on high power. Remove from the microwave, stir the peanut butter into the apples, and mix well. Spread the peanut butter mixture onto the rice cake.

February 24

Apple Cinnamon Tortilla Chips

Serve these chips with a fruit-based salsa or applesauce.

Makes about 4 cups

1 cup dehydrated apple chips
1½ teaspoons ground cinnamon
4½ tablespoons granulated sugar
2 tablespoons butter, melted
10 medium whole-wheat flour tortillas

Preheat the oven to 415° F. Place the apple chips in a food processor and pulse until powdered. Add the cinnamon and sugar and pulse to combine. Transfer to a small bowl.

Brush the melted butter onto both sides of each tortilla, then sprinkle with some of the apple-cinnamon-sugar mixture. Repeat with all tortillas.

Use a pizza cutter to cut the tortillas into 8 wedges.

Place the chips in a single layer on a greased cookie sheet and bake for 5 to 8 minutes, or until the tops are golden brown.

Let cool completely before serving.

Vietnamese Spring Roll with Chicken and Apples

Apples add a nice fresh crunch to these spring rolls, replacing daikon or lettuce.
They also lend a sweetness that beautifully balances the salty ingredients.

Makes 8 rolls

Dipping Sauce

3 tablespoons fish sauce

1 tablespoon soy sauce

1 tablespoon sesame oil

Juice of 1 lime

1 clove garlic, very finely chopped

Spring Rolls

3 to 4 tablespoons hoisin sauce

Juice of 1 lime

About 2 ounces noodles (rice sticks or vermicelli)

12 to 16 fresh chopped basil leaves

¼ cup unsalted chopped peanuts (optional)

8 (8¾-inch) spring roll wrappers (available in Asian markets and some supermarkets), plus more in case of breakage

1 cup shredded cooked chicken, skin and bones removed

1 large apple, peeled, cored and cut into matchstick sized pieces

¼ cup shredded carrot

To make the dipping sauce, combine the fish sauce, soy sauce, sesame oil, lime juice, and garlic in a small bowl, and set aside until ready to serve. (If you like, you can strain out the garlic just before serving.)

Mix the hoisin and lime juice in a mixing bowl. Boil the rice noodles in a large pot of water for about 5 minutes, or until soft. Transfer to a strainer, drain, and rinse under cold running water to stop the cooking process. Add the noodles to the hoisin mixture and toss to coat well. Add the basil and peanuts, if using, and toss gently.

Position a large bowl of warm water near a work surface. Dip 1 spring roll wrapper into the water and let it soften. Hold the wrapper with one hand on either side, lift it out of the water, let it open into a circle, and drain. Place it on the work surface and smooth out any large wrinkles. If a wrapper develops large holes, discard and start over.

To fill, place about 2 tablespoons of the chicken near the side of the circle closest to you, leaving a 1-inch edge. Top with about ⅛ of the apple, ⅛ of the carrot and ⅛ of the noodles. Fold the edge over the filling as tightly as you can, fold the sides in over the filling, and then roll up the spring roll. The wet wrapper will seal itself. Repeat with the remaining wrappers and filling. Serve with dipping sauce.

Asian-Spiced Apples and Pears

Piquant spices give apples and pears a makeover. A tantalizing accompaniment for pork or turkey.

Makes 4 servings

2 teaspoons candied ginger, minced

1 tablespoon Poire Williams

2 large Golden Delicious apples, peeled, cored, and sliced

3 large pears, peeled, cored, and sliced

½ cup brown sugar

½ teaspoon ground star anise or 1 whole star anise, pulverized in a mortar and pestle

2 tablespoons quick tapioca

1 to 2 tablespoons unsalted butter, cut into small pieces

Preheat the oven to 350° F. Soak the ginger in the Poire Williams for about 10 minutes.

Arrange the apples and pears in a baking dish. Add the ginger and sprinkle with the brown sugar, star anise, and tapioca. Toss to mix well. Dot with butter. Bake for about 30 minutes, or until the fruit is tender and the juices are bubbly.

Trail Mix with Dried Apples and Cherries

This snack is perfect any time you're in the mood for a sweet and salty treat, on or off the trail.

Makes about 3 cups

1½ cups raw mixed nuts (almonds, pecans, hazelnuts, cashews, walnuts), roughly chopped

½ cup raw pumpkin seeds

½ cup raw sunflower seeds

1 tablespoon coconut oil

1 tablespoon pure vanilla extract

¼ teaspoon ground cinnamon

¼ teaspoon grated nutmeg

1 teaspoon sea salt

¼ cup honey

¼ cup dried apples, roughly chopped

½ cup dried cherries

Preheat the oven to 350° F. Line a large baking sheet with parchment paper.

In a large bowl, combine the nuts, seeds, coconut oil, vanilla, cinnamon, and nutmeg. Spread on the prepared baking sheet and sprinkle with ½ teaspoon of the salt.

Toast in the oven 2 to 5 minutes, stirring occasionally. Watch to make sure the nuts and seeds don't burn.

Remove the baking sheet from the oven and let cool, about 10 minutes. Add the remaining salt and drizzle with the honey. Toast for an additional 5 minutes, stirring often.

Remove from the oven and transfer to a large bowl. Mix in the chopped apples and cherries; allow to cool completely.

Baked Oatmeal with Apples and Walnuts

If you've never tried baked oatmeal, make this one. It's both creamy and filling on a cold winter morning.

Makes 10 servings

Nonstick vegetable
 oil spray

4 cups milk

½ cup light brown sugar

1 tablespoon butter

½ teaspoon salt

½ teaspoon ground
 cinnamon

2 cups apples, such as
 Fuji, Pink Lady, or
 Honeycrisp, cored
 and diced

1 cup chopped toasted
 walnuts

1 cup dried cherries

3 cups old-fashioned
 rolled oats

Preheat the oven to 350° F. Spray a 2-quart casserole dish with nonstick vegetable oil spray.

In a 3-quart saucepan set over medium heat, combine the milk, brown sugar, butter, salt, and cinnamon. Bring to a simmer. Add the remaining ingredients and stir to combine.

Spoon the oatmeal mixture into the prepared casserole dish. Cover and bake for 45 minutes.

Apple Empanadas

These empanadas, while time consuming, are well worth the effort. If you don't have the time or inclination to make the filling, you can substitute your favorite applesauce, or use the recipe on page 17.

Makes about 12 empanadas

Pastry

2 cups all-purpose flour

1 tablespoon granulated sugar

½ teaspoon salt

1 cup unsalted butter, cold, cut into 1-tablespoon pieces

8 ounces cream cheese, chilled, cut into ½-inch pieces

1 teaspoon pure vanilla extract

Filling

5 Granny Smith apples, peeled, cored, and diced

2 tablespoons unsalted butter

½ cup granulated sugar

¼ cup light brown sugar

2 teaspoons ground cinnamon

1 teaspoon nutmeg

Pinch salt

1 tablespoon cornstarch

2 tablespoons cold water

Finishings

1 egg yolk

2 tablespoons water

Granulated sugar, for sprinkling

To make the pastry dough, combine the flour, sugar, and salt in a food processor bowl. Pulse to mix. Add the butter and pulse several times. Add the cream cheese and pulse until the mixture starts to come together. Add the vanilla and pulse twice more. Gently knead the dough three or four times on a floured surface. Then shape the dough into a disk, place in a plastic bag, and chill for 30 minutes to 1 hour.

To make the filling, combine the diced apples, butter, sugar, brown sugar, cinnamon, nutmeg, and salt in a 2-quart saucepan set over medium heat and cook until the apples are just tender, about 5 to 7 minutes. In a small bowl, combine the cornstarch and cold water and stir until smooth. Add the cornstarch mixture to the apples and cook, stirring, until mixture starts to thicken. Remove the apples from the heat and chill for one hour.

To make the empanadas, cut the dough in half. On a floured surface roll each batch into a rectangle about ¼- to ⅛-inch thick. Cut the rectangles into 5-inch squares. Place 1 tablespoon of filling in the middle of each square. Fold each square in half, forming a triangle, and pinch the edges together to firmly seal. Crimp the flattened edge with the tines of a fork. Mix the egg yolk with 2 tablespoons water to make an egg wash and brush the tops of the empanadas. Sprinkle with sugar.

When you are ready to bake, preheat the oven to 350° F. Place the empanadas on 2 parchment-lined baking sheets. Bake until puffed and golden brown, about 15 to 20 minutes. Serve warm from the oven.

March 2

Carrot Applesauce Muffins

A moist, luscious muffin made with nutritious carrots and applesauce.

Makes 12 muffins

1½ cups all-purpose flour

1½ teaspoons baking powder

½ teaspoon baking soda

1¼ teaspoons ground cinnamon

⅛ teaspoon ground cloves

½ teaspoon ground allspice

¼ teaspoon freshly grated nutmeg

¼ teaspoon salt

2 large eggs, beaten

1 cup light brown sugar, packed

½ cup vegetable oil

1 cup unsweetened applesauce

1 cup finely grated carrot

2 tablespoons granulated sugar

Preheat the oven to 375° F. Line a 12-cup muffin tin with paper liners or grease well with unsalted butter.

Mix the flour, baking powder, baking soda, ¾ teaspoon cinnamon, cloves, allspice, nutmeg and salt in a large bowl.

In another bowl, combine the eggs, brown sugar and oil and beat until well blended. Add the applesauce and carrot and mix just until blended.

Scoop the batter into the muffin tin, filling each cup almost to the top. Mix the sugar and remaining ½ teaspoon cinnamon and sprinkle over the tops.

Bake for 17 to 20 minutes, until the muffins are lightly browned, the tops spring back when pressed gently, and a toothpick inserted into the center of a muffin comes out with just a few moist crumbs.

Apple Art!

Go shopping for apples with an adorable apple tote. Pick a solid-colored tote sack. First insert cardboard inside the tote to keep the paint from bleeding through. Slice an apple in half. Brush fabric paint onto the half with the stem. Press the painted apple and stem onto the sack. Repeat to make a pattern, alternating colors, if you wish. Allow the paint to dry completely. Set a clean cloth atop the tote and heat-set the paint by pressing it with an iron.

Stewed Dried Apples

This versatile compote can be served many ways—as a topping for vanilla ice cream, stirred into oatmeal, or as an accompaniment to pork tenderloin or roasted game hens.

Makes approximately 2½ cups

1½ cups dried apples
½ cup raisins
1½ cups orange juice
½ cup water
⅓ cup light brown sugar
2 cinnamon sticks
2 tablespoons chopped toasted walnuts
2 teaspoons pure vanilla extract

In a 3-quart saucepan, combine the first six ingredients. Set pan on medium-high heat, stirring constantly until the sugar is dissolved.

Reduce the heat to medium and cook, stirring occasionally, for 15 minutes, or until the fruit is plump and softened and the liquid is reduced to a syrup.

Remove from heat and discard the cinnamon sticks. Stir in the walnuts and vanilla.

Mushroom and Apple Soup

The flavors of forest and orchard meld in this soul-warming soup.

Makes 4 to 6 servings

1 tablespoon vegetable oil

1 tablespoon unsalted butter

1 clove garlic, finely minced

2 (10-ounce) packages white mushrooms, brushed and sliced

1 sweet-tart apple, such as Gala or Fuji

3 cups vegetable broth

1 (12-ounce) can evaporated milk

½ teaspoon salt, plus more to taste if needed

Freshly ground black pepper, to taste

2 tablespoons chopped fresh parsley

Heat the oil and butter in a large saucepan set over medium-high heat until the butter is melted and the oil ripples. Add the garlic and cook, stirring, for about 30 seconds or until softened.

Reduce the heat to medium, add the mushrooms and cook, stirring frequently, for about 3 minutes, or until their liquid is released and evaporated. Meanwhile, peel and core the apple and cut it into large chunks. When the mushroom pan is almost dry, add the apples and stir to coat. Cook, stirring occasionally, for 3 minutes, or until the apples begin to soften.

Add the broth and cook, stirring occasionally, until the apples are very soft. Add the milk, season with salt and pepper, and stir to combine. Remove the soup from the heat, let cool a bit, and use an immersion blender to puree, leaving some chunks of apple and mushroom whole. Divide among soup bowls and garnish with parsley.

Sweet Green Juice

Make this refreshing and
nourishing juice whenever you
want a quick pick-me-up.

Makes 4 servings

6 stalks organic kale
6 stalks organic Swiss chard
1 large bunch parsley
12 stalks celery
4 Fuji apples, cored and cut into chunks

Wash the vegetables and apples well.
Add to juicer in the order listed
above. Strain the foam off the top,
pour into tall glasses, and enjoy.

Kiwi Apple Smoothie

Smoothies can accommodate all kinds of ingredients, and this one proves the point. Kiwi, apple, and vanilla ice cream come together to make a satisfying drink.

Makes 2 servings

2 kiwis, peeled

1 apple of your choice

2 cups vanilla ice cream

1 cup ice cubes

2 tablespoons granulated sugar, or to taste

Cut 2 slices off one of the kiwis and reserve for garnish. Cut the rest into rough chunks. Peel and core the apple and cut it into about 8 pieces. Place the apple and kiwi into a food processor or blender and process until smooth. Add the ice cream, ice, and sugar. Process until the ice is crushed and the mixture is smooth and frothy. Taste and add more sugar if necessary, 1 tablespoon at a time. Pulse the processor to combine. Pour into glasses and garnish with the reserved kiwi slices.

Sautéed Chicken with Savory Cider Gravy

This simple but tasty chicken dish gets a little extra zip from the apple cider in the sauce. And no, the sauce is not sweet; the cider melds with the other ingredients to make a savory, satisfying sauce.

Makes 4 servings

¼ cup all-purpose flour

½ teaspoon salt

1½ pounds chicken tenders or skinless, boneless chicken breast cut into 1-inch-thick strips

1 tablespoon olive oil

1½ tablespoons unsalted butter

1 clove garlic, chopped

1 recipe Savory Apple Cider Gravy (see page 75)

1 tablespoon chopped parsley, for garnish

Pour the flour and salt into a shallow bowl and stir. Remove any tough white membrane from the chicken with a sharp knife. Dip the chicken into the flour, turn to coat, and tap off any excess.

Heat the oil and butter in a large skillet set over medium-high heat until the butter is melted and the oil is hot. Carefully add the garlic and cook, stirring, for 30 seconds, or until golden. Place the chicken into the pan in a single layer, working in batches if necessary. Cook, turning occasionally, for 6 or 7 minutes, or until an instant-read thermometer inserted into the chicken reads 165° F. Reduce the heat if necessary so the chicken does not burn. Remove the cooked chicken to a platter.

Make the sauce as directed on the next page, using the same pan you've used for the chicken. (Don't wash it – the flavor left in the pan will improve the sauce.)

Return the chicken to the pan, turn gently to coat with the sauce, and cook for 1 to 2 minutes or until cooked through. To serve, transfer the chicken to serving plates, drizzle with the sauce and sprinkle with parsley.

Savory Apple Cider Gravy

This quick and easy gravy is delicious on chicken, turkey, or pork. If you are sautéing your meat, make the sauce in the same pan after you cook the meat; the sauce will pick up the flavors left in the pan.

Makes about 2 cups

1½ tablespoons butter
3 tablespoons all-purpose flour
1 cup apple cider
2 cups chicken broth

Melt the butter in a skillet set over medium-high heat. Add the flour and stir continually until the flour is completely incorporated into the butter and the consistency is pasty.

Add the cider and stir, scraping up any bits from the bottom of the pan with a wooden spoon. Cook for 30 seconds to 1 minute, or until the sauce has thickened enough for you to draw a line in it with a spoon. Add the chicken broth, reduce the heat to medium, and cook, stirring occasionally, for about 5 minutes, or until the sauce takes on a thick, velvety consistency.

Black Trumpet Mushroom Pudding with Roasted Apple Puree and Cured Venison

If a special occasion is in the works, why not make it extra special? **Chef Scott Anderson's** deluxe dish involves careful preparation and timing, but the results are well worth the effort. Your guests will be raving about this extraordinary meal for months to come.

Makes 6 servings

Cured Venison

1 venison loin
1 cup salt
½ cup freshly ground pepper

Dehydrated Apple Cubes

½ cup granulated sugar
½ cup water
1 apple of your choice

Apple Puree

6 Granny Smith apples
2 tablespoons butter
3 whole cloves
1 tablespoon ground allspice

Black Trumpet Mushroom Pudding

1 (8-ounce) box medium tapioca pearls
2 cups apple cider
4 cloves garlic
1 onion
8 tablespoons butter
1 pound black trumpet mushrooms
Chervil and fennel fronds, for garnish

Two weeks before you intend to serve the dish, cure the venison by seasoning it liberally with the salt and pepper. Store, uncovered, in the refrigerator for 2 weeks to allow the venison to cure.

The day before you intend to serve the dish, preheat the oven to its lowest setting.

Make a simple syrup by combining the sugar and water in a saucepan and bringing the liquid to a boil, stirring to dissolve the sugar. Cut the apple into medium dice and cook it in the boiling syrup for 2 minutes. Drain; spread the apple cubes on a baking sheet and cook until the apples are 90 percent dehydrated, about 2 to 3 hours.

Two hours before you intend to serve the dish, preheat the oven to 250° F. Core and peel the Granny Smith apples and place them in a roasting pan. Add the butter, cloves, allspice, and a scant amount of water to the pan. Cook until the apples are very soft, about 90 minutes. Set aside to cool.

Meanwhile, using apple cider in place of milk, cook the tapioca according to the directions on the package.

In a large heavy skillet, saute the garlic and onion in the butter until translucent. Add the mushrooms and stir to combine. Cook for 10 minutes and let cool slightly. Puree in a blender.

Right before you are ready to serve, wipe the seasonings off the venison loin and cut the meat into paper-thin slices. Puree the cooled roasted apples in a blender.

Mix the mushroom puree into the tapioca and transfer to a large serving platter. Ladle the apple puree over the pudding. Garnish the dish with the dehydrated apple cubes and the chervil and fennel fronds. Arrange slices of the cured venison on top and serve.

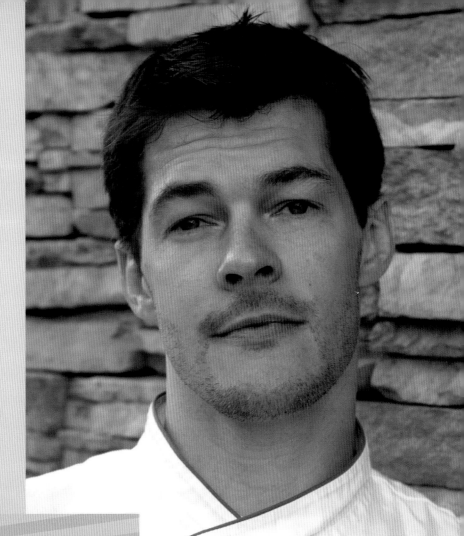

Chef Scott Anderson

CHEF/OWNER AT: elements, Princeton, New Jersey

BELIEVES IN: Sourcing fresh, local, organic ingredients and sustainably raised meats and seafood

RISING STAR: One of *Esquire* magazine's Best New Chefs of 2011

Apple Bran Muffins

Packed with goodness, these muffins make a filling and energizing breakfast for busy people. Grab one on your way out the door.

Makes 12 muffins

Nonstick vegetable oil spray

1 cup milk

½ teaspoon lemon juice

½ teaspoon apple-cider vinegar

1½ cups bran cereal, such as All-Bran

1 cup whole-wheat flour

½ cup old-fashioned rolled oats

½ cup flaxseed meal

2 teaspoons baking powder

1 teaspoon baking soda

¼ teaspoon salt

2 teaspoons ground cinnamon

¼ teaspoon grated nutmeg

1 tablespoon cornstarch

½ cup applesauce (see page 17, or use store-bought)

2 tablespoons light brown sugar

1 teaspoon pure vanilla extract

2 tablespoons vegetable oil

½ cup raisins

1 small apple, such as Fuji, cored and diced

Preheat the oven to 350° F. Spray a 12-cup muffin tray with nonstick vegetable oil spray or line with muffin liners.

In a small mixing bowl, combine the milk, lemon juice, and vinegar. Set aside to allow the milk to curdle.

In a large mixing bowl, whisk the bran cereal, flour, rolled oats, flaxseed, baking powder, baking soda, salt, cinnamon, nutmeg, and cornstarch.

Add the applesauce, brown sugar, vanilla, and oil to the curdled milk. Pour the wet ingredients into the dry ingredients and mix just to combine. Fold in the raisins and diced apple.

Spoon the mixture into the prepared muffin tray, filling each cup to the top. Bake 18 to 20 minutes, or until a toothpick inserted into the center of a muffin comes out clean.

Core Fact:

Many people don't know that the apple muffin is actually the State Muffin of New York! The official recipe, which was adopted in 1987, was actually developed by children in a Syracuse elementary school.

Flatbread Crackers with Sliced Apples and Brie

For this simple snack, use your favorite cracker or crispbread. Feel free to trade out the Brie for another soft cheese, such as Camembert or Paglietta.

Makes 1 serving

½ apple, such as Honeycrisp, cored and thinly sliced

1 teaspoon fresh lemon juice

2 large flatbread crackers or crispbread

1 ounce Brie, thinly sliced

Pinch sea salt

Dip the apple slices in the lemon juice to prevent browning.

Place the crackers or crispbread on a plate. Arrange the slices of Brie on each cracker. Top with the apple slices. Sprinkle with sea salt and serve immediately.

Banana Apple Swirl Loaf

This is a great use for overripe bananas; in fact, it's best if the banana is covered with brown spots, not just a few speckles. If your bananas ripen when you don't have time to bake, freeze them until you do.

Makes 1 (8½- by 4½-inch) loaf cake

Unsalted butter, for greasing

2 large, very ripe bananas, peeled and broken up

1 large apple, peeled, cored, and diced

1 cup plus 2 tablespoons granulated sugar

1 cup chopped walnuts

1¾ cup unbleached all-purpose flour

¾ teaspoon baking soda

½ teaspoon salt

5 tablespoons sour cream

2 large eggs

1 teaspoon pure vanilla extract

Preheat the oven to 350° F. Place the oven rack in the center position. Grease an 8½- by 4½-inch pan with butter and line the bottom with parchment.

In a bowl, covered but vented, microwave the bananas on high power for 3 minute if frozen, or 1 minutes if fresh. Mash the bananas into a very soft paste and drain them over a bowl to catch the juices.

Bring the banana juices to a simmer in a small sauté pan set over medium-high heat. Add the apple and 1 tablespoon sugar and cook, stirring occasionally, for about 3 minutes, or until the juices are reduced and the apples are caramelized. Add the walnuts. Stir for 1 to 2 minutes, or until all the liquid is absorbed, and the mixture is beginning to caramelize. Set aside to cool.

In a large bowl, whisk the flour, baking soda, and salt. In a separate bowl, whisk together ½ cup plus 1 tablespoon sugar, the sour cream, eggs, vanilla, and the mashed bananas. Add the wet ingredients to the dry and stir just to combine. The batter may appear curdled before it is fully mixed. Do not over mix. If it looks lumpy, that's okay.

Scoop ⅓ of the batter into the prepared pan and smooth it to an even layer. Top with half the apple mixture. Top that with ⅓ of the batter and smooth again, covering the apple layer completely. Top with the remaining apple mixture and finish with the last of the batter. Smooth the top. Bake for 1 hour. Let rest in the pan 3 to 5 minutes and carefully turn out onto a rack to cool completely. Serve warm or at room temperature, plain or with sweet butter or cream cheese.

Baked Apples with Blackberry Jam and Crisp Topping

These baked apples taste delicious as is, or with vanilla ice cream and a dollop of whipped cream.

Makes 4 servings

2 tablespoons all-purpose flour

3 tablespoons cold unsalted butter, diced

3 tablespoons light brown sugar

½ cup old-fashioned rolled oats

¼ teaspoon ground cinnamon

Pinch salt

2 apples, such as Fuji or McIntosh, halved lengthwise

4 tablespoons blackberry jam or preserves

Preheat the oven to 350° F.

To make the topping, combine the flour, butter, brown sugar, rolled oats, cinnamon, and salt in a small bowl. Set aside.

Scoop out the seeds of each apple half with a melon baller, creating a hole. Place 1 tablespoon blackberry jam into each cavity.

Press some of the topping mixture on top of each apple, covering jam.

Place the filled apples into a 9- x 13-inch baking dish filled with about ¼ inch of water. Bake until tops are golden brown and the apples are tender, about 35 to 40 minutes.

Chocolate-Caramel Apple Slices

Sweet, gooey, and crunchy, these apples will satisfy any dessert lover's cravings.

Makes 4 servings

Juice of 1 lemon

2 apples of your choice, cored and sliced into 8 wedges each

18 pieces soft caramel candy

1 ounce semi-sweet chocolate chips

½ cup chopped honey-roasted peanuts

16 toothpicks

Fill a large bowl with cold water and mix in the lemon juice. Soak the apple slices in the lemon water while you prepare the caramel-chocolate mixture.

In a double boiler or a bowl set over a saucepan of simmering water (the water should not touch the bowl or the double boiler), combine the caramels and chocolate. Stir until melted; turn off the heat but keep the mixture over the hot water so that it remains soft.

Dry the apple slices on paper towels and skewer each one with a toothpick. Place the slices on wax paper and drizzle with the melted caramel-chocolate mixture. Sprinkle with the crushed peanuts and serve.

Chicken and Apple Caesar Salad Wrap

This is a quick and easy-to-prepare lunch or dinner.

Makes 2 servings

2 boneless, skinless chicken breasts, roasted and cut into strips

Salt

Freshly ground pepper

3 cups romaine lettuce, shredded

1 Granny Smith apple, cored and shredded

2 tomatoes, diced

¼ cup Caesar salad dressing

2 large whole-wheat tortillas

¼ cup grated Parmesan cheese

Place the chicken strips in a medium-size bowl and season with salt and pepper to taste. Add the lettuce, apple, tomatoes, and dressing to the seasoned chicken. Toss to combine.

Divide the filling evenly between the two tortillas. Sprinkle the Parmesan cheese on top.

Roll up the tortillas and cut them in half diagonally. Serve with additional Caesar salad dressing, if desired.

Apple Irish Soda Bread

Enjoy this delectable bread straight from the oven. Serve with plenty of butter and extra maple syrup, if desired.

Makes 16 servings

1 tart apple, such as Braeburn, peeled, cored, and chopped

2 tablespoons unsalted butter

1 teaspoon ground cinnamon

1½ cups all-purpose flour

1 teaspoon baking soda

1 teaspoon salt

2 tablespoons pure maple syrup

½ to 1 cup buttermilk

½ cup raisins

1 cup dried currants

2 tablespoons caraway seeds

Preheat the oven to 350° F. Grease and flour a 9-inch loaf pan.

Place the chopped apple, butter, and cinnamon in a 2-quart saucepan. Cover and cook for 10 to 15 minutes, or until mushy.

In a large bowl, mix together the flour, baking soda, and salt. Stir in the apple mixture, maple syrup, currants, and caraway seeds.

Starting with ½ cup buttermilk, slowly add enough buttermilk to form a soft but easily handled dough. Add a little more of the buttermilk if needed. Mix in the raisins.

Dust your hands with flour and lightly knead the dough until it barely comes together. Don't overknead or the bread will end up tough. Transfer the dough to the prepared cake pan and cut a deep cross in the top. (Scoring the dough lets the heat get to the center of the dough as it cooks.) Bake for 30 to 40 minutes, or until a toothpick inserted in the middle comes out clean.

March 17

Apple Green Devil

When you need something a more adult than green beer to toast St. Patrick, this little devil will do the trick.

Makes 2 cocktails

2 ounces gin

2 ounces green crème de menthe

1 ounce apple brandy

2 teaspoons cream

1 cup ice

4 leaves fresh mint, for garnish

Mix the gin, crème de menthe, brandy, and cream in a blender with ½ cup ice. Blend until frothy.

Divide between 2 cocktail glasses filled with ice. Garnish with fresh mint.

March 18

Braised Red Cabbage with Apples

Make this braised cabbage as a tasty side dish for corned beef or roasted lamb.

Makes 6 servings

4 tablespoons unsalted butter or olive oil

1 medium red onion, thinly sliced

1 head red cabbage, core removed and thinly shredded

2 sweet apples, such as Gala or Fuji, cored and shredded

⅓ cup hard cider

⅓ cup apple cider vinegar

1½ teaspoons sea salt

1 teaspoon freshly ground black pepper

2 tablespoons light brown sugar

1 cup chicken stock

Melt the butter in a large 5-quart sauté pan set over medium heat. Add the onions and sauté until they begin to soften and turn translucent, about 3 minutes.

Add the cabbage, apples, wine or vinegar, salt, pepper, brown sugar, and stock. Stir to coat the ingredients. Cover the pan, reduce heat to low, and cook for 1 hour, stirring occasionally.

Raw Kale, Apple, Cranberry, and Feta Salad with Apple Cider Vinaigrette

For this recipe you don't need to cook the kale. This salad tastes even better the next day.

Makes 6 servings

Vinaigrette

½ cup apple cider vinegar

2 teaspoons honey

2 tablespoons Dijon mustard

½ teaspoon sea salt

½ teaspoon freshly ground black pepper

½ cup extra virgin olive oil

1 tart apple, such as Granny Smith, cored and diced

⅓ cup dried cranberries

⅓ cup toasted pine nuts

½ cup crumbled feta

1 bunch kale, ribs removed, torn into small pieces

To make the vinaigrette, whisk together the vinegar, honey, mustard, salt, and pepper in a large bowl. Slowly whisk in the olive oil, creating an emulsion.

Add the diced apple, cranberries, pine nuts, and feta to the dressing. Toss to combine. Add kale and toss to coat.

Marinate 10 minutes or longer before serving.

March 20

Apple Chutney

Try this chutney as an accompaniment
to roast pork or chicken.

Makes about 2 cups

2 large tart cooking apples, such as
    Braeburn or Cortland, peeled, cored,
    and chopped

½ cup raisins

½ cup chopped sweet onion

¼ cup red wine vinegar

¼ cup light brown sugar

1 tablespoon grated orange peel

1 tablespoon fresh grated ginger

½ teaspoon allspice

½ teaspoon sea salt

½ teaspoon freshly ground
    black pepper

Combine all the ingredients in
a 3-quart saucepan and stir well.
Bring to a boil over high heat;
reduce heat and simmer, covered,
on low heat for 40 minutes.

Uncover and continue to simmer
over low heat 3 minutes longer to
cook off excess liquid. Let cool.

The chutney can be stored in
the refrigerator, covered,
for up to 2 weeks.

Apple Mango Smoothie

Frozen mango chunks make for easy prep, and the result is a luscious, lip-smacking smoothie.

Makes about 2 servings

1 large apple

1 cup frozen mango chunks

1 cup vanilla yogurt

1 cup ice cubes

¼ cup granulated sugar, plus more to taste if needed

Peel and core the apple and cut it into about 8 pieces. Place them into a food processor or blender and add the mango, yogurt, ice, and sugar. Process until smooth and frothy. Taste and add more sugar if necessary, 1 tablespoon at a time. Pulse to combine.

Core Tip:

How can you tell if an apple is fresh? Flick the apple near its stem. A hollow sound indicates the apple is past its prime. What you want is a dull thud. To confirm, take a sniff. A sweet aroma will seal the deal.

Apple Ambrosia

Some say ambrosia is an old-fashioned salad. Others consider it an old-timey dessert. Either way, it's a simple and delicious treat, and apples give it a bright crunch. If you are nostalgic for the ambrosia of the last century, go ahead and add the marshmallows, but the salad works just as well without them.

Makes about 6 servings

4 oranges

2 large apples

2 bananas

⅓ cup sweetened dried shredded coconut

⅓ cup roughly chopped macadamia nuts (optional)

½ cup miniature marshmallows, or to taste (optional)

Peel and section the oranges and trim away as much of the bitter pith as possible. Squeeze the juice from 4 sections into a bowl and discard the pulp. Cut the remaining sections into bite-sized pieces over the same bowl, letting all the resulting juice fall into the bowl along with the pieces and removing any pits or seeds.

Peel and core the apples and cut into ½-inch chunks, placing the chunks into the bowl with the oranges and tossing them a bit with your hands to prevent browning. Peel the bananas and slice into ⅛-inch-thick rounds; place them into the bowl, and toss gently with your hands to prevent browning.

Add the coconut, macadamias, if using, and marshmallows, and toss very gently.

Endive, Apple, and Walnut Salad

This easy but elegant "star" of a salad can be served as
a starter or a light lunch with crusty bread.

Makes 4 servings

1 recipe Walnut Apple Vinaigrette (see page 93)
2 McIntosh or Macoun apples, cored
About 2 cups walnut halves
4 heads red endive, separated, gently washed and patted dry
4 heads white endive, separated, gently washed and patted dry
40 leaves arugula, gently washed and patted dry
½ cup crumbled blue cheese

Prepare the Walnut Apple Vinaigrette in a container with a tight-fitting lid, according to the directions on page 93.

Cut the apples into very thin wedges, immediately placing each wedge into the container with the dressing as you go. Add the walnut halves, seal the container, and shake to coat thoroughly to prevent browning. (If you are using a different vinaigrette, either store-bought or homemade, dip the apples into it to prevent browning.)

Reserve 16 small red endive leaves. Arrange the largest endive leaves on 4 salad plates, in an 8-point star pattern, nesting 2 leaves on each point of the star and alternating between red and white leaves. Nest a small red endive leaf in each white endive leaf. Reserve any remaining endive leaves for future use.

Mound some of the apples and walnuts in the center of each star and on top of the endive, dividing them equally between the plates. Reserve the dressing that remains in the container. Scatter equal portions of arugula and cheese over the top of each salad. Drizzle the endive on each plate with the remaining dressing and serve.

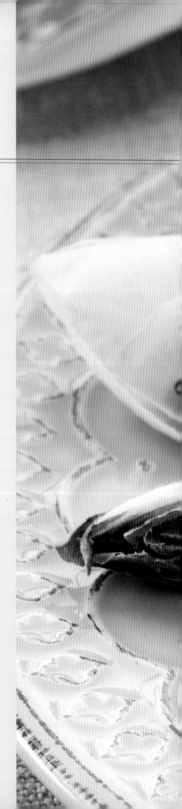

Chicken Apple Sausages with Apples and Cider

Serve these hors d'oeuvres at your next dinner party and watch your guests devour them.

Makes 6 to 8 servings

1 teaspoon extra virgin olive oil

½ cup diced sweet onion

3 chicken apple sausages, sliced into 1-inch segments

1 sweet firm apple, such as Honeycrisp or Fuji, cored and sliced into 12 segments

1¼ cups apple cider

1 teaspoon fresh sage, chopped

¼ teaspoon sea salt

In a large nonstick sauté pan set over medium high heat, heat the olive oil. Add the onion and sauté for 3 minutes, or until softened and lightly browned. Add the sausage and cook for 3 minutes, stirring occasionally.

Add the apple slices, apple cider, sage, and salt. Turn the heat to high and cook until the cider begins to thicken, about 3 minutes longer.

Serve hot speared on toothpicks.

Walnut Apple Vinaigrette

Walnut oil gives this vinaigrette a nutty flavor and aroma. Use it on any green salad, but it's particularly good on salads with nuts in them.

Makes about 2 dozen

⅔ cup walnut oil

2½ tablespoons white balsamic vinegar

2 tablespoons apple juice

1½ tablespoons Dijon mustard

2 teaspoons chopped fresh chives

Mix the walnut oil, vinegar, juice, mustard, and chives in a container with a tight-fitting lid. Seal and shake to combine well.

Cinnamon Apples in the Microwave

This quick-and-easy side dish can easily double as a dessert.

Makes 4 servings

1 cup apple cider

4 apples, peeled, cored, and cut into wedges

¼ teaspoon ground cinnamon

Pour the cider into a shallow, microwavable container that is big enough to hold all the apple wedges.

Peel the apple wedges, placing each one into the cider as you go and turning to coat. Sprinkle the apples with the cinnamon and turn to coat again.

Microwave on high power, uncovered, 3 to 3½ minutes, or longer if you like the apples softer. (Test them with a fork.) Serve warm.

Apple Tip:

Beneath a McIntosh apple's red and green skin is tart, tender white flesh. McIntosh is a popular pick for apple ciders and pies.

Apple Grape Crisp

A variation on the tried and true apple crisp. The grapes add a sweet-tart zing.

Makes 4 servings

¼ cup unsalted butter, chilled, plus more for greasing

¾ cup all-purpose flour

¾ cup plus 2 tablespoons granulated sugar

½ teaspoon ground cinnamon

¼ teaspoon salt

3 large sweet-tart apples, such as Gala or Fuji

1 teaspoon cornstarch

1 cup green grapes, peeled and stems removed

Preheat the oven to 375° F. Butter a glass or ceramic baking dish or 4 dessert-sized ramekins.

Mix the flour, ¾ cup sugar, the cinnamon, and salt in a bowl. Cut in the chilled ¼ cup butter and mix with your fingertips until coarse crumbs form.

Core and peel the apples and cut them into ½-inch chunks. In a separate bowl, mix them with the remaining 2 tablespoons sugar and the cornstarch. Pour the apples and grapes into the prepared baking dish or ramekins and even out the surface with a spatula. Top with the crumbs.

Bake for 50 to 55 minutes, or until the crumbs have baked into a golden brown crust.

March 28

Grilled Cheese and Apple Sandwiches with Cilantro Pesto

Apple slices and pesto turn these grilled cheese sandwiches into something special.

Serves 4 services

1 cup fresh cilantro leaves

⅓ cup walnuts

½ teaspoon sea salt

½ teaspoon freshly ground black pepper

3 tablespoons extra virgin olive oil

8 (½-inch-thick) slices Italian bread

6 ounces melting cheese, such as such as Monterey jack or cheddar, thinly sliced

1 small red apple, Honeycrisp or Fuji, thinly sliced into 8 pieces

In a food processor, process the cilantro, walnuts, salt, and pepper; pulse until finely chopped. Slowly add in 2 tablespoons of the extra virgin olive oil and process until almost smooth.

Lightly brush each bread slice with the remaining olive oil. Turn the slices over and cover four of them with half the cheese. Arrange the apple slices on top of the cheese. Then place the remaining cheese on top of the apples. Spread the pesto on the remaining bread slices and close the sandwiches.

Set a large nonstick skillet over medium heat. Cook the sandwiches, turning once, until the cheese is melted and the bread is golden brown and crisp, about 5 minutes per side.

Warm Red Potato, Apple, and Corn Salad with Bacon

Dig into this substantial salad the next time you crave a medley of flavors.

Makes 8 servings

2 pounds red potatoes, cut into 1-inch pieces

¼ teaspoon salt

1½ cups corn kernels

½ pound haricot verts, trimmed and cut in half

4 ounces thick-cut smoked bacon, diced

1 red onion, chopped

⅓ cup apple cider vinegar

2 tablespoons whole-grain mustard

⅓ cup chicken broth

1 teaspoon sea salt

¼ teaspoon crushed red pepper

1 tart apple, such as Granny Smith, cored and diced

½ cup flat-leaf parsley, chopped

In a large 5-quart pot, combine the potatoes and salt with enough cold water to cover. Set the pan over high heat and bring to a boil. Reduce heat to medium, cover, and simmer 8 to 10 minutes or until potatoes are almost tender.

Add the corn and haricot verts and cook for 2 minutes longer. Drain well, transfer to a large bowl, and set aside.

Meanwhile, for the dressing, in a 4-quart skillet set over medium heat, cook the bacon until crisp, about 5 to 7 minutes. Remove the bacon and drain on paper towels, reserving drippings in the skillet.

Add the onion to the drippings in the skillet and cook over medium heat until the onion is tender, about 5 minutes.

Carefully add the vinegar, mustard, broth, sea salt, and crushed red pepper. Bring to a boil, reduce the heat to medium low, and simmer, uncovered, for 5 minutes. Stir in the apple and parsley.

Pour the dressing over the potatoes and toss to coat. Serve warm.

Chickpea and Apple Salad

This light, refreshing salad will go well with just about anything from the grill.

Makes 2½ to 3 cups

1 tablespoon vegetable oil

2 teaspoons seasoned rice vinegar, plus more to taste if needed

1 large apple

1 (15-ounce can) chickpeas (garbanzo beans), rinsed and drained

¼ cup chopped red onion

¼ cup finely chopped fresh parsley

Freshly ground black pepper to taste

Mix the oil and rice vinegar in a container with a tight fitting lid. Peel and core the apple and cut into ¼-inch pieces. Immediately add to the dressing, cover, and toss to coat, to prevent browning.

Add the chickpeas, onion, and parsley, season with black pepper, and mix with a wooden spoon to distribute the ingredients. Taste and add a bit more vinegar if needed. Serve cold or room temperature.

Apple-Cinnamon Waffles

These waffles are great for Sunday brunch or an after-school snack.

Makes 12 waffles

Nonstick vegetable oil spray

2 large eggs, separated

2 cups all-purpose flour

1 tablespoon baking powder

¼ teaspoon salt

1 teaspoon ground cinnamon

1 cup milk

1 teaspoon pure vanilla extract

1 apple, such as Fuji, cored and shredded

½ cup vegetable oil

Applesauce (see page 17, or use store-bought)

Pure maple syrup

Preheat and grease a waffle iron according to the manufacturer's instructions.

In a medium bowl, use an electric mixer to beat the egg whites until foamy and stiff peaks form. Set aside.

Mix the flour, baking powder, salt, and cinnamon in a large bowl.

In another medium bowl, whisk together the egg yolks. Add the milk, vanilla, shredded apple, and vegetable oil; pour wet ingredients into dry ingredients. Stir to just combine.

Fold the stiff egg whites into the batter, leaving some lumps.

Pour about ½ cup batter into each side of the waffle iron. Cook until golden brown and crispy, about 5 minutes. Repeat with remaining batter.

Serve hot with applesauce and maple syrup.

Apple Almond Macaron Pastries

This cookie combines the best of several treats: sweet, tender pastry on the outside and melt-in-your mouth apple-almond-macaron filling on the inside, finished with an almond-brown sugar coating.

Makes about 2 dozen

Dough

2⅓ cups unbleached, all-purpose flour

⅔ cup light brown sugar

⅛ teaspoon kosher salt

1 teaspoon baking powder

¾ cup cold unsalted butter, cut into 1-teaspoon pieces

1 egg

1 teaspoon pure vanilla extract

Filling

⅔ cup slivered blanched almonds

⅓ cup granulated sugar

¼ teaspoon almond extract

1 extra large egg white

1 small apple, cored and finely chopped

Coating

½ cup sliced or slivered almonds

¼ cup light brown sugar

Combine the flour, brown sugar, salt, and baking powder in a food processor fitted with a metal blade. Pulse 4 or 5 times. Add the butter and pulse 10 or 12 times.

Whisk the egg and vanilla in a small bowl. Drizzle the egg mixture over the flour mixture. Pulse 6 to 10 times, or until the dough just begins to come together. It should not form a ball, but just start to clump.

Place the dough onto a large piece of plastic wrap, press it together, and flatten it into a disk so it will chill thoroughly. Wrap it in plastic and refrigerate for at least 1 hour or up to 1 day.

To make the filling, combine the almonds and sugar in a food processor and process for 45 to 60 seconds, or until finely ground. Add the almond extract and egg white and pulse about 10 times, until the mixture comes together. You may need a few drops of water to make it come together. It should be the consistency of marzipan. If crumbly, add water by drops until it becomes a thick paste. Scrape the filling out of the processor onto a work surface and knead the apple into it.

Make the coating: Combine the almonds and brown sugar in a food processor and pulse until finely chopped.

When you are ready to bake, preheat the oven to 400° F. Place the rack in the center position of the oven and line 2 baking sheets with parchment paper.

To form the cookies, keep the dough cold; take out only a portion at a time. If the dough sticks to your hands, dampen them slightly. Shape half the dough into a long rope or rectangle and slice into 12 even pieces. Flatten them with your palm and add about 1 teaspoon of the filling to the center of each. Shape the dough around the filling to enclose it completely. With your palms, roll each cookie into a smooth ball. Roll each in the coating thoroughly.

Flatten the balls slightly on one side by pressing gently. Place them on the baking sheets with the flattened edges to one side (not on the bottom). Space them about 1 inch apart. Bake 1 sheet at a time for 10 to 12 minutes, or until golden and firm to the touch. Cool for 1 minute, remove with a spatula and cool completely on a rack.

Apple Cider Jalapeno Jelly

Use the freshest jalapenos you can find. If you want a hotter jelly, include the jalapeno seeds. Otherwise, discard.

Makes about 6 cups

1 large red bell pepper, seeded and cut into chunks

3 jalapeno peppers, seeded and cut into chunks

6 cups granulated sugar

1½ cups apple cider vinegar

1 (6-ounce bottle) liquid pectin

In a food processor, process the bell and jalapeno peppers until finely ground.

In a 2-quart saucepan set over high heat, combine the pureed peppers, sugar, and cider vinegar. Bring to a rolling boil. Boil 1 minute, stirring constantly until sugar has dissolved. Remove from the heat and let cool for a few minutes. Add the pectin and mix well. Pour into glass jars and seal.

This will last refrigerated for up to one month.

Apple-Strawberry Jam

The high amount of pectin found in apples helps the strawberries jell. Try this pleasingly tart jam with flaky homemade biscuits.

Makes about 1½ cups

1 pound fresh strawberries, hulled and quartered

⅔ cup granulated sugar

1 large Granny Smith apple, peeled, cored, and grated

1½ tablespoons fresh lemon juice

Combine the ingredients in a large saucepan set over medium low heat. Stir until the sugar dissolves, about 5 minutes. Use a potato masher to mash the fruit. Simmer until the jam has thickened, about 10 to 15 minutes.

Remove from heat and allow to cool. Transfer to a container and chill until set, about 2 hours.

Store in a covered container 3 to 4 weeks or freeze for up to 1 year.

April 4

Apple and Blueberry Turnovers

Apples and blueberries make a tasty filling for these old-timey treats.

Makes 6 turnovers

½ recipe Quick Puff
   Pastry Dough (see
   Apple Apricot Bistro
   Tart, page 26)

Filling

1 large Golden Delicious,
   apple peeled, cored,
   and finely chopped

1½ cups blueberries

2 tablespoons granulated
   sugar

2 teaspoons unsalted
   butter, melted

2 teaspoons cornstarch

Zest of ½ medium lemon

1 teaspoon fresh lemon
   juice

1 egg white

2 teaspoons water

1 to 2 teaspoons
   granulated sugar

Prepare and chill the dough according to the directions on page 26. When you are ready to bake, flour a work surface and roll the dough a little, to get it pliable enough to fold. Fold the dough from each long end into the middle. Fold again as if closing a book, to form a 4 ⅔-inch by 4-inch rectangle. If it has softened, chill it again. Roll the dough out to a 6- by 15-inch rectangle, fold in thirds, folding the ends in to again form a rectangle about 6 inches by 5 inches. Wrap well and chill while you prepare the filling.

Preheat the oven to 400° F. Position an oven rack in the center of the oven. Line a baking sheet with parchment paper.

To make the filling, mix the apple, blueberries, sugar, butter, cornstarch, lemon zest, and juice. Let stand for 15 minutes to allow the juices to release and dissolve the sugar. Stir before using.

Roll out the dough to form a 9- by 13½-inch rectangle about 1/8 inch thick. Cut it into six 4½- by 4½-inch squares. Spoon about ¼ cup filling onto 1 square, placing it just off center. Fold the dough on a diagonal to form a triangle and press the edges together to seal. Repeat with the remaining turnovers, placing them on the baking sheet.

Make an egg wash by mixing the egg white with the water and brush all the turnovers with it. Sprinkle them with the sugar. Cut a couple of small slits in the top of each to allow steam to escape. Bake for 9 to 12 minutes, until the turnovers are golden and the juices are bubbling. Immediately turn from the pan and cool on racks.

Core Fact:

Where to store your apples? If you plan to eat them within two days, they're fine at room temperature. For longer storage, place apples in the fruit drawer of your refrigerator. They'll keep for up to 3 weeks.

Dining in Style:

Reinforce an apple-inspired meal by incorporating apples into your table settings. Tie dried apple slices onto pretty twine for napkin rings destined to give any table rustic charm.

April 5

Cardamom Apple Oatmeal Chewies

This soft cookie is mildly spiced with cardamom and made chewy with dried apples, oatmeal, and brown sugar.

Makes about 34 cookies

Cookies

¼ cup apple juice concentrate (not diluted)

¾ cup finely chopped dried apples

2 cups all-purpose flour

½ teaspoon cardamom

¼ teaspoon grated nutmeg

½ teaspoon baking soda

Small pinch of salt

1¼ cups old-fashioned rolled oats

1 cup unsalted butter, at room temperature

¾ cup light brown sugar

1 large egg

Icing

1 cup confectioners' sugar

1 tablespoon milk

½ teaspoon pure vanilla extract

Spoon the apple juice concentrate into a microwavable container and microwave until liquefied. Add the dried apples and microwave for 1 more minute, until they are soft but not mushy. Set aside to cool.

Sift the flour, cardamom, nutmeg, baking soda, and salt into a mixing bowl and whisk. Stir in the oats.

In a separate bowl, cream the butter with an electric mixer set at medium speed for about 1 minute, or until very soft. Add the brown sugar and continue beating for 3 more minutes.

Beat in the egg. By hand, stir in the softened apples. Stir in the flour and oatmeal mixture to form a dough.

Set the dough aside for 15 to 20 minutes. Preheat the oven to 350° F. Position the oven rack in the center of the oven. Line a baking sheet with parchment.

When you are ready to bake, scoop out about 2 tablespoons of the dough and lightly shape into a rough ball. Place on the baking sheet. Repeat with the remaining dough, spacing the balls about 2 inches apart. Press the dough balls down with your palm to flatten. Bake for 8 to 11 minutes. Cool for 3 to 5 minutes on the baking sheet and then transfer to a rack to cool completely.

While the cookies are baking, make the icing. Sift the confectioners' sugar into a bowl. Stir in the milk and vanilla to make a smooth icing. Drizzle the icing over the cooled cookies.

Spinach, Apple, and Blue Cheese Salad with Honey-Glazed Pecans

The crisp tartness of the apple combines with the spicy sweetness of the pecans and the richness of the blue cheese to tantalize your taste buds.

Makes 6 servings

Honey-Glazed Pecans

½ cup whole pecans

2 tablespoons honey

¼ teaspoon sea salt

¼ teaspoon cayenne pepper

Salad

9 ounces baby spinach

1 tart apple, such as Granny Smith, cored and thinly sliced

½ cup crumbled blue cheese

½ cup Apple Cider-Honey Vinaigrette (see page 31)

To make the honey-glazed pecans, combine the pecans, honey, sea salt, and cayenne in a small non-stick sauté pan set over medium heat. Cook, stirring, 5 minutes or until the nuts are lightly toasted. Transfer the pecans to a foil-lined baking sheet and place in the freezer to cool completely.

When ready to serve, combine the spinach, sliced apple, blue cheese, and pecans in a large bowl. Pour the vinaigrette over the salad. Toss gently to distribute the vinaigrette. Divide the salad among 4 salad plates and serve immediately.

Apple Tip:

Garnish an apple-based cocktail. With a sharp knife, cut an apple slice ½-inch thick. Then cut a circle within the slice, about 1 inch in diameter. Remove the circle and fill the hole with a maraschino cherry. Float the apple-cherry garnish in your cocktail glass.

April 7

Jack Rose Cocktail

Some say the Jack Rose cocktail was named for the applejack on the ingredient list and the rosy color imparted by the grenadine. Others say it was named for the defendant in a notorious murder case in the early years of the 20th century. Either way, it's a classic.

Makes 2 cocktails

4 ounces applejack (apple brandy)
Juice of 1 lime
1 ounce grenadine
Ice
2 lime twists, for garnish
2 thin slices apple dipped in lime juice, for garnish

Mix the brandy, lime juice, and grenadine with ice; shake well. Strain into 2 cocktail glasses, garnish each with a twist of lime and an apple slice.

April 8

Curried Chicken Salad with Apples and Dried Fruit

A spicy, fruity twist on chicken salad that can be served in a sandwich, over lettuce leaves as a luncheon salad, or as an hors d'oeuvre topping.

Makes 4 to 6 servings

2 cups chopped cooked chicken
2 stalks celery, trimmed and finely chopped
½ cup raisins
8 dried apricots, finely chopped
2 or 3 scallions, trimmed and finely chopped
1 large apple of your choice
½ cup mayonnaise, plus more to taste if needed
1 tablespoon curry powder, plus more to taste if needed

Combine the chicken, celery, raisins, apricots, and scallions in a bowl. Core the apple and chop it finely.

Mix the mayonnaise and curry powder and add to the chicken mixture.

April 9

Whole-Grain Apple Muffins

A not-too-sweet whole-grain muffin, perfect for breakfast on the run.

Makes 12 muffins

2 eggs

⅔ cup vegetable oil

⅓ cup honey

½ cup whole milk

¼ cup plain Greek-style yogurt

½ teaspoon pure vanilla extract

1 cup plus 3 tablespoons rolled oats (quick or old-fashioned)

1¼ cup crushed bran cereal

1½ cups unbleached, all-purpose flour

1 teaspoon baking powder

1 teaspoon baking soda

½ teaspoon kosher salt

1 large Golden Delicious or Granny Smith apple, peeled, cored, and coarsely grated

Preheat the oven to 375° F. Line a 12-cup muffin tin with paper liners.

Mix the eggs, oil, honey, milk, yogurt, and vanilla in a large bowl until well blended. Add 1 cup oats and the bran and let them soak for 10 minutes.

In a separate bowl, whisk the flour, baking powder, baking soda, and salt. Add the wet ingredients to the dry ingredients and mix just until well blended. The batter will be thick. Stir in the grated apple.

Scoop the batter into the muffin tin, filling each cup almost to the top. Sprinkle the tops of muffins with the remaining oats. Bake for 15 to 20 minutes, or until a toothpick inserted into the center of a muffin comes out clean.

Upside-Down Apple Cake

Turn the tables on an upside-down cake by using apples instead of the usual pineapple.
Cinnamon whip makes an easy, elegant accompaniment.

Makes 1 (9-inch) cake

Cake

½ cup plus 2 tablespoons
  unsalted butter, room
  temperature

¾ cup granulated sugar

¼ cup light brown sugar

1 tablespoon apple brandy or
  apple juice

2 medium apples, peeled,
  cored, and each cut into 6
  wedges

2 tablespoons raisins (optional)

1 egg

1 yolk

½ teaspoon pure vanilla extract

2 tablespoons milk

1 cup all-purpose flour

1 teaspoon baking powder

⅛ teaspoon salt

Cinnamon Whip

1 cup chilled heavy cream

1 to 2 tablespoons superfine
  sugar

¼ teaspoon pure vanilla extract

¼ teaspoon ground cinnamon

Preheat the oven to 350° F. Position an oven rack in the bottom third of the oven.

Combine 2 tablespoons butter, ¼ cup granulated sugar, the brown sugar, and brandy or juice in a 9-inch oven-proof sauté pan or cast-iron skillet and set over medium-high heat until the butter is melted and the sugar dissolves. Add the apples and cook, stirring gently, for about 2 minutes or until just slightly softened. Remove from the heat and, with tongs, arrange the apples in an attractive pattern on the bottom of the pan. If you wish, scatter the raisins over them. Set aside.

With an electric mixer set at medium-high speed, mix ½ cup butter and ½ cup sugar for about 4 minutes. Add the egg and yolk and beat for 1 more minute.

In a small bowl, mix the vanilla and milk. In a separate bowl, sift the flour, baking powder, and salt. Add half the flour mixture to the egg mixture and beat with the mixer for 20 seconds. Add the vanilla mixture and beat for 20 more seconds. Add the remaining flour mixture and beat for 20 to 30 seconds, until well combined.

Drop scoops of the batter over the apples in the pan. Smooth with a spatula to even out the batter and cover all the apples. Bake for 30 to 35 minutes, or until the cake is golden and puffed and a toothpick inserted into the cake (not the apples) comes out clean.

While the cake is baking, make the Cinnamon Whip: With a clean mixer, beat the cream, sugar, vanilla, and cinnamon until very soft peaks form.

Apple-Walnut Charoset

Made of fruits and nuts, Charoset is a sweet paste typically eaten at the Passover Seder. Its name comes from the Hebrew word for "clay." Take a bite of its dark, dense consistency and you'll know why.

Makes about 4 cups

3 medium apples, such as Gala or Fuji, cored and grated

½ cup coarsely chopped walnut halves, lightly toasted

½ cup golden raisins (optional)

½ cup chopped black mission figs

½ cup sweet red wine, such as Manischewitz

1½ teaspoons ground cinnamon

1½ tablespoons light brown sugar

In a large bowl, add all the ingredients and stir to combine. Serve on matzah bread or your favorite cracker.

Brisket with Apples

Braising requires little effort yet produces succulent results. This recipe makes a brisket so tender it will melt in your mouth.

Makes 8 servings

2 tablespoons olive oil

1 (4- to 5-pound) beef brisket

1 tablespoon sea salt

1 teaspoon freshly ground black pepper

2 onions, sliced

6 cloves garlic, smashed with the back of a knife

3 cups apple cider

3 sprigs fresh rosemary

3 sprigs fresh thyme

3 Granny Smith apples, cored and sliced

Preheat the oven to 325° F.

In a 5-quart Dutch oven set over medium-high heat, heat the olive oil. Trim the outer fat from the brisket and season on both sides with salt and pepper. Place the brisket in the Dutch oven and sear on both sides until golden brown, about 5 minutes. Transfer the brisket to a platter.

Add the sliced onions and garlic cloves and sauté until softened, about 5 minutes. Pour in a few tablespoons of the apple cider and deglaze, scraping up any browned bits from the bottom.

Return the brisket and any accumulated juices to the Dutch oven and add the rosemary, thyme, and the rest of the cider. Bring to a boil over high heat, cover, and transfer to the preheated oven.

Cook for 2½ hours or until tender. Add the apple slices and cook for an additional 30 minutes.

Remove the meat, apples, and onions to a platter. Over high heat bring the sauce to a boil, and, stirring occasionally, reduce until it has thickened. Remove the rosemary and thyme sprigs and season with salt and pepper if needed.

Slice the brisket against the grain and serve with the apples, onions, and gravy.

Apple Tip:

Gala and Fuji are two popular apple varietals. Both taste sweet. Gala has a grainy texture and is resistant to bruising, while Fuji is distinctively crisp with a long shelf life. When properly refrigerated, this hardy apple can last up to a year.

Waldorf Salad

This refreshing salad makes a mouth-watering first course. If you would like to serve it as a main meal, add cooked cubed chicken or turkey.

Makes 2 servings

3 tablespoons mayonnaise or yogurt

1 tablespoon fresh lemon juice

1 teaspoon honey

1 sweet apple, such as Fuji or Honeycrisp, cored and chopped

½ cup coarsely chopped walnuts, toasted

½ cup sliced celery

½ cup sliced seedless red grapes

1 head butter lettuce, leaves separated

In a medium-size bowl, whisk together the mayonnaise or yogurt, lemon juice, and honey. Mix in the apples, walnuts, celery, and grapes. Serve on top of lettuce.

Dutch Apple Betty

Known for her signature cocktails, **Bartender Mary Hulse** tends bar at the award-winning restaurant Muriel's Jackson Square, right in the heart of New Orleans. Sample her unique take on the apple toddy.

Makes 1 cocktail

1½ ounces hot apple juice

1½ ounces Boulard Calvados

¼ ounce St. Elizabeth Allspice Dram (rum-based liqueur)

¼ ounce Tuaca (Italian liqueur)

1 teaspoon McIlhenny Farms honey

¼ teaspoon ground cinnamon

Cinnamon stick, for garnish

Pour the hot apple juice, Calvados, St. Elizabeth Allspice Dram, and Tuaca in a heat-resistant mug. Stir in the honey and ground cinnamon. Garnish with a cinnamon stick.

The clear, pure flavor of apple can take many cocktails to the next level. Apple cider makes a wonderful base for hot cocktails in the chilly fall. Apple-infused brandies, rums, and vodkas do wonders for mixologists year-round. Sour apple liquors and schnapps make for less expensive yet still delightful flavor additions to mixed drinks.

The Crabby Apple

Both sweet and sour, this cocktail will make your lips pucker--and leave you craving another sip.

Makes 1 cocktail

Simple Syrup

½ cup granulated sugar

½ cup water

1 ounce cranberry jelly

1 ounce applesauce

1½ ounces Stoli Vanilla vodka

1 ounce DeKuyper Apple Pucker schnapps

½ ounce fresh lemon juice

To make the simple syrup, put the sugar and water into a saucepan and bring to a boil. Reduce the heat to a simmer and stir until the sugar dissolves. Cool to room temperature. Reserve 1¼ ounces and refrigerate the remainder in an airtight container. It will keep for up to 1 month.

Blend together the cranberry jelly and 1 ounce of the simple syrup. Combine the cranberry puree and the applesauce, vodka, Apple Pucker schnapps, lemon juice, and 1 ounce of the simple syrup in a shaker filled with ice. Shake well and pour into a martini glass. Garnish with a green apple slice.

Bartender Mary Hulse

BAR SUPERVISOR AT: Muriel's Jackson Square, New Orleans

EXPERIENCE: Seventeen years in the bar and restaurant industry

SPECIALTY: Signature cocktails

Turkey Enchiladas with Apples

A tasty way to use up leftover roasted turkey.

Makes 4 servings

1 teaspoon olive oil

1 Pink Lady or Honeycrisp apple, cored and thinly sliced

1½ cups thinly sliced onion

2 cups roasted and shredded turkey

6 cups baby spinach

3 green onions, chopped

1 tablespoon ground cumin

2 garlic cloves, minced

1½ tablespoons all-purpose flour

1¼ cups chicken broth

⅓ cup cilantro leaves, chopped

3 ounces cream cheese

½ teaspoon sea salt

½ teaspoon freshly ground black pepper

8 (6-inch) corn tortillas

Low-fat sour cream, for serving

Preheat the oven to 350° F. Heat the olive oil in a large nonstick sauté pan set over medium-high heat. Add the apples and onions and cook 10 minutes or until golden brown, stirring frequently.

Remove half the apple-onion mixture and transfer to a medium bowl. Add the shredded turkey to the bowl. Set aside.

Add the spinach to sauté pan containing the remaining onions and apples. Cover and steam over medium heat 3 minutes or until wilted. Add the green onions, cumin, and garlic and cook for 3 minutes longer.

In a small bowl, combine the flour and broth, whisking to incorporate. Add the flour-broth mixture, cilantro, cream cheese, and salt to the sauté pan and stir 3 minutes longer, or until the cheese has melted and the sauce has thickened. Transfer the sauce mixture to a blender or a food processor and puree until smooth.

Pour ½ the spinach sauce in bottom of a 9- x13-inch baking dish.

Divide the turkey mixture evenly among the 8 tortillas and roll up, arranging the filled tortillas.

Arrange the filled tortillas on top of the spinach sauce, and pour remaining spinach sauce over the tortillas.

Cover with foil and bake at 350° F for 10 minutes or until enchiladas are heated through.

Serve with a dollop of low-fat sour cream.

Roasted Cauliflower with Apples

Roasting transforms cauliflower, giving it a nutty flavor. Paired with sweet apple, the combo makes an out-of-the-ordinary side dish.

Makes 6 servings

1 head of garlic, cloves separated and unpeeled

1 large cauliflower, cut into small florets

2 firm, sweet apples, such as Honeycrisp, cored and chopped into bite-sized pieces

2 tablespoons olive oil

1 teaspoon sea salt

½ teaspoon freshly ground black pepper

¼ cup chopped fresh parsley

½ tablespoon fresh lemon juice

½ cup coarsely chopped walnuts, toasted (optional)

Preheat the oven to 425° F.

Bring a 2-quart saucepan of water to a boil. Add the garlic cloves and cook for 15 seconds, drain, and peel.

Toss the cauliflower florets and chopped apple with the garlic cloves, 1 tablespoon of the olive oil, salt, and pepper. Spread out on a large baking pan and roast for 30 minutes, or until the cauliflower is just tender and lightly brown, stirring occasionally to prevent burning.

Transfer the mixture to a large bowl and add the parsley, lemon juice, and the remaining olive oil. Toss to combine and sprinkle with the walnuts, if using.

Figgy Apple-Brie Quiches

These make great hors d'oeuvres
to pass at a cocktail party.

Makes 30 mini quiches

30 mini phyllo shells

1 apple, such as Honeycrisp or Fuji, peeled, cored, and finely diced

¾ cup fig jam

Filling

4 eggs

1 tablespoon Dijon mustard

½ teaspoon sea salt

½ teaspoon freshly ground black pepper

½ teaspoon pumpkin pie spice

4 ounces Brie, cut into 30 slices

Preheat the oven to 350° F. Arrange the phyllo shells on a large parchment-lined baking sheet. Divide the diced apples evenly among them. Spoon about 1 teaspoon of the jam on top of each apple-filled shell.

To make the egg filling, in a small bowl, whisk together the eggs, mustard, salt, pepper, and pumpkin pie spice. Pour over the apples to the top of each shell. Place a slice of Brie in each shell.

Bake 15 minutes, or until the egg is set and the dough is brown around the edges. Cool slightly before serving.

April 18

Apple Pie Milkshake

This shake is like sipping apple pie a la mode through a straw.

Makes 2 servings

½ cup apple cider
½ cup apple pie filling
1 cup French vanilla ice cream
Whipped cream
Ground cinnamon, for sprinkling

Place the cider, apple pie filling, and ice cream in a blender and process until smooth. Pour the milkshake into two glasses and top with whipped cream and sprinkle with cinnamon.

April 19

Sautéed Apples, Fennel, and Sweet Onions

This easy sauté is an excellent accompaniment to pork chops, pork tenderloin, roasted chicken, or potatoes.

Makes about 1½ cups

1 tablespoon olive oil
1 bulb fennel, cored and thinly sliced
2 Golden Delicious apples, peeled and thinly sliced
1 sweet onion, thinly sliced
½ teaspoon sea salt
½ teaspoon freshly ground black pepper
½ cup apple cider

In a large nonstick sauté pan set over medium-high, heat the olive oil. Add the fennel, apples, onion, salt, and pepper. Lower the heat to medium and sauté for 10 minutes or until the mixture begins to caramelize.

Add the apple cider and continue to cook for 10 minutes longer, or until the mixture has thickened.

April 20

Potato, Leek, and Apple Soup

Toasted garlic bread is the perfect accompaniment
for this filling soup.

Makes 8 to 10 servings

6 Yukon Gold potatoes, chopped

6 cups chicken stock

2 sprigs fresh thyme, tied
together with kitchen twine

2 cloves garlic, peeled

4 ounces bacon, cut into 1-inch
pieces

1 tablespoon olive oil

2 Granny Smith apples, peeled,
cored and diced

2 leeks, white part only, cut in
half lengthwise, washed, and
finely sliced

½ cup plain Greek-style yogurt

Salt, to taste

Pepper, to taste

In a 5-quart soup pot set over high heat, combine the potatoes,
chicken stock, thyme, and garlic cloves and bring to a boil.
Reduce the heat and simmer, uncovered, until the potatoes are
tender, about 15 minutes.

While the potatoes are simmering, heat a 4-quart sauté pan over
medium high heat. Cook the bacon until browned and crispy.
Remove from pan and drain on paper towels.

Add the olive oil to the bacon fat and sauté the apples and leeks over
medium high heat until they are golden brown and slightly crispy,
about 10 minutes. Return the bacon to the pan with the apple-leek
mixture and stir to combine.

When the potatoes are tender, remove the thyme sprigs and discard.
Add the yogurt to the potato mixture and stir. Using a handheld
immersion blender or transferring the mixture in batches to a regular
blender, puree the soup until smooth. If using a regular blender,
transfer the pureed soup back to the soup pot. Stir the apple mixture
into the pureed soup, season with salt and pepper to taste, and serve.

April 21

Apple Kebabs with Chocolate Dipping Sauce

Turn dessert time into family fun time. Kids (and adults) will enjoy dipping pieces of crisp apple into this velvety smooth chocolate sauce.

Makes 4 servings

1 cup whipping cream

1 tablespoon apple juice

9 ounces milk chocolate, broken into squares

2 sweet crisp apples, such as Pink Lady, cored and cut into bite-sized pieces

12 mini skewers

In a small 2-quart saucepan set over medium-high heat, combine the cream and apple juice and bring to a boil. Remove from heat and stir in the chocolate squares. Let stand for 1 minute and then stir until smooth. Pour the dipping sauce into a small serving bowl.

Thread the cut-up apples onto mini bamboo skewers; serve with the dipping sauce.

April 22

Apple and Banana Smoothie

A frozen banana endows a smoothie with wonderful sweetness and creaminess. You probably won't even need to add sugar.

Makes 2 servings

1 large apple

1 frozen banana

1 cup vanilla ice cream

1 cup ice cubes

¼ cup apple juice

¼ cup granulated sugar, plus more to taste if needed (optional)

Peel and core the apple, cut it into rough chunks, and place them into a food processor or blender. Peel the banana, cut it into chunks, and add to the apple. Add the ice cream, ice, and juice and process until smooth and frothy. Taste and add sugar if necessary.

Liver with Apples and Onions

Don't overcook the liver. It should be a rosy pink when you cut it.

Makes 6 servings

2 tablespoons olive oil

2 sweet onions, peeled and thinly sliced

3 Granny Smith apples, cored and thinly sliced

1 teaspoon chopped thyme leaves, plus several
  sprigs for garnish

2 tablespoons apple cider vinegar

1 teaspoon granulated sugar

¼ cup dry white wine

2 tablespoons unsalted butter

1 teaspoon sea salt

½ teaspoon freshly ground black pepper

1½ pounds calf's liver, patted dry and cut into
  ½-inch slices

¼ cup finely chopped parsley

Heat the olive oil in a large skillet set over medium heat. Add the onions and cook, stirring, for 5 minutes, or until the onions have softened and turned golden. Add the apple slices and cook 5 minutes longer. Add the thyme, vinegar, sugar, and wine and bring the mixture to a boil. Cook 5 minutes or until the mixture has thickened. Transfer the apple-onion mixture to a platter.

Clean the skillet and add the butter. Melt over medium-high heat. Season the liver well with the salt and pepper. Add the liver and sauté for about 2 minutes per side. Liver is done when it is golden brown on the outside but still pink inside.

Arrange the liver over the apple-onion mixture. Sprinkle with chopped parsley. Garnish with the thyme sprigs.

Rice Pilaf with Apples and Raisins

A pilaf is a grain dish that is sautéed in oil before being simmered. In this one, the rice is seasoned with onion, apple, raisins, and curry powder. The result is a fragrant, delicious dish.

Makes 4 servings

2 to 3 tablespoons olive oil

½ cup chopped onion

2 tablespoons raisins

½ large apple, cut into ½-inch chunks

1 cup rice

2 cups chicken stock

½ teaspoon curry powder

½ teaspoon salt

¼ teaspoon freshly ground black pepper

Heat 2 tablespoons oil in a large saucepan or Dutch oven set over medium-high heat. Add the onion, raisins, and apples and mix gently to coat. Cook, stirring, for about 5 minutes, or until just beginning to soften.

If the pan looks dry, add 1 tablespoon oil; add the rice and mix gently to coat. Reduce the heat to medium-low, add the stock, curry powder, salt, and pepper and mix to incorporate. Cover and cook for 20 to 25 minutes. Let stand off the heat for about 10 minutes, or until soft and cooked through.

Apple Cinnamon Popcorn

Make a batch of this addictive snack and keep it on hand for those times when the munchies hit.

Makes about 14 cups

2 cups coarsely chopped dried apples

10 cups air-popped popcorn

2 cups chopped walnuts

5 tablespoons melted butter

1 teaspoon ground cinnamon

2 tablespoons light brown sugar

½ teaspoon pure vanilla extract

Preheat the oven to 250° F. Place the apples in a large baking pan and bake 20 minutes. Remove the pan from the oven and stir in the popcorn and nuts.

In a small bowl, combine the melted butter, cinnamon, brown sugar, and vanilla. Pour over the popcorn mixture and toss to coat.

Return the pan to the oven and bake 30 minutes, stirring occasionally so the mixture doesn't burn. Cool completely before storing in an airtight container.

Fresh Fruit Muesli with Yogurt

Muesli is a traditional breakfast from Sweden. Since the oats aren't cooked, they must soften overnight in a liquid; in this recipe apple juice is used.

Makes 2 servings

1 cup quick-cooking rolled oats

1 cup apple juice

2 tablespoons honey, plus more for drizzling

½ cup dried cherries

1 cup plain whole yogurt

1 apple of your choice, cored and shredded

½ cup sliced banana

¼ cup blueberries

In a medium bowl, combine the oats, apple juice, honey, and dried cherries. Stir to mix well and refrigerate overnight.

In the morning, add the yogurt, shredded apple, banana slices, and blueberries to the mixture. Stir gently to combine and serve topped with a drizzle of honey.

Cranberry Apple Quencher

For a grown-up version, add a shot of vodka to each glass.

Makes 6 drinks

2 cups apple juice
2 cups cranberry juice
12 ounces pineapple juice
2 ounces lemonade or limeade concentrate, thawed
Mint leaves, for garnish

Combine the apple, cranberry, and pineapple juice in a large container or punch bowl. Stir in lemonade or limeade concentrate. Serve in tall glasses with plenty of ice, and garnished with mint leaves.

Mulligatawny Soup

Highly seasoned, this aromatic curry soup is loaded with flavor. For a vegetarian version, use vegetable broth instead of chicken broth and omit the cooked chicken.

Makes 8 to 10 servings

2 tablespoons vegetable oil

2 cups chopped onion

½ cup diced carrots

2 tablespoons garam masala (available in Asian markets and most supermarkets)

1¾ teaspoons sea salt

¾ teaspoon freshly ground black pepper

2 tablespoons minced garlic

2 tablespoons minced fresh ginger

2 cups cored and diced Granny Smith apples

6¼ cups chicken broth

1 cup, peeled and diced Yukon Gold potatoes

1 cup peeled and diced sweet potatoes

1 cup dried red lentils

1 cup baby spinach

1 (14-ounce can) unsweetened coconut milk

1 cup chopped tomatoes

2 cups diced cooked chicken

2 cups cooked basmati rice

¼ cup finely chopped fresh cilantro

Heat vegetable oil in a 5-quart Dutch oven over medium-high heat. Add the onions and carrots and sauté until lightly caramelized, about 4 to 5 minutes. Add the garam masala, salt, pepper, garlic, and ginger and stir 1 minute.

Add the apples and ¼ cup of the chicken broth and sauté about 5 minutes. Add the potatoes and lentils and stir to incorporate.

Add the rest of the chicken broth. Bring the soup to boil, reduce the heat to medium low, and simmer about 8 to 10 minutes or until the potatoes are tender.

Stir in the spinach, coconut milk, and tomatoes. Simmer until the lentils and vegetables are tender, 10 to 15 minutes. Stir in the chicken. Taste and adjust seasoning if needed.

Divide rice among bowls and pour soup over the rice. Garnish with cilantro and serve.

Apple Baklava

The traditional Greek dessert is combined with a traditional American one—apple pie—for a flaky, sticky-sweet new classic.

Makes 24 servings

Nut Filling

2½ cups chopped pecans

½ cup brown sugar

1 teaspoon lemon zest

½ teaspoon ground cinnamon

Apple Filling

2 tablespoons unsalted butter

6 Golden Delicious apples, peeled, cored, and chopped

6 Granny Smith apples, peeled, cored, and chopped

6 tablespoons granulated sugar

½ teaspoon ground cinnamon

24 sheets phyllo dough, thawed

½ cup unsalted melted butter

½ cup honey

Preheat the oven to 400° F.

To make the nut filling, combine the pecans, sugar, lemon zest, and cinnamon in a food processor and pulse until the mixture is finely ground, about 20 seconds. Set aside.

To make the apple filling, melt the butter in a heavy-bottom pot set over medium-high heat, then add the apples, sugar, and cinnamon. Cook about 15 to 20 minutes, or until the apples are tender and form a jammy consistency. Set aside to cool.

To prepare the baklava, unroll the phyllo sheets and trim to fit a 13- x 9-inch baking pan.

Brush the baking dish with some of the melted butter. Place 1 pastry sheet in the dish, keeping the remaining sheets covered, and brush it with butter. Add 5 more layers of phyllo and butter.

Spread ½ the nut mixture over the pastry. Layer 6 more sheets pastry over the nuts, spreading each with butter. Spread all the apple mixture on top. Layer 6 more sheets phyllo and butter over the apples. Make another layer using the remaining nut mixture, and top with 6 more phyllo sheets and butter.

With a sharp knife, cut into 16 squares. Bake for 35 to 40 minutes or until golden-brown. Remove from the oven and drizzle with the honey. Bake 5 minutes.

Cool to room temperature before serving.

Little Apple and Caramel Cheesecakes

A little goes a long way when it comes to these sweet, decadent cheesecakes.
Use less caramel sauce—or none at all—if you prefer a less sweet result.

Makes 6 (4-ounce) cheesecakes

1 small Golden Delicious apple

¼ cup plus 2 teaspoons granulated sugar

½ recipe Apple Caramel Sauce (see page 15) or ¾ cup bottled caramel sauce

12 ounces cream cheese, room temperature

¼ cup brown sugar, lightly packed

2 teaspoons all-purpose flour

1 tablespoon apple brandy

2 tablespoons heavy cream

2 eggs

Grapes, halved, for garnish

Preheat the broiler. Line a baking sheet with aluminum foil. Core the apple and cut it into ⅛-inch wedges. Place them on a baking sheet and sprinkle with 2 teaspoons sugar. Broil for about 3 minutes, or until the apples are just beginning to brown. Watch these carefully, as broilers vary. Remove from the broiler and set aside to cool. (If you wish, you can use a small kitchen torch to sear the apples instead of broiling.)

If you are making your own caramel sauce, prepare it according to the directions on page 15.

Preheat the oven to 325° F. Spoon about 2 tablespoons of the caramel sauce into each of 6 (4-ounce) ramekins. Put a pot of water on and bring to a simmer.

With an electric mixer or a stand mixer fitted with a paddle attachment, beat the cream cheese at medium speed until very smooth, with no lumps remaining. Add the brown sugar, flour, brandy, and cream and beat until smooth. Beat in the eggs, one at a time, until well combined

Divide the batter among the prepared ramekins and place them in a baking pan. Pour enough simmering water into the pan to come halfway up the sides of the ramekins. Place the pan in the oven and bake for 25 to 30 minutes, or until the edges of the cheesecake are firm but the very center is still a bit jiggly but not liquid. Carefully remove the ramekins from the hot water bath. Use heatproof silicone oven mitts (cloth mitts can get wet and the cause burns) and/or a strong spatula or silicone-coated tongs.

Risotto with Porcini Mushrooms and Apple

When cooked very slowly with broth, the starch in Arborio rice is released and forms its own lovely sauce. Take your time preparing this dish; stirring constantly and adding the broth in small increments will ensure success, especially when the rice is accompanied by luscious apples and porcini mushrooms.

Makes 4 servings

5 cups chicken broth

1 cup apple cider or apple juice

2 tablespoons vegetable oil

2 tablespoons unsalted butter

½ large apple of your choice

1 or 2 cloves garlic, finely chopped

8 ounces porcini mushrooms, trimmed and cut into chunks

2 tablespoons fresh lemon juice

¼ teaspoon salt

⅛ teaspoon white pepper, plus more to taste

1½ cups Arborio rice

Fresh thyme or rosemary sprigs, for garnish

Combine the broth and cider or juice in a saucepan set over medium-low heat. Bring to a simmer and keep simmering during the entire cooking process. Reduce the heat, if necessary.

In a large saucepan or Dutch oven, heat 1 tablespoon of the oil and 1 tablespoon of the butter over medium heat until the butter is melted. Tilt to coat the pan. Meanwhile, core the apple and cut into ⅛-inch slices. Add them to the pan and cook, stirring occasionally, for about 5 minutes, or until the apple is softened and golden.

Add the garlic, and cook, stirring, for 30 seconds to 1 minute, or until softened. Add the remaining butter and oil, the mushrooms, lemon juice, salt, and pepper and toss to coat. Cook, stirring, for 5 to 8 minutes, or until just beginning to soften. Remove the mushrooms from the pan and set aside, leaving any juices in the pan.

Return the pan to medium heat, add the rice, and stir to coat. Add ½ cup of the warm broth mixture and stir constantly until the liquid is absorbed by the rice; then add another ½ cup of broth and repeat. Continue the process of adding broth, ½ cup at a time; stir constantly for about 20 minutes, allowing the rice to absorb the liquid. Then begin adding ¼ cup of broth at a time until all the broth has been added and the rice has absorbed the liquid and is soft and cooked through. It will take about 10 more minutes. Add the mushrooms back to the rice and stir gently to combine. Taste and season with white pepper, if necessary. (If the broth is salted, you probably won't need more salt.)

Divide the risotto among 4 soup bowls, top each with some of the reserved apples, and garnish with fresh herb sprigs.

Apple-Berry Oat Crisp

This easy-to-prepare dessert is so tasty the family will forget about all the healthful ingredients that go into it.

Makes 4 servings

1 tablespoon unsalted butter, melted, plus more butter for greasing and serving

½ cup old-fashioned rolled oats

½ cup granulated sugar

¾ teaspoon ground cinnamon

4 large sweet-tart apples, such as Gala or Fuji

½ cup blueberries

1 tablespoon cornstarch

4 pats of butter (optional)

Preheat the oven to 350° F. Butter a glass or ceramic baking dish.

Combine the oats in a bowl with the melted butter, 1 tablespoon sugar, and ½ teaspoon cinnamon. Toss gently to coat.

Core, peel, and cut the apples into ½-inch chunks. In a separate bowl, mix them with the remaining sugar and cinnamon, the blueberries, and cornstarch. Pour into the prepared baking dish and even out the surface with a spatula.

Sprinkle the oats over the apples and even the surface with a spatula. Bake for 50 to 55 minutes, or until the fruit is softened. Serve warm with a pat of butter on each serving, if you wish.

Fennel, Apple, and Carrot Slaw

Instead of the usual cabbage slaw, try this knockout combination. The sweetness of the apples and carrots balances the fennel for a superb side dish.

Makes 6 servings

½ cup fresh lemon juice

2 tablespoons honey

1 tablespoon granulated sugar

1 teaspoon kosher salt

¾ cup olive oil

1 fennel bulb, shredded

3 carrots, peeled and coarsely shredded

1 Fuji apple, cored and shredded

1 Granny Smith apple, cored and shredded

¼ cup dried cranberries

In a large bowl, whisk together the lemon juice, honey, sugar, and salt. Slowly add the oil, whisking as you go, until incorporated. Add the fennel, carrots, apples, and cranberries. Toss to combine and refrigerate for 30 minutes to 1 hour to let the flavors blend.

Cinnamon Apple Slices

Keep a bag of these in the fridge. Children can dip in and help themselves whenever hunger pangs strike.

Makes about 2 servings

1 large eating apple, such as Gala or Granny Smith, cored and cut into wedges

1½ teaspoons ground cinnamon

1½ teaspoons granulated sugar

Put the apples, cinnamon, and sugar in a ziplock bag. Shake and refrigerate 1 hour to 2 days.

Apple-Scented Ornaments

Enjoy the sweet scent of apple and cinnamon even when you're not baking. Mix together equal parts cinnamon and applesauce. Flatten the "dough" with a roller and cut shapes with cookie cutters. Arrange the shapes on a plate. Poke a hole into the top of each shape with a pencil or straw. Allow the shapes to dry completely. Hang from ribbons around your home.

Apple Torta

This variation on the Spanish omelet works for breakfast, lunch, or dinner.

Makes 4 servings

2 tablespoons unsalted butter

1 Fuji apple, peeled, cored, and thinly sliced

2 large eggs, separated

3 tablespoons all-purpose flour

¼ teaspoon baking powder

½ teaspoon sea salt

Freshly ground black pepper, to taste

3 tablespoons milk

¼ cup chopped ham (optional)

¼ cup grated Cheddar

Preheat the oven to 350° F.

Melt 1 tablespoon butter in a large, ovenproof skillet. Add the apple slices and sauté just until they begin to soften, 2 to 3 minutes. Remove to a plate and set aside.

In a medium bowl, beat the egg whites with a handheld mixer until stiff peaks form.

In a separate bowl, combine the flour, baking powder, salt, and pepper. Combine the milk and egg yolks in a measuring cup and add to the flour mixture. Stir until blended. With a rubber spatula, gently fold the egg whites into the batter.

Melt the remaining butter in the same skillet over medium heat; remove from heat. Spread the batter evenly in the pan. Layer the apple slices over the batter and sprinkle with the ham, if using, and grated cheese.

Place the skillet on the top rack in the oven and bake for 15 minutes, or until the cheese is golden brown. Cut into wedges and serve.

Grilled Kielbasa with Apple Sauerkraut

The blend of sweet apple and sour cabbage makes for a memorable sauerkraut.

Makes 4 servings

2 tablespoons salted butter

1 medium sweet onion, thinly sliced 2 medium Granny Smith apples, peeled and shredded

1 tablespoon fresh lemon juice

8 ounces sauerkraut, drained

½ cup apple juice or apple cider

1 teaspoon caraway seeds

1 teaspoon fennel seeds, crushed

½ teaspoon freshly ground black pepper

1 pound kielbasa

Preheat a grill.

Meanwhile, melt the butter in a large skillet over medium-high heat. Add the onion and sauté for 15 minutes or until caramelized.

In a medium bowl, toss the shredded apples with the lemon juice. Add the apples, sauerkraut, apple juice or cider, caraway seeds, fennel, and pepper to the skillet. Bring to a boil, reduce heat to low, and simmer for 15 minutes.

While the sauerkraut is simmering, cut the kielbasa into 3-inch sections. Butterfly lengthwise and place on the grill. Cook the sausages until charred and cooked through, about 4 minutes per side. Cut the grilled kielbasa into 1-inch pieces and add to the skillet. Toss with the apple sauerkraut. Transfer to a platter and serve with your favorite mustard.

Apple Swirl Bundt Cake

There's a yummy surprise inside this Bundt cake: delicious swirls of apples, nuts, and cinnamon!

Makes 1 Bundt cake

Apple Swirl

1 large apple of your choice

½ teaspoon fresh lemon juice

1 cup coarsely chopped pecans or walnuts, toasted

2 teaspoons ground cinnamon

Bundt Cake

1 cup unsalted butter, softened at room temperature

1¼ cups granulated sugar

2½ cups sifted pastry or bleached all-purpose flour

1 teaspoon baking powder

1 teaspoon baking soda

¼ teaspoon salt

3 eggs

1 teaspoon pure vanilla extract

1 cup sour cream (full fat only)

Preheat the oven to 350° F. Position the oven rack to the bottom third of the oven.

Grease and flour a Bundt pan.

To prepare the swirl, peel, core, and dice the apple and toss with the lemon juice. Add the nuts and cinnamon and toss gently to combine.

To prepare the batter, with a an electric mixer or stand mixer set at medium, speed mix the butter and sugar together for 6 to 7 minutes or until very light. In a large bowl, sift the flour, baking powder, baking soda, and salt. In a separate bowl, whisk the eggs, vanilla, and sour cream until smooth.

With the mixer at low speed, add about one-third of the flour mixture and beat for 15 to 20 seconds. Add about half of the egg mixture and beat for 15 to 20 seconds. Repeat with the remaining flour and egg mixtures, alternating between the two, adding another third of the flour mixture (half of the remaining mixture), half the egg mixture and ending with the remaining flour mixture; beat for 15 to 20 seconds between each addition and scrape down the bowl each time. Beat for another 30 to 40 seconds to fully combine the batter.

Scoop about one-third of the batter (it will be thick) into the prepared pan. Top with half the apple mixture, being careful not to let the apples touch the pan's sides or tube to avoid sticking or it might cause the cake to stick. Repeat with another third of the batter, the remaining apple mixture, and the last of the batter. Smooth the surface with a spatula.

Bake for 50 to 60 minutes, or until the top is golden and springs back when gently pressed. Cool the cake in the pan for 5 to 7 minutes and then turn out onto a rack. Serve warm or at room temperature.

Apple and Golden Raisin Tart

Impress your guests with this easy-to-prepare dessert.

Makes 8 to 12 servings

Pastry

1½ cups all-purpose flour

½ cup cold, unsalted butter, cut in pieces

¼ cup confectioners' sugar

⅛ teaspoon salt

Filling

2 large Honeycrisp or Fuji apples, peeled, cored, and thinly sliced

¼ cup golden raisins

2 tablespoons apple brandy, such as Calvados

2 tablespoons granulated sugar

Topping

8 ounces cream cheese, softened

½ cup granulated sugar

2 tablespoons fresh lemon juice

2 large eggs

1 teaspoon pure vanilla extract

Preheat the oven to 375° F.

To make the pastry, place the flour, butter, confectioners' sugar, and salt in the bowl of a food processor. Pulse 5 to 7 times or until the mixture is crumbly and the butter is incorporated. Do not over process. Press the pastry into a fluted tart pan with a removable bottom.

To make the filling, overlap the apple slices on top of the pastry, creating a concentric design. Sprinkle the raisins, apple brandy, and sugar over the apples.

To make the topping, beat together the cream cheese, sugar, lemon juice, eggs, and vanilla with a hand held mixer until blended. Pour topping over the apples.

Bake for 40 minutes. Cool and refrigerate before serving.

Wasabi Pea and Dried Apple Trail Mix

Hot, spicy wasabi peas make this trail mix utterly addictive.

Makes 18 servings

¾ cup wasabi peas

¾ cup chopped dried apples

¾ cup dried cranberries

1 cup unsalted peanuts

1 cup cashews

Mix all the ingredients in a large bowl. Store in an airtight container.

Apple Blueberry Smoothie

Blueberries not only pair nicely with tart apples, they are loaded with powerful antioxidants.

Makes 2 servings

1 Granny Smith apple, cored and coarsely chopped

1 cup blueberry yogurt

½ cup apple juice

½ cup fresh or frozen blueberries

4 to 5 ice cubes

Place all the ingredients in a blender and process until smooth. Serve in a tall glass.

Carrot, Apple, and Ginger Soup

Carrot, apple, ginger, and onion make
sweet harmony in this zesty soup. It's good hot
out of the pot, or chilled.

Makes 4 servings

2 apples of your choice

¼ cup apple juice

1 tablespoon butter

1 tablespoon olive oil

2 small onions, coarsely
   chopped

1 tablespoon grated fresh
   ginger

8 carrots (about 1 pound),
   peeled and coarsely chopped

3 cups chicken broth

½ teaspoon salt

¼ teaspoon white pepper

Cut 1 apple in half and reserve half for garnish, removing the
core, and dipping the cut side into the apple juice to keep it from
browning. Peel and core the remaining 1½ apples and chop them.

Heat the butter and oil in a large pot set over medium-high heat
until the butter melts and the oil ripples. Add the chopped apple,
onion, ginger, and carrot and cook for 6 to 10 minutes, stirring
occasionally, until the onions are softened and translucent but not
browned. Reduce the heat, if necessary.

Add the chicken broth, salt, and pepper. Cook for 20 to 25
minutes, or until the carrots and apples are soft.

Meanwhile, cut the reserved apple into ½-inch pieces, leaving the
skin on if you like. Immediately toss to coat in the apple juice.

Remove the soup from the heat, let it cool a bit and use an
immersion blender to puree it until very smooth. Divide among
4 soup bowls and garnish with the reserved apple chunks.

Celery-Apple Juice with Ginger

If you have trouble getting started in the morning, try this tangy, refreshing drink.

Makes 1 serving

2 stalks celery, cut into thirds

1 Granny Smith apple, cored
and quartered

1 (1-inch) piece fresh ginger,
peeled

6 sprigs parsley

1½ tablespoons fresh lemon
juice

¼ teaspoon ground
cinnamon (optional)

Add the ingredients to a
juicer in the order listed.
Serve at room temperature.

Fennel, Apple, and Pancetta Pizza

The recipe for the dough is enough for two pies. Freeze half to use on another day.

Makes 8 servings

Dough

2½ cups all-purpose flour

2 teaspoons SAF Instant Yeast

1 teaspoon kosher salt

1 tablespoon dried fennel seeds

1 to 1¼ cups lukewarm water

Olive oil

Cornmeal, for sprinkling

Topping

4 ounces diced pancetta

1 fennel bulb, thinly sliced

1 small onion, thinly sliced

1 Granny Smith apple, cored and thinly sliced

3 garlic cloves, minced

½ teaspoon sea salt

½ teaspoon freshly ground black pepper

1 tablespoon fresh chopped rosemary

¼ cup shredded Parmesan cheese

¼ cup shredded Manchego cheese

½ cup shredded mozzarella cheese

To make the dough, place the flour, yeast, salt, and fennel seeds in the bowl of a food processor fitted with a steel blade. Process for a few seconds, then, with the motor running, slowly pour the water into the chute, ¼ cup at a time. Process until the dough comes together into a ball and then starts to ride around on the blade. The dough should be somewhat dry, but not too stiff.

Turn the dough out onto a board. Divide the dough into two balls. Roll each ball in some olive oil and place each in a separate bowl. Cover with plastic wrap and allow to rise in a warm spot until doubled, about 1½ hours.

Sprinkle a rimless cookie sheet with a little cornmeal to prevent the dough from sticking. Once the dough has doubled in size, stretch one ball to a circle the size of the pizza stone. Lay it on the cookie sheet, giving it a little shake to make sure it doesn't stick. Cover with a clean kitchen towel and allow to rest an additional 30 minutes.

Meanwhile, place a pizza stone or baking sheet in the oven and preheat to 450° F. To make the topping, add the pancetta to a large nonstick sauté pan set over medium-high heat. Sauté, stirring occasionally, for 5 minutes, or until crispy and browned.

Add the fennel, onion, and apple and sauté for 5 to 7 minutes, stirring frequently, until the mixture is caramelized. Add the garlic and sauté 30 seconds. Season with salt, pepper, and rosemary and stir to combine. Spread the topping on the pizza dough and sprinkle with cheese.

Carefully slide pizza the onto the preheat pizza stone or baking sheet and bake for 15 to 18 minutes or until the dough is brown and crispy and the cheese is melted.

Slice into 8 pieces and serve.

The New Pink Lady

This update on the classic Pink Lady uses pomegranate juice instead of the grenadine (which was originally made with pomegranate juice). The classic drink got its frothiness from a raw egg white added to the mix, but these days, a pasteurized egg white is the way to go.

Makes 2 cocktails

3 ounces gin

2 ounces pomegranate juice

4 ounces apple brandy, such as Calvados

2 egg whites

Lemon twists or yellow apple peels dipped in pomegranate juice, for garnish (optional)

Combine the gin, juice, brandy, and egg white in a shaker with 2 cups crushed ice. Shake very well.

Strain into small martini glasses. Garnish with lemon twist or apple peel, if desired.

Apple Quesadilla

Apples aren't typical Mexican fare, but they go nicely in these simple quesadillas, which can be served as a light lunch or supper, or cut into small wedges as an hors d'oeuvre.

Makes 4 quesadillas

2 cups shredded Monterey Jack, Cheddar, or Mexican-blend cheese

1 green onion, trimmed and finely chopped

1 apple, cored

4 (8-inch) flour tortillas

Preheat the oven to 450° F.

Pour the cheese into a small bowl and add the scallion. Chop the apple and toss with the cheese.

Place a sheet of foil on a work surface and place 1 tortilla on it. Spoon about ½ cup of the cheese mixture onto the half closest to you, leaving a ¼-inch edge. Fold the other half of the tortilla over the cheese and wrap in the foil. Repeat with the remaining tortillas and filling.

Bake for about 15 minutes, or until the cheese is melted and adheres to the tortillas and the tortillas begin to crisp. Remove from the oven and let cool for a minute. Cut in half or quarters and serve. (If you are making this as an hors d'oeuvre, cut into smaller wedges.)

Apple and Maple Syrup Turkey Burgers

A mixture of white and dark turkey meat will produce
the most flavorful burgers.

Makes 4 servings

Sauce

¼ cup mayonnaise or yogurt
2 tablespoons pure maple syrup
1 tablespoon Dijon mustard
¼ teaspoon sea salt
¼ teaspoon freshly ground black pepper

Topping

1 tablespoon olive oil
1 sweet onion, thinly sliced
1 small apple of your choice, cored and chopped

Burgers

1 pound ground turkey
1 small apple of your choice, cored and chopped
1 large egg, lightly beaten
2 tablespoons pure maple syrup
½ cup bread crumbs
1 tablespoon fresh chopped rosemary
½ teaspoon sea salt
½ teaspoon freshly ground black pepper
Nonstick vegetable oil spray
4 sandwich rolls, split and toasted

To make the sauce, whisk all the ingredients in a small bowl. Set aside.

To make the topping, heat the olive oil in a nonstick sauté pan set over medium heat. Add the onion and chopped apple and cook until soft and caramelized, about 10 minutes. Set aside.

To make the burgers, mix the ground turkey, chopped apple, egg, maple syrup, bread crumbs, rosemary, salt, and pepper in a medium bowl. Shape the turkey mixture into 4 uniform patties.

Coat a large nonstick sauté pan with vegetable cooking spray. Cook the patties over medium-high heat until browned on each side, 4 to 6 minutes per side.

To assemble, place a turkey burger on each roll and top with the sautéed apples and onions. Serve the sauce on the side.

Apple Slices with Mimolette and Prosciutto

Quickly put together, this elegant hors d'oeuvre will both satisfy your guests and free your time in the kitchen. If you can't find mimolette cheese, you may substitute aged Cheddar.

Makes 4 servings

1 apple of your choice, cored and cut into 8 slices
8 wedges mimolette cheese
8 slices prosciutto

Place a wedge of cheese on each apple and wrap with a slice of prosciutto. Secure with toothpicks and serve.

Gingery Apple Fizz

The hot spiciness of the ginger liquor combines with the sweetness of the apple juice to make this refreshing cocktail a winner.

Makes 1 cocktail

2 ounces ginger liquor
1 ounce light rum
2 ounces apple juice
3 ounce club soda
Basil leaf, for garnish

Combine the ginger liquor, rum, apple juice, and club soda in a highball glass filled with ice. Stir once and garnish with basil.

Red Braised Pork Sandwich with Pickled Crimson Gold Apples

Chef Linton Romero's spice-based pork sandwich makes the perfect party fare.

Makes 15 sandwiches

Red-Braised Pork Belly

3 pounds Kurobuta pork belly

3 (1-inch) pieces fresh ginger, crushed

5 ounces rock crystal sugar

2 ounces maltose sugar (available in Asian markets)

6 green onions, chopped in half

1 cinnamon stick

3 whole cloves

6 pieces star anise

1 tablespoon Szechuan peppercorns (available in Asian markets)

1 teaspoon coriander seeds

1 cup dark soy sauce

½ cup light soy sauce

2 quarts water, or as needed

1½ quarts Shao-hsing cooking wine (available in Asian markets)

2 dry Thai bird chilies (available in Asian markets)

Pickled Crimson Gold Apples

1 cup white wine vinegar

1 tablespoon salt

1 cup granulated sugar

1 cup water

1 bay leaf

1 teaspoon mustard seed

1 teaspoon coriander seed

1 teaspoon pink peppercorns

1 teaspoon white peppercorns

2 pounds Crimson Gold apples, sliced or julienned

Assembly

15 pita loaves

Sliced green onion

Cilantro leaves

For the Red-Braised Pork: Blanch the pork belly in boiling water for 10 minutes. Rinse the pork and set aside. Combine the remaining ingredients in a large pot and bring to a simmer. When the sugar is dissolved, add the pork and braise over medium-low heat until caramelized and tender, about 4 hours. Remove the pork and compress it between two flat baking pans overnight. Strain liquids, discard solids, and chill.

For the Pickled Crimson Gold Apples: Combine the vinegar, salt, sugar, and water in a saucepan and bring to a boil. Add the bay leaf, mustard seeds, coriander seeds, and pink and white peppercorns. Place the apple slices in a mason jar. Pour the hot vinegar mixture over the apples and let cool. Seal the jar and marinate in the refrigerator overnight or up to one month.

To assemble the dish, slice the braised pork into thin strips and combine with the desired amount of pickled apples. Season to taste with the salt and pepper. Garnish with the green onions and cilantro leaves. Serve with the pita bread and allow guests to stuff their own sandwiches.

Chef Linton Romero

STUDIED AT: Le Cordon Bleu California School of Culinary Arts

HAS COOKED AT: Caesar's Palace, Las Vegas, Nevada and The Ritz-Carlton, Los Angeles, California

TODAY: Oversees all food and beverage outlets for the JW Marriott Hotel Los Angeles at L.A. LIVE

Apple, Orange, and Rum Compote

Use your slow cooker to make this grown-up dessert.

Makes 12 servings

6 cups peeled Cortland apple slices

¼ cup dried figs

¼ cup raisins

¼ cup currants

¼ cup light brown sugar

2 teaspoons orange zest

1 tablespoon quick-cooking tapioca

3 tablespoons dark rum

¼ cup orange juice

Whipped cream, for topping

¼ cup toasted walnuts, for topping

Put the apples, dried fruit, brown sugar, orange zest, tapioca, rum, and orange juice in a slow cooker. Cover and cook on low 7 to 8 hours or on high for 3 to 4 hours. Spoon compote into bowls and top with whipped cream and walnuts.

Apple Brown Betty

A traditional American dessert, Apple Brown Betty is a great way to use up slightly stale bread.

Makes 8 servings

Nonstick cooking spray

6 slices white bread, cubed

5 Fuji apples, peeled, cored, and sliced

1 cup granulated sugar

2 teaspoons ground cinnamon

½ cup unsalted butter, melted

1 cup orange juice

Sauce

¼ cup unsalted butter, softened

¾ cup confectioners' sugar

1 teaspoon pure vanilla extract

1 tablespoon whiskey

Preheat the oven to 350° F. Spray an 8- x 8-inch baking dish with cooking spray.

Arrange the bread cubes on a baking sheet and toast in the oven for 10 minutes or until golden brown and crispy. Set aside.

In a medium bowl, combine the apples, sugar, and cinnamon; toss to coat.

To assemble, layer ⅓ of the bread cubes in the bottom of the baking dish. Drizzle with ⅓ of the melted butter. Layer ½ of the sugared apple slices on top of bread and drizzle with ½ of the orange juice. Repeat until the baking dish is almost filled. Then place a final layer of bread cubes on the top. Bake about 30 minutes or until apples are tender.

Meanwhile, prepare the sauce. In a medium bowl use an electric mixer to combine the softened butter, confectioners' sugar, vanilla, and whiskey. Process until smooth.

Cut the Brown Betty into squares, top with the sauce, and serve.

Baby Spinach Salad with Strawberries, Green Apples, and Pecans

Strawberries are one of the true delights of springtime. Celebrate this luscious fruit by pairing it in a salad with tart green apple wedges.

Makes 6 servings

1 (9-ounce) package fresh baby spinach

1 recipe Apple Cider-Raspberry Vinaigrette (see page 151)

1 cup hulled and quartered strawberries

1 cup coarsely chopped pecans, toasted

1 Granny Smith apple

Put the spinach into a large bowl.

Make the vinaigrette in a small bowl, according to the directions on the next page. Core the apple and cut it into ⅛-inch wedges. Place each piece immediately into the vinaigrette and turn to coat to prevent browning.

Transfer all the apple wedges into the bowl with the spinach. Add the strawberries. Pour the remaining vinaigrette over the salad. Toss gently to distribute the vinaigrette. Add the pecans, toss gently, and divide the salad between 4 salad plates. Serve immediately.

Apple Cider– Raspberry Vinaigrette

This vibrant vinaigrette works especially well with nut- and fruit-based salads.

Makes about ¾ cup

2 tablespoons apple cider

2 tablespoons raspberry vinegar

1/3 cup extra virgin olive oil

1 tablespoon Dijon mustard

1 tablespoon honey

½ teaspoon sea salt

½ teaspoon freshly ground black pepper

Whisk the vinegars, oil, mustard, honey, salt, and pepper until thoroughly combined. Taste and adjust the salt, if necessary.

Herbed Crab Cakes with Apple Horseradish Sauce

Fresh herbs enliven these crab cakes. Served with a green salad, they make a satisfying lunch.

Makes 4 servings

Herbed Crab Cakes

2 tablespoons sour cream

1 large egg, lightly beaten

1 cup panko bread crumbs

2 tablespoons fresh lemon juice

1¼ teaspoons seafood seasoning, such as Old Bay

2 tablespoons chopped fresh parsley

1 tablespoon chopped fresh basil

1 tablespoon chopped fresh tarragon

½ teaspoon sea salt

½ teaspoon freshly ground black pepper

1 pound fresh lump crabmeat, drained and picked through

Apple Horseradish Sauce

½ cup crème fraîche

¼ cup diced Granny Smith apple

2 tablespoons horseradish, drained

1 teaspoon lemon zest

¼ teaspoon sea salt

½ teaspoon freshly ground black pepper

1 tablespoon unsalted butter

2 tablespoons olive oil

To make the crab cakes, combine the sour cream, egg, bread crumbs, lemon juice, seafood seasoning, parsley, basil, tarragon, salt, and pepper in a large bowl. Gently fold in the crabmeat. Shape the mixture into 4 (4-inch) cakes; chill 1 hour in the refrigerator.

To make the sauce, combine the crème fraîche, diced apple, horseradish, lemon zest, salt, and pepper in a small bowl. Refrigerate until needed.

When the crab mixture is ready, melt the butter and oil in a large skillet over medium-high heat. Cook the crab cakes until golden brown, about 4 to 6 minutes per side. Serve with the crème fraîche sauce.

Apple Lime Cooler

Summer is around the corner. Kick off your shoes and sip this refreshing cocktail under a shady tree.

Makes 8 cocktails

2 cups water

2 cups granulated sugar

½ cup packed mint leaves, plus a few sprigs for garnish

¾ cup fresh lime juice

1½ cups gin

2 Granny Smith apples, cored and thinly sliced

1 lime, thinly sliced

1 liter club soda

Make a simple syrup by bringing the water, sugar, and mint to a boil in a 4-quart saucepan. Reduce heat, simmer 5 minutes, and let cool; strain out the mint.

To make the apple lime coolers, mix the simple syrup, lime juice, gin, apple and lime slices in a large pitcher or jar. Add ice.

To serve, pour into drinking glasses filled with ice cubes and top with club soda and a sprig of mint.

May 26

Apples Baked in Wine

This dessert goes well with a dollop of whipped cream or vanilla ice cream.

Makes 4 servings

4 apples of your choice
4 tablespoons honey
1 teaspoon ground cinnamon
4 teaspoons unsalted butter
¾ cup dry white wine

Preheat the oven to 350° F.

Core the apples and place them in a glass baking dish. Put 1 tablespoon honey in each hole and top each apple with 1 tablespoon of butter. Sprinkle cinnamon evenly over the apples. Pour the wine over the apples and place in the oven. Occasionally spoon the wine over the apples as they cook. Apples are done when they are soft, about 30 to 45 minutes. Serve either hot or cold.

May 27

Apple Spread

Smear some of this spread on a stack of pancakes and dig in.

Makes about 2 cups

2 pounds cooking apples, such as Granny Smith, Cortland, or Jonagold, peeled, cored, and cut into chunks
1 (6-ounce) can apple juice concentrate, thawed
1 teaspoon ground cinnamon
1 teaspoon pure vanilla extract

Preheat the oven to 300° F.

Put all the ingredients in a food processor and blend until smooth. Place the pureed apple mixture in a 9- x 13-inch glass baking dish and cook for 1 hour, stirring occasionally. Let cool, then refrigerate in an airtight container up to 1 week.

Apple Tip:

What do you get when you crossbreed a McIntosh with a Ben Davis? A Cortland! Its sweet white flesh makes it an ideal dessert apple.

Apple Slices with Goat Cheese, Pistachios, and Dried Apricots

Dried fruits can be difficult to cut. Before you start chopping the apricots, grease your knife with cooking spray.

Makes 8 servings

2 Honeycrisp apples, cored and cut into 24 slices
1 tablespoon fresh lemon juice
¼ cup goat cheese
2 tablespoons finely chopped pistachios
2 tablespoons finely chopped dried apricots

Toss apple slices with lemon juice to prevent browning. Spread ½ teaspoon goat cheese onto the end of each apple slice and arrange on a platter. Sprinkle cheese end with pistachios and dried apricots; serve immediately.

Turkey Burgers with Apple

Ground turkey is low in fat, but that quality can cause it to dry out. The apples and onions in
these burgers keep the meat nice and juicy without requiring added fat or making it sweet.
Apple Chipotle Sauce is a spicy condiment, but if it's too spicy for you,
it can be turned into a milder—but still lively—Apple Chipotle Mayonnaise.

Makes 4 burgers

1 small onion

2 cloves garlic

½ large apple, peeled, cored, and coarsely chopped

1 pound ground turkey

2 tablespoons grated cheese

4 good-quality hamburger buns or other rolls

Apple slices dipped in orange juice, for garnish

1 recipe Apple Chipotle Sauce (optional) (right)

Tomato ketchup, for serving (optional)

Grate the onion, garlic, and apple in a food processor fitted with a metal blade, or chop them finely with a sharp knife. Place the turkey in a mixing bowl and add the cheese and the chopped ingredients. Mix with your hands until all the chopped ingredients are thoroughly integrated into the meat. Form into 4 patties.

Grill or broil for about 5 minutes per side, or until the meat is light brown with no traces of pink and an instant-read thermometer inserted into the burger reads at least 165° F. Serve with the rolls, garnished with apple slices. Serve the condiments on the side.

Apple Chipotle Sauce

This hot, spicy condiment, rich with layers of flavor, is not for the timid. The sauce makes a nice condiment for the burgers on the previous page, as well as for beef, pork, and poultry dishes.

Makes 1½ to 2 cups

2 canned chipotle peppers packed in adobo sauce

½ tablespoon adobo sauce from the canned chipotles, or to taste

½ large sweet onion, such as Vidalia, coarsely cut

½ large apple, peeled and cut in pieces

2 tablespoons tomato ketchup

⅛ cup apple cider

1 tablespoon brown sugar

Combine the chipotles, adobo, onion, apple, ketchup, cider, and brown sugar in a food processor fitted with a metal blade. Process until very smooth.

Apple Chipotle Mayonnaise

A milder version of the Apple Chipotle Sauce that is equally delicious but not quite as hot.

Makes about 2 to 2½ cups

1 recipe Apple Chipotle Sauce (see above)

1 cup mayonnaise

Prepare the Apple Chipotle Sauce as directed above, adding the mayonnaise to the processor as well. Process until smooth and coral-colored.

Blackberry Apple Pie

Apples give a summertime berry pie an extra dimension. Fresh berries are best, but you can make this pie with frozen berries, too.

Makes 1 (9-inch) pie

1 recipe Pate Brisée (Flaky Pastry Dough) (see Apple Dumplings, page 12)

3½ cups blackberries

1 cup plus 2 teaspoons granulated sugar

2 teaspoons fresh lemon juice

3 tablespoons cornstarch

2 cups peeled, cored, and grated Empire apples

1 to 2 teaspoons heavy cream

Prepare the dough as directed on page 12. Divide the dough into two pieces, using slightly more than half for one disk (which will be the bottom crust). Chill as directed on page 12.

When you are ready to bake, preheat the oven to 400° F. Position the rack in the lower third of the oven. Roll out half the dough to a thickness of ⅛ inch, rolling it around the rolling pin. Place the rolling pin on a 9-inch pie pan and unroll the dough over it. Line the pie pan with the dough, leaving a 1-inch overhang all around. Refrigerate until you are ready to fill and bake the pie.

To make the filling, use a potato masher or fork to mix the berries, 1 cup sugar, lemon juice, and cornstarch in a large bowl to break up the berries and release their juices. Add the apples and toss gently to mix well.

Remove the pastry-lined pan from the refrigerator and prick the bottom with a fork a few times. Roll out the other half of the dough so that it will be slightly larger than the pan. Pile the filling into the pan, mounding it in the center. Arrange the remaining dough on top, tuck the edges under, pinching to seal them, and crimp. Cut 2 or 3 small steam vents in the top crust. Brush with the cream and sprinkle with the remaining sugar.

Bake immediately for 20 minutes. Reduce the heat to 375° F and bake for another 25 to 35 minutes, until the crust is golden and the juices are bubbly. Cool on a rack.

Apple Strawberry Smoothie

Whip up this nourishing smoothie for breakfast. If you'd like to make it a dessert, substitute strawberry ice cream for the yogurt.

Makes 2 servings

1 large apple

1 cup frozen strawberries

½ cup milk

½ cup strawberry yogurt

½ teaspoon pure vanilla extract

1 teaspoon honey, or to taste, depending on sweetness of strawberries

Peel and core the apple, cut it into chunks, and place them into a food processor or blender. Add the remaining ingredients and process until smooth.

Tuna Apple Pocket

Crunchy apples bring a touch of sweetness to this lunch staple.

Makes 2 servings

1 (6⅛-ounce) can chunk white tuna, drained

½ cup diced Gala or Honeycrisp apple

⅓ cup golden raisins

¼ cup diced celery

2 tablespoons plain Greek-style yogurt

1 teaspoon Dijon mustard

2 teaspoons lemon juice

¼ teaspoon sea salt

¼ teaspoon freshly ground black pepper

2 (7-inch) whole wheat pitas, cut in half

1 cup baby spinach

In a medium bowl, mix together the tuna, apple, raisins, and celery. Stir in the yogurt, Dijon, lemon juice, salt, and pepper; blend thoroughly.

Line each pita half with spinach leaves and then stuff with the tuna mixture, dividing equally.

Crispy Rice and Apple Treats

The addition of dried apples turns this favorite treat into something special.

Makes about 15 treats

Nonstick cooking oil spray

3 tablespoons unsalted butter

10 ounces marshmallows

5 cups crisp rice cereal

1 cup dried apples, chopped in ¼-inch pieces

Spray an 11- by 7-inch baking pan with cooking oil spray. Melt the butter with the marshmallows in a large saucepan or stockpot set over medium heat until it becomes a liquid that is easy to pour. Work carefully to make sure the mixture does not burn; reduce the heat if necessary. Add the cereal and apples and mix gently until thoroughly coated.

Working quickly, pour the mixture into a pan. Press with a greased spatula to make an even layer and let stand until hardened. Cut into 15 (2-inch) squares.

Pork and Apple Meatballs with Balsamic Glaze

Sweet and savory, try serving these meatballs with a side of polenta and a green salad.

Makes 24 meatballs

Meatballs

Olive oil cooking spray

1 pound ground pork

1 Granny Smith apple, peeled and diced

¼ cup finely diced shallots

3 garlic cloves, minced

2 eggs, lightly beaten

⅓ cup fresh bread crumbs

1 tablespoon honey

1 teaspoon dried rosemary

¾ teaspoon sea salt

¾ teaspoon freshly ground black pepper

Glaze

½ cup balsamic vinegar

¼ cup honey

¼ cup sugar

¼ teaspoon sea salt

½ teaspoon freshly ground black pepper

Preheat the oven to 375° F. Lightly spray a baking sheet with olive oil spray.

In a large bowl, combine the pork, apple, shallots, garlic, eggs, bread crumbs, honey, rosemary, salt, and pepper. Mix thoroughly. Using wet hands, form mixture (about 1 tablespoon) into 24 meatballs and arrange on prepared baking sheet.

Bake 15 minutes, or until meatballs are browned on the outside and cooked through on the inside.

While the meatballs are baking, make the glaze. In a 2-quart saucepan, combine the vinegar, honey, sugar, salt, and pepper; bring to a boil, reduce heat to low, and simmer for 5 to 7 minutes or until thickened.

To serve, arrange meatballs on a platter and drizzle with glaze.

Apple Butter Turnovers

Chef Catherine McCord knows how to make baking fun. In this recipe, she uses cookie cutters to create turnovers in all kinds of shapes. Let your imagination go wild!

Makes 8 to 10 small turnovers

8 tablespoons unsalted butter, chilled and cubed

8 tablespoons vegetable shortening or lard, chilled and cubed

2½ cups all-purpose flour

1 teaspoon salt

5 to 6 tablespoons ice water

½ cup apple butter

1 tablespoon honey

1 tablespoon water

Place the first 4 ingredients in the bowl of a food processor and pulse until the mixture resembles coarse cornmeal.

Sprinkle ice water, 1 tablespoon at a time, into the bowl and pulse a few times until the dough starts to come together.

Place the dough on a piece of parchment or plastic wrap, gather it into a ball, and flatten into a disk. Refrigerate the dough for 30 minutes, or until chilled. Roll out the dough until it is ¼ inch thick.

Using cookie cutters, cut out the dough into desired shapes. (If you are making 8 turnovers, you'll need 16 cut-outs, one for the top and one for the bottom.)

Place one cut-out on a parchment- or silicone-lined baking sheet and top with about 2 teaspoons of apple butter (depending on the size of your shape). Be sure to leave a ¼-inch border around the cut-out.

Combine the honey and water in a separate bowl. Brush the ¼-inch border with the honey water. Place a matching pastry shape on top of the apple butter and, using the tines of a fork, gently press down to seal the dough. Repeat the process with the remaining cut-outs.

When all the turnovers have been assembled, brush the remaining honey water on top of each turnover. Using the tip of a knife, cut several slits through the dough to allow steam to escape.

Bake at 400° F for 20 minutes, or until the dough begins to turn golden brown.

Chef Catherine McCord

FOUNDER OF: Weelicious.com

AMBITION: To help parents turn kids
into great eaters

FANS OF HER NEW COOKBOOK, *ONE
FAMILY, ONE MEAL*:
Jennifer Garner & Heidi Klum

June 7

Apple Cream Popsicles

This is an easy recipe for homemade popsicles. The proportions below are based on a popsicle mold with cups that hold ⅓ cup each, but you can tweak them to fit any size mold that you might have.

Makes 8 (⅓-cup) popsicles

1 cup vanilla ice cream
1 cup apple juice

Mash the ice cream and juice in a bowl to incorporate thoroughly. (The ice cream will become a bit soupy, but don't worry because it will freeze again.)

Use a funnel to fill the popsicle molds. Seal and freeze until hardened.

Perfect Prep

Peel an apple: Circle the apple's circumference with a sharp swivel peeler and remove its skin.

Core an apple: Push apple corer into center of the apple. Twist and remove seeds and membranes.

Halve an apple: Place the apple, stem up, on a cutting board. Slice down its middle.

Quarter an apple: Place the apple halves, cut side down, on a cutting board. Slice each half down its middle.

June 8

Green Apple, Cheese, and Bacon Panini

For a vegetarian—but not vegan—version of this recipe, simply omit the bacon.

Makes 4 sandwiches

¼ cup goat cheese
¼ cup cream cheese
¼ cup cooked bacon, chopped
¼ teaspoon sea salt
¼ teaspoon freshly ground black pepper
8 slices 12-grain bread
1 Granny Smith apple, cored and thinly sliced
2 tablespoons olive oil

Preheat a panini press or a grill pan.

Combine the goat cheese, cream cheese, bacon, salt, and pepper in a food processor and blend until mixed. Spread 4 slices of the bread with the mixture. Top with apple slices. Close the sandwiches with the other 4 slices of bread.

Brush both sides of the bread with the olive oil. Press the sandwiches in the panini press, about 5 minutes. Cut the sandwiches in half, transfer to plates, and serve.

Apple and Mango Fruit Salad

This fruit salad combines tart apples with sweet, tropical mangos and rich macadamia nuts.

Makes 6 servings

¾ cup coarsely chopped macadamia nuts

1 Granny Smith apple, cored and diced

1 mango, peeled, seeded, and diced

1 tablespoon fresh lime juice

¼ teaspoon ground ginger

¼ teaspoon sea salt

1 tablespoon chopped fresh basil

Lightly toast the macadamia nuts in a nonstick skillet, taking care they don't burn.

In a medium bowl, toss together all the ingredients, including the toasted nuts. For full flavor serve at room temperature.

Pork Chops Smothered with Mushrooms and Apples

A hearty dish that's packed with flavor. If you prepare the mushrooms and apples first, and then proceed to cook the pork chops and sauce in the same pan, you get layers of rich, luscious flavor.

Makes 4 servings

1 recipe Mushrooms and Apples (see page 167)

Pork chops

4 (7-ounce, 1-inch thick) bone-in rib pork chops

¼ teaspoon salt

¼ teaspoon freshly ground black pepper

1 to 2 tablespoons butter

1 tablespoon oil

Sauce

2 tablespoons apple brandy, such as Calvados

½ cup low-salt chicken broth

½ cup apple cider or apple juice

1 sprig fresh thyme

1 tablespoon butter

1 tablespoon all-purpose flour

Prepare the Mushrooms and Apples as directed and transfer to a bowl to keep warm. Reserve the juice in the skillet.

Pat the chops dry and season with salt and pepper. Heat the butter and oil in the skillet until the butter is melted. Add the pork chops in a single layer and brown one side, uncovered, for 5 to 8 minutes. Turn, cover, reduce the heat to low, and brown the other side for 4 more minutes, or until the pork is cooked to 140° F.

Transfer the chops to a platter and cover loosely with foil, reserving all the browned bits in the pan. Let the chops rest while finishing the sauce.

Return the pan to the heat, add the apple brandy and cook, stirring to scrape up the browned bits. Add the broth, cider or juice, and thyme and simmer until reduced to ½ cup. Transfer to another container and set aside.

Add 1 tablespoon butter to the same pan and let melt, stirring to scrape up any remaining browned bits. Add the flour and cook, stirring, until deeply browned. Return the broth mixture to the pan and whisk well for about 2 minutes, or until smooth and thickened. Remove the thyme sprig.

Return the mushroom mixture to the pan, along with any juices. Stir to reheat and coat with sauce. Season to taste with salt and pepper. Place the pork chops on serving plates, smother with the mushrooms, apples, and sauce, and serve immediately.

Mushrooms and Apples

A tasty blend of mushrooms and apples that will go well with the pork chops on page 166 or any pork, poultry, or beef dish.

Makes 4 servings

1 tablespoon unsalted butter

1 tablespoon vegetable oil

1 medium onion, chopped

¼ teaspoon salt, or to taste

1 large apple of your choice, peeled, cored, and cut into chunks about the size of the mushroom pieces

10 ounces white mushrooms, cut in half or quarters if large

Heat the butter and oil in a large sauté pan set over medium-high heat until the butter is melted. Add the onion and season with the salt. Cook, stirring frequently, for about 4 minutes, or until soft and translucent.

Add the apples and cook for 5 to 6 minutes, until softened and golden brown. Add the mushrooms and cook for 1 to 2 minutes, until just beginning to soften.

June 12

Apple Salsa

This zingy salsa goes well with grilled meats.

Makes about 2 cups

2 Granny Smith apples, cored and finely diced

¼ cup fresh lime juice

1 jalapeno pepper, seeded and minced

½ teaspoon cayenne pepper

¼ cup finely diced red onion

2 tablespoons chopped cilantro

½ cup chopped pecans, toasted

2 tablespoons grated ginger

½ teaspoon sea salt

To prevent browning, toss the apples with the lime juice in a large bowl. Add the rest of the ingredients and mix thoroughly. Chill in a covered container in the refrigerator for at least 1 hour to give flavors a chance to blend.

June 13

Apple Margarita

While many margarita recipes rim the glasses with salt, this version uses a spicy cinnamon-sugar mixture.

Makes 4 cocktails

¼ cup coarse sugar

1 teaspoon ground cinnamon

1 lime, cut into 4 wedges

1 cup gold tequila

1 cup fresh apple cider

⅓ cup fresh lime juice

½ cup triple sec, such as Cointreau

Ice cubes

4 apple slices, for garnish

Mix the cinnamon and sugar in a small bowl and transfer to a plate. With the lime wedges, moisten the rims of 4 glasses. Dip the glasses in the cinnamon-sugar mixture.

In a pitcher, combine the tequila, apple cider, lime juice, and triple sec. Stir to mix.

Fill the glasses with ice and pour in the margarita mixture. Garnish each cocktail with an apple slice and serve.

June 14

Apple, Fig, and Feta Salad

Welcome summer with a delicious and easy salad that pairs fresh figs with crispy apples and tangy feta cheese.

Makes 4 servings

12 fresh figs, quartered, stems removed

2 Honeycrisp apples, cored and sliced

½ cup crumbled feta cheese

Sea salt, to taste

½ cup torn basil leaves

Freshly ground black pepper, to taste

2 teaspoons balsamic vinegar

1 tablespoon extra virgin olive oil

Arrange the figs and apples on a platter and top with crumbled feta cheese and torn basil leaves. Season to taste with salt and pepper. Drizzle with the vinegar and olive oil. Serve immediately.

Apple Tip:

A bushel of apples weighs about 42 pounds.

A peck of apples weighs about 10.5 pounds.

Twenty-five percent of an apple's volume is air.

The average American eats about 45 pounds of apple annually.

Apple, Strawberry, and Peach Free-Form Tarts

Apples combine surprisingly well with warm-weather fruits, and these luscious tarts are proof. If you prefer, instead of six individual tarts, you can make one or two large ones.

Makes 6 tarts

1 recipe Pate Brisée (Flaky Pastry Dough) (See Apple Dumplings, page 12)

4 cups strawberries, hulled, cut into chunks or thick slices

2 medium ripe peaches, peeled and finely diced

¼ cup plus 2 tablespoons strawberry preserves or jam

4 large Golden Delicious or other baking apples, peeled, cored and diced

¼ cup apple jelly

2 tablespoons cornstarch

Finely grated zest and the juice from 1 medium lemon

1 egg, beaten

2 teaspoons heavy cream

2 tablespoons granulated sugar

Prepare and chill the dough as directed on page 12.

When you are ready to bake, preheat the oven to 375° F. Position the oven rack in the lower third of the oven. Line a baking sheet with parchment paper.

Combine 2 cups berries, the peaches, and ¼ cup strawberry jam in a bowl and toss. Set aside.

Combine the apples, apple jelly, cornstarch, lemon juice and zest, and the remaining berries in another bowl. Stir to mix well and coat the apples thoroughly.

Divide the dough into 6 equal pieces and roll them out into circles, 6½ to 7 inches in diameter. Place 2 or 3 dough circles onto the prepared baking sheet. Keep the unused circles in the refrigerator until needed.

Spread 1 teaspoon strawberry jam or preserves in the middle of each of the 3 circles, leaving an uncovered edge of 1½ inches all around.

Divide the apple-strawberry-lemon juice mixture evenly, using about 1 cup per tart, and pile into the center of the dough circle on top of the jam. Bring the edges of each dough circle up around the filling to make a tart about 5 inches in diameter, pleating the dough to shape it to the filling. The center will not be covered. Repeat with the remaining dough and filling. Six (5-inch) tarts should fit on one sheet, but if they don't, proceed in two batches.

Make an egg wash by mixing the egg and cream and brush the pastry gently with it. Sprinkle with 1 teaspoon sugar per tart.

Bake for 20 to 24 minutes, or until the pastry is cooked and golden, the juices are bubbling up, and the apples are soft enough to pierce easily with the tip of a knife. (They should not be mushy.) Remove the tarts from the oven and immediately top each with ¼ to ⅓ cup of the reserved uncooked strawberries and peaches. The heat of the tart will soften the berries, peaches, and jam just enough to glaze the tarts. Serve warm or at room temperature.

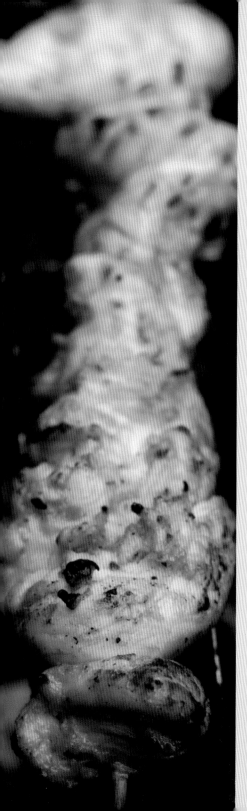

Grilled Chicken and Apple Satay with Peanut Sauce

Surprise dad on Father's Day with this spicy satay and addictive peanut sauce.

Makes 4 servings

Marinade

2 garlic cloves, minced

½ teaspoon curry powder

½ teaspoon chili powder

½ teaspoon sea salt

1 tablespoon coconut milk

1 tablespoon fresh lime juice

Peanut Sauce

¼ cup coconut milk

2 tablespoons smooth peanut butter

¼ tablespoon curry powder

¼ teaspoon sea salt

½ tablespoon apple cider vinegar

½ tablespoon honey

¼ cup water

2 boneless, skinless chicken breasts, sliced into strips

1 Granny Smith apple, cored and cut into chunks

16 mini bamboo skewers, soaked in water for 30 minutes

To make the marinade, combine the garlic, curry powder, chili powder, salt, coconut milk, and lime juice in a medium bowl. Pour over the chicken strips and toss to coat. Marinate for at least 1 hour or overnight in the refrigerator.

To make the peanut-curry sauce, place the sauce ingredients in a small 1-quart saucepan. Bring to a boil over medium heat and whisk constantly. Lower heat and simmer 3 to 5 minutes to thicken, stirring frequently to prevent burning.

When you are ready to grill, heat the grill to medium. Core the apple and cut it into chunks. Thread a piece of chicken and apple on each mini skewer. Grill skewers 3 to 5 minutes per side, or until cooked through. Serve the chicken satay with the sauce on the side.

Apple-Beet Salad

*The variety of flavors—sweet, tart, sharp, and mild—
and textures—the crunch of the nuts and the pop of quinoa—
make for a salad to remember.*

Makes 4 to 6 servings

8 small baby beets, trimmed

2 tablespoons honey

1 tablespoon apple cider vinegar

2 tablespoons orange juice

2 tablespoons Dijon mustard

1 tablespoon minced shallot

¼ teaspoon sea salt

½ teaspoon freshly ground black pepper

2 teaspoons extra virgin olive oil

2 cups cooked quinoa

1 cup chopped Honey Crisp or Fuji apple

¼ cup shelled dry-roasted pistachio nuts, chopped

4 cups arugula

4 ounces crumbled goat cheese

Preheat the oven to 400° F.

Scrub the beets and wrap each one in foil. Place them on a baking sheet and roast until the beets are tender when pierced with a knife, 30 to 40 minutes. Remove from the oven and allow to cool. Peel the beets and cut into bite-size pieces; set aside.

To make the dressing, whisk together the honey, vinegar, orange juice, mustard, shallot, salt, and pepper. Slowly drizzle in the olive oil, whisking until emulsified.

Combine the beets, quinoa, apples, and pistachios in a bowl and toss with the dressing. Place the arugula on a platter and top with the beet salad; sprinkle the goat cheese on top and serve.

Center of Attention

Simple to make, this inexpensive table centerpiece will brighten any summertime meal or party. Find a tall vase with a flared top. Fill the bottom of the vase about 3 inches deep with marbles or pebbles. Pour water to a few inches from the top of the vase. Nestle small branches with pretty leaves (freshly picked from your yard or obtained at a florist's shop) into the stone base. Slide skewers into Granny Smith apples. Stand the apples in the base, arranging them attractively within the branches.

Spicy Coconut Apple Soup

If you'd like a less spicy soup, omit the chili pepper seeds.

Makes 4 servings

2 tablespoons olive oil

1 medium onion, diced

3 cloves garlic, minced

2 teaspoons grated fresh ginger

2 red or green chili peppers with seeds, finely chopped

2 teaspoons ground cumin

1 teaspoon turmeric

1 teaspoon ground coriander

1 Granny Smith apple, cored, peeled, and diced

1 cup diced peeled sweet potato

2 boneless, skinless chicken breasts, diced

1 (14-ounce) can coconut milk

3½ cups chicken broth

Juice of 1 lime

½ teaspoon sea salt

½ teaspoon white pepper

¼ cup chopped cilantro

Heat the oil in a large 5-quart stock pot over medium heat. Add the onion and sauté 3 minutes, stirring occasionally. Add the garlic, ginger, and chilies; sauté 5 more minutes.

Stir in the cumin, turmeric, coriander, apple, sweet potato, chicken, coconut milk, and chicken broth. Bring to a boil, reduce heat, cover, and simmer 15 minutes or until potato and chicken are cooked through. Add the lime juice, salt, and pepper. Ladle into soup bowls, garnish with cilantro, and serve.

Apple Coffee Cake

What could be better than an old-fashioned coffee cake with a swirl of apples, pecans, cinnamon, and brown sugar? Two of them! Eat one now and freeze the other, well-wrapped, for up to a month.

Makes 2 (10-inch) coffee cakes

Cake

2¼ teaspoons instant yeast

½ teaspoon honey

¾ cup warm water (100° F on an instant-read or candy thermometer)

1 cup warm whole milk (100° F on an instant-read or candy thermometer)

½ cup plus 2 tablespoons unsalted butter, cut into pieces

½ cup plus 2 tablespoons granulated sugar

3 large eggs

1 teaspoon kosher salt

1½ teaspoons pure vanilla extract

5 to 5½ cups unbleached, all-purpose flour

Filling

2 medium apples, peeled, cored, and cut into small dice

1 teaspoon fresh lemon juice

2 cups finely chopped, toasted pecans

4 teaspoons ground cinnamon

1⅓ cups light brown sugar

Icing

1 cup confectioners' sugar, sifted

2 tablespoons heavy cream, water, or apple juice

Proof the yeast by dissolving it in a small bowl with the water and honey. Let it sit for 10 minutes or until it bubbles.

Pour the warm milk into a large bowl and let ½ cup of the butter melt in it. Add ½ cup sugar, the eggs, salt, and vanilla and whisk well. Stir in 3 cups flour. With a mixer set at medium speed, beat well for 1 minute. Add 2 to 2½ cups more flour and knead it in to form a soft dough. Knead 4 to 5 minutes with a mixer or 8 minutes by hand, until the dough is smooth and springs back when pressed lightly.

Place the dough in a covered container or a bowl covered tightly with plastic wrap and let rise at room temperature (68° to 70° F) for about 2 hours or until doubled in volume.

Meanwhile, make the filling. Mix the apple, lemon juice, toasted pecans, cinnamon, and brown sugar in a bowl.

When the dough has risen, press it down and turn it out onto the counter. Flatten it slightly, divide it into 2 pieces, and roll each one out to form a 10- by 20-inch rectangle. Let rest for 20 minutes.

Preheat the oven to 375° F. Position the oven rack in the center of the oven. Grease 2 (10-inch) cake pans or spring-form pans.

Spread each rested dough rectangle with 1 tablespoon butter, leaving 1 inch uncoated around the edges. Divide the filling in half and cover each buttered area with filling.

Roll up the dough and filling tightly to form two 20-inch ropes. Seal the seams by pinching them together. Starting in the center of one pan, coil the rope loosely, tucking the end under and pinching to seal. Press the dough down to flatten it to about ¾ inch. Repeat with the other pan and rope of filled dough. Cover the coffee cakes with greased plastic wrap and let rise at room temperature until the dough is about 1¼ inches high. Remove the plastic.

Bake for 10 minutes at 375° F; then reduce the heat to 350° and bake for another 25 to 30 minutes, until golden and an instant-read thermometer inserted into the cake reads 190° F.

Remove the coffee cakes from the pans and cool completely on a rack.

Make the icing by mixing the confectioners' sugar with the cream, water, or apple juice. Drizzle the icing over the cooled cakes.

Apple and Vanilla Roll-Ups with Honey Yogurt

Keep prepared crepes and fresh apples on hand and you can make this dessert whenever the mood hits.

Makes 2 servings

3 Gala apples, cored and cut into 8 wedges each

¾ cup granulated sugar

½ teaspoon ground cinnamon

1 vanilla bean

6 (9-inch) prepared crepes

Honey Yogurt

2 cups plain Greek-style yogurt

½ teaspoon ground cinnamon

¼ cup honey

In a 3-quart saucepan, combine the apples, sugar, and cinnamon. Split the vanilla bean in half lengthwise and scrape the seeds into the pan; add the pod to the pan. Stir over medium heat for 8 to 10 minutes or until the apples are soft. Remove from the heat and allow to cool. Remove and discard the vanilla pod.

To make the honey yogurt, combine the yogurt, cinnamon, and honey in a small bowl.

To make the roll-ups, arrange 4 apple pieces down the center of each crepe and roll up. Place each crepe seam side down on an individual dessert plate. Serve with honey yogurt.

Soft Tacos with Chicken and Apples

South of the border never tasted so good. Apples might seem out of place in a taco, but they add a mellow sweetness that counters the jalapeno's heat.

Makes 4 servings

8 (4-inch) corn tortillas

2 tablespoons olive oil

1 pound boneless, skinless chicken breasts, diced into 1-inch cubes

½ teaspoon sea salt

Freshly ground black pepper, to taste

1 jalapeno, seeded and thinly sliced

1 cup thinly sliced red onion

1 cup thinly sliced sweet onion

2 cups thinly sliced Granny Smith apples

2 garlic cloves, minced

¼ cup chopped cilantro

1 lime, cut into 4 wedges

Preheat the oven to 350° F. Wrap the tortillas in foil and heat them in the oven while you make the filling.

Heat 1 tablespoon of the oil in a large nonstick sauté pan set over medium-high heat. Season the chicken with salt and pepper. Sauté the chicken until lightly brown, about 5 to 10 minutes. Remove from pan and set aside.

In the same sauté pan, add the remaining oil over medium-high heat. Add the jalapeno and onions. Cook 5 minutes or until lightly browned and tender, stirring frequently. Add the apples and cook an additional 5 minutes. Add the garlic and cook 30 seconds, stirring constantly.

Return the chicken to the sauté pan and cook until heated. Remove the tortillas from the oven. Spoon in some of the chicken and apple mixture and top with the chopped cilantro. Fold in half and serve immediately with the lime wedges.

Corn and Apple Salad

Freshly picked corn is one of the delights of summer. This crunchy salad goes well with grilled pork or beef.

Makes 4 to 6 servings

Juice of 1 lime, plus more to taste if needed

3 tablespoons olive oil

¼ teaspoon salt

⅛ teaspoon freshly ground black pepper

1 large apple of your choice

4 ears cooked corn or 2 cups canned or frozen and defrosted corn kernels

½ cup chopped red bell pepper, seeds and pith removed

½ cup chopped red onion

1 to 2 tablespoons chopped fresh flat-leaf parsley

Mix the lime juice, oil, salt, and pepper in a bowl until thoroughly combined.

Peel and core the apple and cut it into ¼-inch chunks, placing them into the dressing and tossing lightly to prevent browning.

If you are using fresh corn, scrape the kernels off the cob with a sharp knife. Pour the corn into the mixing bowl. Add the red pepper, onion and parsley. Toss lightly to incorporate all the ingredients and coat with the dressing.

White Wine Punch with Apples

An easy, festive quaff for a summer picnic. Choose a wine that is a bit fruity and has not been aged in oak.

Makes about 1¼ quarts

1 (750-milliliter) bottle white wine (unoaked), well chilled

1¾ to 2 cups lemon-lime soda, well chilled

1 orange, thinly sliced

1 large apple, cored, halved, and cut into 1/8-inch wedges

Ice cubes, to taste

Combine the wine, soda, orange and apple slices, and ice in a punch bowl and stir gently.

Apple Tip:

When choosing a wine to pair with your apple-based dish, look to whites. Ideal choices include wines that have apple flavors in them—such as Chardonnay, Riesling, and Viognier. Also consider sparkling wines, which are clean and light.

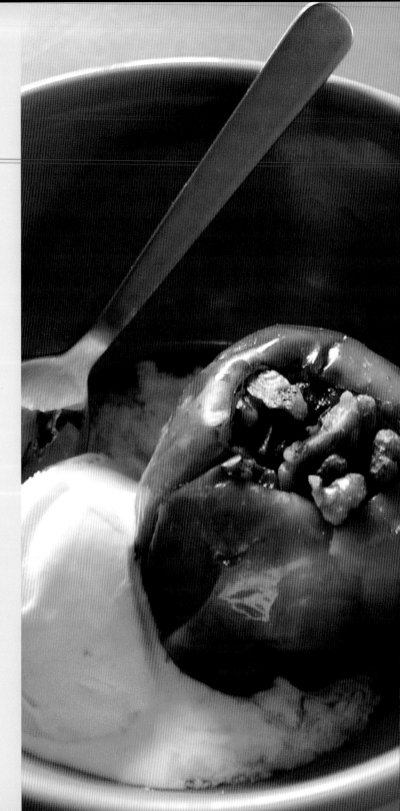

Grilled Baked Apples

If you put these apples on the grill as you start to eat, by the time dinner is finished, they'll be ready.

Makes 4 servings

4 baking apples, such as Gala or McIntosh
¼ cup coarsely chopped walnuts
4 teaspoons brown sugar
1 teaspoon ground cinnamon
½ teaspoon grated nutmeg
4 tablespoons unsalted butter
Vanilla ice cream

Preheat the grill.

Core the apples. Place each cored apple on its own square of aluminum foil. Divide the walnut pieces evenly and stuff inside each apple. Combine the brown sugar, cinnamon, and nutmeg in a small bowl and sprinkle evenly over the apples. Place 1 tablespoon butter on top of each apple.

Wrap each apple in the foil, leaving a small vent at the top, and place in the grill. Close the grill lid and let the apples cook until they have softened, about 30 to 40 minutes.

Serve immediately with vanilla ice cream.

Apple, Cheddar, and Onion Crostini

Crostini means "little toasts" in Italian. This appetizer pairs slices of crispy baguette with sweet onions, apples, and melted cheese.

Makes 24 crostini

2 tablespoons olive oil

1 large sweet onion, thinly sliced

2 Gala or Golden Delicious apples, cored and thinly sliced

1 tablespoon apple cider vinegar

½ teaspoon sea salt

¼ cup honey

2 stems fresh thyme, plus more leaves for garnish

24 (½-inch thick) baguette slices, cut on the diagonal

2 tablespoons whole-grain mustard

8 ounces sharp Cheddar or Gruyere cheese, shredded

Preheat the oven to 400° F. Cover two large baking sheets with parchment paper or foil.

In a large sauté pan, warm the oil over medium heat. Add the onion and apples. Cook a few minutes, until they begin to soften. Reduce the heat to medium-low and add the vinegar, salt, honey, and thyme. Cook, stirring occasionally, until the apples and onions are very soft, 30 to 35 minutes. Remove the thyme stems.

Arrange the bread slices on the baking sheets and spread lightly with mustard. Distribute the onion and apple mixture evenly over the bread. Top with the shredded cheese.

Bake for 8 to 10 minutes or until the cheese melts. Transfer the crostini to a platter and garnish with fresh thyme.

Honeyed Fruit Kebabs with Toasted Coconut

The start of summer is the perfect time for fresh fruit desserts.

Makes 8 fruit kebabs

1 cup cubed apple of your choice

1 tablespoon fresh lemon juice

1 cup cubed pineapple

1 cup cubed mango

1 cup red grapes

¼ cup honey

⅓ cup shredded coconut, toasted

8 bamboo skewers

Toss the apple in the lemon juice to prevent browning.

Thread the cubes of apple, pineapple, and mango and the grapes alternately onto skewers. Arrange the skewers on a serving platter and drizzle honey over the fruit. Sprinkle with coconut and serve immediately.

Roasted Beet, Apple, and Fennel Salad

This colorful and versatile salad can be featured either as a vegetarian main course or as a side dish for roast pork or chicken.

Makes 6 servings

4 medium beets, peeled and quartered

4 Honeycrisp apples, cored and quartered

1 fennel bulb, cored, cut into ½-inch slices

1 tablespoon olive oil

½ teaspoon sea salt

Freshly ground black pepper, to taste

4 cups arugula

Chunk of Pecorino Romano cheese

¼ cup salted, shelled, and chopped pistachio nuts

Vinaigrette

¼ cup apple cider vinegar

2 tablespoons Dijon mustard

1 tablespoon honey

½ teaspoon sea salt

½ teaspoon freshly ground black pepper

2 tablespoons extra virgin olive oil

Preheat the oven to 400° F. Place the beets, apples, and fennel in a large roasting pan. Toss with the oil, salt, and pepper. Roast in the oven for 1 hour or until the beets are tender; cool slightly.

Arrange the arugula on a platter and top with the roasted beets, apples, and fennel. With a cheese or vegetable slicer, shave the cheese into large pieces. Add the shaved pecorino and chopped pistachios to the salad.

To make the vinaigrette, mix together the vinegar, mustard, honey, salt, and pepper in a small bowl. Slowly drizzle in olive oil, whisking until emulsified. Drizzle over prepared salad.

White Pizza with Apple Slices

Instead of the traditional tomato based pie, why not try an all-white pizza with the extra surprise of tart-sweet apple.

Makes 8 servings

2 tablespoons extra virgin olive oil

1 garlic clove, minced

½ teaspoon sea salt

½ teaspoon freshly ground black pepper

1 (10-ounce) prepared whole wheat pizza shell

½ cup thinly sliced Granny Smith apple

6 ounces chopped fresh mozzarella cheese

3 ounces crumbled goat cheese

½ cup ricotta cheese

¼ cup grated Parmesan cheese

¼ cup basil leaves, torn

Place a pizza stone in the oven and preheat to 450° F.

In a small bowl, combine the olive oil, garlic, salt, and pepper.

Brush the garlic-infused olive oil onto the pizza shell. Top with apple slices, then mozzarella, then goat cheese, then ricotta, then Parmesan. Sprinkle with torn basil leaves.

Carefully transfer the pizza on the preheated stone and bake for 15 minutes or until the cheese melts and the crust is crisp. Remove from oven and let cool for 2 minutes. Cut into 8 wedges and serve.

Grilled Salmon, Apple, and Spinach Salad

Tangy feta cheese and tart apple rounds provide a tasty foil for the rich smokiness of the grilled salmon.

Makes 4 servings

4 (6-ounce) salmon filets

1 Granny Smith apple, cored and sliced into ¼ inch-thick rounds

1 teaspoon olive oil

½ teaspoon sea salt

½ teaspoon freshly ground black pepper

12 ounces baby spinach

1 cup peeled and sliced cucumber

1 avocado, sliced

⅓ cup crumbled feta cheese

Vinaigrette

1 tablespoon Dijon mustard

1 tablespoon honey

2 tablespoons apple cider vinegar

¼ teaspoon sea salt

½ teaspoon freshly ground black pepper

¼ cup extra virgin olive oil

Preheat a grill to medium-high heat; oil the grill rack.

Season the salmon and apple slices with olive oil, salt, and pepper. Place the salmon and apple slices on the preheated grill and cook 3 to 5 minutes per side, or until salmon reaches desired doneness and apple slices are tender with grill marks. Remove skin from the salmon. Transfer the salmon and apples to a plate and let cool while you assemble the salad.

Arrange the spinach, cucumber slices, and avocado slices on a platter. Sprinkle with crumbled feta cheese.

To make the vinaigrette, combine the mustard, honey, apple cider vinegar, salt, and pepper in a small bowl. Slowly drizzle in the olive oil until the dressing is emulsified.

Top the salad with the grilled salmon and apples. Drizzle with the vinaigrette and serve immediately.

Pretzel Crisps with Apple Slices, Mozzarella, and Basil

Play around with different varieties of apples and cheese until you find the combination you like best.

Makes 2 servings

12 pretzel crisps

1 Honeycrisp apple, cored and cut into 12 slices

12 basil leaves

12 slices fresh mozzarella

Arrange the pretzel crisps on a microwave-safe plate. Top each one with a slice of apple, a basil leaf, and a mozzarella slice. Microwave on high in 20-second intervals or until the cheese is melted and bubbly.

Serve piping hot.

July 1

Spicy Apple Cabbage Slaw

This slaw tastes best when it has been marinated overnight, so plan ahead.

Makes 12 servings

1 head green cabbage, thinly shredded (about 10 cups)

2 carrots, grated

1 Granny Smith apple, cored and grated

1 red onion, thinly sliced

3 green onions, chopped

1 red jalapeno pepper, seeded and thinly sliced

¾ cup mayonnaise

¾ cup nonfat Greek yogurt

¼ cup whole-grain mustard

2 tablespoons apple cider vinegar

½ cup fresh lemon juice

1 tablespoon honey

1 tablespoon celery seed

1 tablespoon hot sauce

1 teaspoon sea salt

1 teaspoon freshly ground black pepper

In a large bowl, combine the cabbage, carrots, apple, red and green onions, and jalapeno pepper; toss to mix.

In a medium bowl, combine the mayonnaise, yogurt, mustard, vinegar, lemon juice, honey, celery seed, hot sauce, salt, and pepper; whisk together until blended.

Pour the dressing over the cabbage mixture and toss gently to thoroughly mix. Transfer to a large container with a tight fitting lid. Refrigerate overnight. Serve chilled.

July 2

Apple and Peanut Butter S'mores

Apple slices and peanut butter give a new twist to this old campfire favorite.

Makes 4 servings

4 large marshmallows

4 graham cracker sheets, split in half (8 squares)

4 teaspoons peanut butter

1 Granny Smith apple, cored and sliced into 12 slices

Over an outdoor fire or an open flame, |toast the marshmallows on skewers until lightly browned.

While the marshmallows are toasting, spread peanut butter onto 4 of the graham crackers, about 1 teaspoon per cracker. Arrange apple slices on top of the peanut butter, 3 per square. Top with the marshmallow and the remaining graham cracker squares. Serve immediately.

Apple Tip:

Apples dunked in peanut butter make an excellent post-workout snack. The apples provide your body with essential energy-boosting (and glycogen-replenishing) carbohydrates. The peanut butter provides a protein punch.

Apple Cider and Molasses Baked Beans

Make up a batch of these slow-cooked beans for your Fourth of July barbeque. If you have a slow cooker, instead of transferring the beans to the oven, place the beans in the cooker for the same amount of time.

Makes 8 servings

3 cups dried pinto beans

3 cups apple cider

1 cup water

4 ounces salt pork, thinly sliced

1 large sweet onion, peeled and cut into chunks

1 Fuji apple, cored and cut into chunks

½ cup ketchup

⅓ cup blackstrap molasses

2 tablespoons Worcestershire sauce

2 tablespoons brown sugar

1 tablespoon dry mustard

2 teaspoons salt

Pick over the beans, discarding any stones and wrinkled beans. Rinse them well and place them in a large bowl. Add enough cold water to cover by 3 inches and soak for 12 hours.

Drain the beans and discard the water. Transfer the beans to a 5-quart Dutch oven. Add the apple cider and water; bring to a boil over high heat. Lower the heat to medium and gently boil for 1½ hours, or until the beans are tender. Remove from the heat and drain, reserving the cooking liquid (reduced to about 1 cup).

Preheat the oven to 300° F. Layer the salt pork slices on the bottom of the Dutch oven and add the drained beans, onions, and apples.

In a 2-quart saucepan, combine the ketchup, molasses, Worcestershire, brown sugar, and dry mustard. Place over medium heat and cook until the brown sugar and mustard dissolve, about 3 minutes. Pour the mixture over the beans. Add the reserved cooking liquid and enough hot water (about 4 cups) to cover the beans. Cover the pot and bake for 4 hours. Add more water if the beans seem too dry, and season with the salt. Serve hot.

All-American Apple Pie

This combination of different apple varieties, applesauce, and apple juice concentrate produces a decidedly apple-y pie. You can vary the kinds of apples you use, but the combination should include about half Granny Smith or another variety that retains some firmness when baked.

Makes 1 (9-inch) pie

1 recipe Pate Brisée (Flaky Pastry Dough; see Apple Dumplings, page 12)

4 medium Granny Smith apples

2 large Golden Delicious apples

2 large Rome apples

Zest of 1 small lemon

1 teaspoon fresh lemon juice

2 tablespoons apple juice concentrate (undiluted)

¼ cup granulated sugar, plus more for sprinkling

½ teaspoon ground cinnamon

2 tablespoons cornstarch

1½ cups unsweetened applesauce

2 tablespoons unsalted butter, dices

1 egg white mixed

1 tablespoon cream

When you are ready to bake, preheat the oven to 400° F. Position the rack in the lower third of the oven. Roll out half the dough to a thickness of 1/8 inch, rolling it around the rolling pin. Place the rolling pin on a 9-inch pie pan and unroll the dough over it. Line the pie pan with the dough, leaving a 1-inch overhang all around. Refrigerate until you are ready to fill and bake the pie. Reserve any dough scraps to use for making apple-shaped decorations for the top crust.

To make the filling, peel and core the apples and cut them into ⅛-inch-thick slices. (You should have 8 to 9 cups.) Toss the apples gently with the lemon zest and juice, juice concentrate, ¼ cup of the sugar, the cinnamon, and cornstarch. Let stand for 15 to 20 minutes. Gently stir in the applesauce.

Remove the pastry-lined pan from the refrigerator and prick the bottom with a fork a few times. Pile the filling into the pan, mounding it in center. Dot with the butter.

Roll out the other half of the dough so that it will be slightly larger than the pan and cover the apples with it, easing the dough onto the apples and pressing slightly to warm the top dough just enough to conform it to the apple mound. (This will help prevent a gap between the apples and the crust once they are baked.) Seal the edges and crimp as desired. Cut two or three slits in the top for steam to escape. Use any dough scraps to fashion apple-shaped decorations for the top of the pie. To make egg wash, combine egg white and cream. Brush dough with egg wash and sprinkle with sugar.

Bake for 25 minutes. Reduce the heat to 375° F and bake for another 20 to 30 minutes, until the crust is a deep golden color and the juices are bubbly. Cool on a rack.

Roast Beef, Cheddar, and Apple Sandwich

Flaky croissants make a perfect foil for melted cheddar, crisp apple slices, and peppery watercress.

Makes 2 sandwiches

2 croissants, each sliced in half
2 tablespoons honey mustard
2 ounces sharp Cheddar, sliced
4 ounces roast beef, thinly sliced
½ Granny Smith apple, cored and thinly sliced
1 cup watercress
¼ teaspoon sea salt
¼ teaspoon freshly ground black pepper

Preheat the broiler. Line a baking sheet with foil.

Spread ½ tablespoon of mustard on each croissant half. Arrange all 4 halves on the baking sheet and top the 2 bottoms with the cheese.

Place the baking sheet under the broiler for 30 seconds to 1 minute, until the bread is lightly browned and the cheese is melted.

Remove the baking sheet from the oven and top each cheese half with 2 ounces of roast beef, half of the apple slices, and half of the watercress; season with salt and pepper. Make into sandwiches and serve immediately.

Dried Fruit and Dark Chocolate Trail Mix

Dark chocolate is packed with antioxidants. Enjoy this fruit and nut trail mix studded with bits of dark chocolate goodness.

Makes about 5½ cups

½ cup roasted peanuts
½ cup choped almonds
½ cup chopped cashews
½ cup roasted sunflower seeds
½ cup dark chocolate chips or chunks
½ cup dried cherries
½ cup chopped dried apples
½ cup chopped dried apricots
½ cup toasted coconut

Mix ingredients in a large bowl. Store in an airtight container in a cool, dry place for up to 2 weeks.

Minty Pineapple-Apple Juice

Serve this refreshing juice on hot summer days and cool down immediately.

Makes 4 drinks

½ pineapple, cored and cut into chunks

2 apples of your choice, cored and cut into chunks

6 tablespoons fresh mint, finely chopped

½ cup fresh lime juice

Juice the pineapple and apple in a juicer. Pour the pineapple-apple juice into a pitcher and add the mint and lime juice. Mix well and serve in tall glasses with plenty of ice.

Fresh Fruit Salad with Walnuts, Pecans, and Coconut

Utilize the luscious fruits of summer in this easy-to-make salad.

Makes 8 servings

1 Honeycrisp apple, cored and sliced

1 white or yellow peach, pitted and sliced

1 kiwi, peeled and sliced

½ cup strawberries, hulled and sliced

½ cup raspberries

¼ cup chopped toasted walnuts

¼ cup chopped toasted pecans

½ cup toasted coconut

In a large bowl, combine all ingredients and toss to combine. Serve with frozen yogurt or ice cream, if desired.

Fish Roasted in Parchment with Apples

Cooking in parchment paper sounds more complicated than it is—and it makes an elegant, tasty dish.

Makes 4 servings

2 tablespoons plus 2 teaspoons olive oil

1 medium onion, sliced very thinly

1 red bell pepper, sliced very thinly

1 large Gala or Fuji apple, cored and cut in matchstick-sized slices

4 tablespoons roughly chopped fresh parsley

4 (4 to 6-ounce) fillets of tilapia, flounder, or other white-fleshed fish

Juice of 2 small limes

1 teaspoon curry powder

Salt and freshly ground black pepper to taste

Preheat the oven to 400° F. Cut 4 (12- by 12-inch) squares of parchment paper or aluminum foil.

Place one square on a work surface and drizzle the center with 1 teaspoon of the oil. Arrange about ⅛ of the onion, red pepper, apple, and parsley in the center of the square on top of the oil. Place 1 fillet on top. Drizzle the fillet with 1 teaspoon oil and the juice of ½ lime. Sprinkle with about ¼ teaspoon curry powder and season with salt and pepper. Scatter ⅛ of the onion, red pepper, apple, and parsley on top.

Fold all 4 edges of the square in over the fish to make a rectangle and place, seam side down, on a baking sheet. Repeat with the remaining ingredients to make 3 more parcels.

Bake for 12 to 22 minutes, or until the fish is cooked through and no longer pink and the vegetables and apples are nicely softened. The timing will depend on the thickness of the fillets.

Apple Tip:

Apples make the perfect accompaniment to any fruit salad. But once an apple is cut, tyrosinase, an enzyme, reacts to oxygen, turning the apple's polyphenols into melanin—and starting the browning process. If you want to keep apples from turning brown:

Cut and store apples in water until serving time.

Cover cut apples in plastic wrap.

Soak apples in lemon juice to delay/prevent browning.

July 10

Apple Cantaloupe Smoothie

Make this tasty refresher for a summer day. Process the melon last and only briefly, as its high water content will thin the smoothie if processed for too long.

Makes about 2 cups

1 large apple, peeled, cored, and cut into large chunks

1 cup ice

2 cups vanilla ice cream

2 tablespoons granulated sugar, or to taste

1 cup cantaloupe chunks

Combine the apple, ice, ice cream, and sugar in a food processor and process until smooth. Add the melon last and process briefly until smooth. Taste and add more sugar if necessary.

Apple-Berry Pavlova

Pavlova, named after the famous Russian ballet dancer Anna Pavlova, is a meringue dessert. Crispy outside and soft and airy within, it's an ideal way to end a summer meal.

Makes 8 servings

Meringue

3 large egg whites, room temperature

1 cup superfine granulated sugar

1 teaspoon cornstarch

1 teaspoon white vinegar

1 teaspoon pure vanilla extract

Filling

3 Granny Smith apples, peeled, cored, and thinly sliced

2 tablespoons unsalted butter

2 tablespoons light brown sugar, packed

½ teaspoon ground cinnamon

⅛ teaspoon salt

1 cup blackberries, strawberries, or raspberries, cut in half or quarters depending on size

Whipped Cream

1½ cups heavy cream

Preheat the oven to 250° F. Trace out a 7-inch circle of parchment paper. Place on a baking sheet and set aside.

To make the meringue, place the egg whites in a large glass or metal bowl and beat with an electric mixer on high speed until soft peaks form, about 3 to 5 minutes. Slowly add in half the sugar, beating until stiff peaks form and egg whites are glossy. Slowly beat in the remaining sugar, reserving 1 tablespoon, until it has fully dissolved.

In a small bowl, combine the reserved tablespoon sugar, cornstarch, vinegar, and vanilla. Add into meringue and beat until incorporated, about 1 minute.

Spoon the meringue on top of the prepared parchment circle on the baking sheet. Spread the mixture to the edges of the circle, creating a well in the center.

Bake the meringue for 45 minutes to 1 hour, or until crisp on the outside and slightly marshmallowy on the inside. Let cool on the baking sheet. Once cool, transfer to a plate and remove the parchment paper.

To prepare the filling, place the apples, butter, brown sugar, cinnamon, and salt in a large skillet over medium-high heat. Cook, stirring occasionally, until the apples are tender and slightly caramelized, about 7 to 10 minutes. Stir in the blackberries and set aside to cool completely.

To make the whipped cream, place the heavy cream in a medium bowl and whip with a handheld mixer on high for 3 to 5 minutes, or until stiff peaks form. Set aside.

To assemble, place the whipped cream in the middle of the meringue and spoon the apple-berry mixture on top. Serve immediately.

Grilled Steak Salad with Apples, Blue Cheese, and Pecans

A grilled steak is one of the treats of summer. Thinly sliced and arranged over a salad of mixed greens and apples, it makes for a no-fuss dinner.

Makes 4 servings

1 pound flank steak

1 teaspoon olive oil

1 teaspoon sea salt

1 teaspoon freshly ground black pepper

8 cups mixed baby greens

1 Honeycrisp apple, cored and thinly sliced

1 cup chopped toasted pecans

½ cup crumbled blue cheese

Apple Cider Vinaigrette (See page 197)

Preheat a grill to medium high.

Season the flank steak with the olive oil, salt, and pepper. Grill the steak 5 to 6 minutes per side for medium rare or longer if you want it more thoroughly cooked. Allow the steak to rest for 10 minutes, tented with foil.

On a platter, arrange the baby greens and top with the apple slices, pecans, and blue cheese.

Slice the steak thinly, against the grain. Arrange the sliced steak on top of the salad and drizzle with some of the vinaigrette. Serve with extra dressing on the side.

July 13

Apple Cider-Mustard Vinaigrette

This versatile dressing is delicious on both meat and vegetable salads.

Makes about ½ cup

2 tablespoons Dijon mustard

1½ tablespoon honey

2 tablespoons apple cider vinegar

2 tablespoons apple cider

½ teaspoon sea salt

½ teaspoon freshly ground black pepper

⅓ cup extra virgin olive oil

In a small bowl, whisk together the mustard, honey, vinegar, cider, salt, and pepper. Slowly drizzle in the olive oil and whisk to form an emulsion.

July 14

Widow's Kiss

This flavorful cocktail dates back to the '90s—the 1890s, that is. With its blend of apple brandy and two herbal liqueurs, it's a kiss you'll long remember.

Makes 2 cocktails

4 ounces apple brandy, such as Calvados

2 ounces yellow Chartreuse

1 ounce Benedictine

2 dashes Angostura bitters

Ice

Mix the brandy, Chartreuse, Benedictine, and bitters in a shaker with ice. Strain into 2 cocktail glasses.

Corn Upside-Down Cake with Apples

A mix of corn muffin and apple pie, this cake is delicious as is or with a scoop of whipped cream.

Makes 1 (9-inch) cake

Nonstick cooking spray

Apple Layer

3 Granny Smith apples, peeled, cored, and
   cut into bite-sized pieces
⅓ cup granulated sugar
½ teaspoon ground cinnamon
¼ teaspoon salt
1 teaspoon pure vanilla extract

Batter

3 large eggs
½ cup granulated sugar
⅓ cup olive oil
¼ cup applesauce
¼ water
1 teaspoon pure vanilla extract
¾ cup all-purpose flour
¼ cup corn flour, such as
   Bob's Red Mill brand
1 teaspoon baking powder
¼ teaspoon salt

Preheat the oven to 350° F. Prepare a 9-inch springform pan by spraying it with nonstick cooking spray. Cut a piece of parchment paper to fit the pan and place it on the bottom; set aside.

To make the apple layer, combine the apples, sugar, cinnamon, salt, and vanilla in a medium bowl. Pour into the prepared pan.

To make the batter, beat the eggs and sugars in a large bowl for about 3 minutes, or until light and creamy. Add the olive oil, applesauce, water, and vanilla; beat another 2 minutes.

In a small bowl, whisk together the flours, baking powder, and salt.

Add the dry ingredients into the wet and mix on medium for 2 minutes, or until well blended. Pour the batter over the apple layer.

Transfer the pan to the oven (place a piece of foil on the rack beneath the springform pan for easy clean-up). Bake for 35 to 45 minutes, or until a toothpick inserted in the center comes out clean. Cool for 10 minutes.

When ready to serve, place a plate on top of the cake and flip it over so the apples are on top. Release from the pan and serve warm.

July 16

Sautéed Escarole with Apples, Garlic, and Pecorino

The sweet tartness of the apples offset the slight bitterness of the escarole to make this a side dish you'll go to again and again.

Makes 4 servings

2 teaspoons olive oil

1 Granny Smith apple, cored and diced

4 to 6 cloves garlic, minced

8 cups chopped escarole

¼ cup chicken broth

½ teaspoon sea salt

1 teaspoon freshly ground black pepper

2 tablespoons grated Pecorino Romano

Heat the olive oil in a large sauté pan set over medium high heat. Add the apples and sauté for 5 minutes, or until lightly browned and softened. Add the garlic and stir for 30 seconds or until fragrant. Add the escarole, chicken broth, salt, and pepper. Steam for 3 to 5 minutes, stirring frequently, until the escarole is wilted. Stir in the grated cheese and serve immediately.

July 17

Lentil, Feta, and Apple Salad

Makes 2 servings

2 cups French lentils, cooked

1 Honeycrisp apple, cored and diced

½ stalk celery, diced

¼ cup crumbled feta, crumbled

¼ cup fresh flat-leaf parsley, chopped

¼ cup fresh basil leaves, torn

1 tablespoon extra virgin olive oil

2 teaspoons red wine vinegar

¼ teaspoon sea salt

½ freshly ground black pepper

Combine the cooked lentils, apples, celery, feta, parsley, and basil in a medium bowl. Drizzle with the olive oil and red wine vinegar and season with salt and pepper. Toss gently and divide the salad between 2 salad plates. Serve immediately.

July 18

Apple Gazpacho

A perfect start to a summer meal, this no-cook soup is light and refreshing.

Makes 8 servings

1 cup cubed stale white crustless country bread

½ cup apple juice

1¼ cups blanched sliced almonds

1 cup chopped cucumber

1 Granny Smith apple, peeled, cored, and chopped

1 cup seedless green grapes

¼ cup basil leaves

1 clove garlic

3 tablespoons apple cider vinegar

¼ cup extra virgin olive oil

½ cup low-fat buttermilk

½ teaspoon sea salt

½ teaspoon freshly ground black pepper

Basil leaves, for garnish

Preheat the oven to 350° F.

Combine the stale bread and apple juice in a small bowl and let soak for 5 minutes.

Meanwhile, spread the almonds onto a baking sheet and bake for 6 minutes or until golden brown. Transfer 1 cup of the toasted almonds to a blender, reserving ¼ cup for garnish.

Add the soaked bread and apple juice mixture, cucumber, apple, grapes, basil, garlic, apple cider vinegar, olive oil, buttermilk, salt, and pepper to the blender. Puree until smooth. If necessary, strain the mixture to ensure smoothness. Refrigerate for 30 minutes. Ladle the chilled soup into bowls, garnish with the reserved almonds and basil leaves, and serve immediately.

Chilled Apple Soup

Refreshing and lightly spiced, this dessert soup is delicious to the last spoonful.

Makes 8 servings

8 Golden Delicious apples, peeled, cored, and quartered

2 cups apple cider

¼ cup fresh lemon juice

1 tablespoon granulated sugar

3 cinnamon sticks

1 teaspoon freshly grated nutmeg

2 teaspoons pure vanilla extract

2 cups orange juice

2 cups vanilla yogurt

1 cup light cream

Lemon slices, for garnish

In a 5-quart saucepan, combine the apples, apple cider, lemon juice, sugar, cinnamon sticks, and nutmeg. Bring to a boil, reduce heat, cover, and simmer until the apples are tender, about 20 minutes.

Remove from heat and add the vanilla extract. Transfer to a glass bowl and let cool. Cover and refrigerate overnight.

Remove cinnamon sticks and puree until smooth in a blender. Add the orange juice, yogurt, and cream. Stir to combine. To serve, ladle the soup into bowls and garnish with lemon slices.

Apple-licious Taquitos

Chef Yvette Garfield is determined to introduce children to the world's vast cuisines, one recipe at a time. Here she shares a Mexican-based recipe that combines apples, cinnamon, and tortillas. But you certainly don't have to be a kid to enjoy the results!

Makes 6 servings

1 large apple of your choice

1 cup unsweetened applesauce

1 teaspoon ground cinnamon plus
¼ teaspoon for sprinkling

6 (8-inch) whole wheat tortillas

¼ cup vegetable oil

6 scoops vanilla ice cream (optional)

Preheat the oven to 350° F.

Core and dice the apple. In a medium bowl, combine the diced apple, applesauce, and cinnamon.

Use a pastry brush to lightly coat both sides of the tortillas with vegetable oil.

Place 1 heaping tablespoon of the apple mixture in the center of each tortilla.

Roll the tortillas to make a flute shape, and place them on a baking sheet. Bake for 20 minutes, or until the tortillas become crispy. Remove them from the oven and let cool.

Sprinkle cinnamon on top of each warm taquito. Add a scoop of vanilla ice cream onto the taquitos, if desired.

Chef Yvette Garfield

OWNER AND FOUNDER: Handstand Kids, a company that produces globally-inspired cookbook kits for children

MISSION: To teach children about different cultures through recipes they make themselves

WHERE: Featured on CNN, The Today Show, and *People* magazine

White Sangria

Celebrate the lazy days of summer with this sparkling sangria. If you'd like a less sweet sangria, omit the sugar.

Makes 6 cocktails

1 nectarine, pitted and cut into bite-sized pieces

1 tangerine, peeled and cut into bite-sized pieces

1 apple of your choice, cored and cut into bite sized pieces

1 cup seedless green grapes, sliced in half

1 lemon, sliced

2 (750 ml) bottles Sauvignon Blanc or other dry white wine

½ cup Calvados

1 cup white grape juice

¼ cup superfine granulated sugar (optional)

8 ounces club soda

6 mint sprigs, for garnish (optional)

Place the fruit in a large pitcher. Add the wine, Calvados, grape juice, and sugar if desired. Chill in the refrigerator for 1 hour to allow flavors to blend. Right before serving, add the club soda.

Baked Caramel Apples

This gooey dessert is a kid pleaser. Serve with plenty of napkins.

Makes 4 servings

4 Fuji or Honeycrisp apples, cored with a melon baller

¼ cup light brown sugar, packed

¼ cup caramel sauce

½ teaspoon ground cinnamon

4 scoops vanilla ice cream

Chopped toasted pecans

Preheat the oven to 350° F.

Place the cored apples in a 9- x 13-inch baking dish. Divide the brown sugar, caramel, and cinnamon among the apples. Bake for 30 to 45 minutes, or until tender.

To serve, place each apple with some of the sauce from the bottom of the pan on a serving dish, top with a scoop of vanilla ice cream and sprinkle with the pecans.

Chicken, Avocado, and Apple Salsa Wrap

Use the zesty apple salsa on page 168 to make this quick and easy wrap.

Makes 4 servings

1 ripe avocado

⅓ cup fresh lime juice

¼ teaspoon sea salt

4 whole wheat tortilla wraps

2 boneless, skinless chicken breasts, grilled and sliced

1 cup apple salsa (See page 168)

½ cup Boston lettuce, chopped

Scoop out the avocado into a small bowl and add the lime juice and sea salt. Mash the avocado into a paste.

Place the tortillas on a work surface. Spread ¼ of the avocado mixture in the middle of each tortilla. Top with ¼ of the grilled chicken, ¼ cup salsa, and ¼ of the lettuce.

Fold the bottom and top portions of the tortilla up and over the filling and then fold the right and left sides on top of that. Serve immediately.

Fruity Oatmeal Cookie Pie

Kids will love this huge cookie topped with fresh fruit.

Makes 12 servings

Cookie

¼ cup applesauce

¼ cup unsalted butter

¾ cup light brown sugar, packed

1 large egg

2 teaspoons pure vanilla extract

1 cup all-purpose flour

1 cup old-fashioned rolled oats

1 teaspoon ground cinnamon

1 teaspoon baking soda

½ teaspoon baking powder

½ teaspoon salt

⅓ cup dried apples, finely chopped

Topping

8 ounces cream cheese, softened

¼ cup apple juice concentrate, thawed (not diluted)

2 tablespoons orange zest

2 teaspoons pure vanilla extract

2 kiwis, peeled and thinly sliced

1 Honeycrisp apple, cored and thinly sliced

1 nectarine, pitted and thinly sliced

1 cup thinly sliced strawberries

½ cup orange marmalade

Preheat the oven to 350° F.

To make the crust, cream the applesauce, butter, and brown sugar in a large bowl. Add the egg and vanilla; mix to combine.

In another large bowl, whisk together the flour, oats, cinnamon, baking soda, baking powder, and salt. Add the dry ingredients to the wet and stir to combine. Fold in the chopped dried apples.

Spread the batter on a baking sheet lined with parchment paper. Wet your hands first. This helps spread the cookie dough without it sticking to your hands.

Bake for 20 to 25 minutes, or until browned and crispy. Remove from the oven and let cool for 15 to 20 minutes.

While the cookie is baking, make the topping. In a small bowl, beat the cream cheese with the apple juice concentrate, zest, and vanilla until fluffy. Spread the mixture on top of the cooled cookie crust. Arrange the fruit over the top.

In a 2-quart saucepan, heat the marmalade until just melted. Brush the melted marmalade on top of the fruit. Cut into wedges and serve.

Smoked Trout and Apple Salad

This easy-to-prepare meal makes a filling lunch or a light supper.

Makes 6 servings

1 cup crème fraîche

½ cup horseradish, drained

2 teaspoons extra virgin olive oil

2 tablespoons apple cider vinegar

2 teaspoons chopped dill

¼ teaspoon sea salt

8 cups watercress, arugula, dandelion, or other sharp-tasting green

¼ cup thinly sliced red onion

2 Fuji or Honeycrisp apples, cored and thinly sliced

1 smoked trout, skin and bones removed and flaked

½ teaspoon freshly ground pepper

In a small bowl, whisk together the crème fraîche, horseradish, olive oil, vinegar, dill, and salt. Set aside.

On a large platter, arrange the watercress, red onion, and apple slices. Top with the flaked trout. Drizzle the crème fraîche dressing over the salad and season with black pepper. Serve immediately.

Apple Tip:

To counteract the sweetness of the other fruits in your smoothie, add a tart apple, such as Braeburn, Granny Smith, or Pink Lady. For a sweeter smoothie, add a Fuji, Gala, or Sonya.

Apple Honeydew Smoothie

The taste of midsummer in a tall glass. Add the melon last and process briefly, as its high water content will thin the smoothie if processed for too long.

Makes about 2 servings

1 large apple, peeled, cored, and cut into large chunks

1 cup ice

2 cups vanilla ice cream

2 tablespoons granulated sugar, or to taste

1 cup honeydew melon chunks

Combine the apple, ice, ice cream, and sugar in a food processor and process until smooth. Add the honeydew and process again until smooth. Taste and add more sugar if necessary.

Salt-Topped Cardamom Apple Oatmeal Cookies

Coarse-grained salt, in combination with apple, cardamom,
and oats, separates this cookie from the rest.

Makes about 34 cookies

¼ cup apple juice concentrate (not diluted)

¾ cup dried apples, finely chopped

2 cups all-purpose flour

¾ teaspoon cardamom

¼ teaspoon nutmeg

½ teaspoon baking soda

Pinch of salt

1¼ cups old-fashioned rolled oats

1 cup unsalted butter, at room temperature

¾ cup light brown sugar

1 large egg

1 teaspoon coarse-grained salt

Spoon the apple juice concentrate into a microwavable container and microwave until liquefied. Add the dried apples and microwave for 1 more minute, until they are soft but not mushy. Set aside to cool.

Sift the flour, cardamom, nutmeg, baking soda, and salt into a mixing bowl and whisk. Stir in the oats.

In a separate bowl, cream the butter with an electric mixer set at medium speed for about 1 minute, or until very soft. Add the brown sugar and continue beating for 3 more minutes.

Beat in the egg. By hand, stir in the softened apples. Stir in the flour and oatmeal mixture to form a dough.

Set the dough aside for 15 to 20 minutes. Preheat the oven to 350° F. Position the oven rack in the center of the oven. Line a baking sheet with parchment paper.

When you are ready to bake, scoop out about 2 tablespoons of the dough and lightly shape into a rough ball. Place on the baking sheet. Repeat with the remaining dough, spacing the balls about 2 inches apart. Press the dough balls down with your palm to flatten. Bake for 8 to 11 minutes, rotating the pan halfway through. When the cookies are done, remove from the oven, sprinkle lightly with the salt and cool for 3 to 5 minutes on the baking sheet. Transfer to a rack to cool completely.

Apple Peach Sauce

A seasonal twist on traditional applesauce that tastes of summer and sunshine. Taste before you add sugar; the sweetness of your fruit will determine whether you need any and how much.

Makes about 3 cups

¾ cup apple juice

2 large apples of your choice

2 peaches

Granulated sugar to taste (optional)

Pour the juice into a large pot. Peel and core the apples and cut them into chunks. Place them into the juice as you go to prevent browning.

Peel the peaches and remove the pits. Add to the apples. Set the pot over medium heat and bring to a simmer. Simmer for 30 to 35 minutes, until the fruit is soft and mushy and the liquid is absorbed into it. (The timing will depend on the ripeness of the fruit.) Taste, add sugar if necessary, and stir well to combine.

July 29

Iced Apple Tea

Keep a pitcher of this refreshing tea at hand all summer long.

Makes 6 drinks

6 cups water

6 apple tea bags

⅓ cup honey, or to taste

1 small sweet apple of your choice, cored and thinly sliced

1 lemon, washed and thinly sliced

Fresh mint leaves, for garnish

In a 5-quart saucepan, bring the water to a boil. Remove the saucepan from the heat and add the tea bags. Steep for 1 hour before removing the tea bags.

Stir the honey into the steeped tea and pour into a glass pitcher.

Add the apple and lemon slices and refrigerate for 1 hour. Serve in tall glasses over ice. Garnish each glass with mint leaves.

Spiked Apple Punch

The grenadine turns this punch a delicate shade of rose. Mix up a batch for your next party.

Makes 8 cocktails

8 cups ice cubes

8 ounces vodka

8 ounces apple schnapps

8 cups lemon-lime soda

¼ cup grenadine

1 Granny Smith apple, cored and thinly sliced

Fill a large punch bowl with ice. Pour in vodka, schnapps, and soda. Add the grenadine and stir briefly to mix. Float apple slices on top and serve.

Apple Tip:

Pinova, which also goes by the festive monikers "Pinata" and "Sonata," is a firm and heavy apple with taut skin. The versatile Pinova is especially delicious juiced, poached, roasted, sauced— or eaten out of hand.

Pinova Apple and Mixed Baby Green Salad with Queso Fresco Cheese

The Pinova apple is crisp and juicy with a tropical flavor. If you can't find it, substitute your favorite eating apple.

Makes 4 servings

Vinaigrette

¼ cup chopped fresh cilantro

2 tablespoons fresh lime juice

1 tablespoon apple cider vinegar

1 tablespoon honey

¼ teaspoon sea salt

½ teaspoon freshly ground black pepper

¼ cup extra virgin olive oil

Salad

8 cups mixed baby greens

2 Pinova apples, cored and sliced

¼ cup crumbled queso fresco cheese

2 tablespoons roasted pumpkin seeds

In a small bowl, whisk together the cilantro, lime juice, vinegar, honey, salt, and pepper. Drizzle in the olive oil, whisking to create an emulsion.

To plate the salad, arrange the greens on a large platter. Top with the apple slices, cheese, and pumpkin seeds. Drizzle with the vinaigrette and serve.

Chilled Carrot and Apple Soup

A refreshing vegetable soup, perfect for hot summer days.

Makes 6 servings

1 tablespoon olive oil

1 cup chopped sweet onion

2 cloves garlic, minced

1 teaspoon ground cumin

3 cups chopped carrots

2 cups chopped Fuji or Honeycrisp apples

3 cups vegetable or chicken broth

2 bay leaves

8 ounces nonfat Greek yogurt

½ cup apple cider

1 teaspoon salt

½ cup chopped green onions, green part only, for garnish

In a 5-quart Dutch oven, heat the olive oil over medium-high heat. Add the chopped onion and sauté for 5 minutes or until softened and translucent. Add the garlic and cumin and stir continually until fragrant, about 1 minute.

Add the carrots and apples and sauté until lightly caramelized, about 5 minutes. Add the broth and bay leaves and bring to a boil. Lower heat and simmer until the carrots and apples are tender, about 20 minutes. Cool for 10 minutes.

Transfer the soup to a blender. Add the yogurt, apple cider, and salt. Puree until smooth. Chill for several hours. To serve, ladle into soup bowls and garnish with chopped green onions.

August 2

Croque-Monsieur Pommes

The classic sandwich of the French café gets an update. You can substitute any shredded cheese you like for the Gruyere and Swiss.

Makes 4 sandwiches

Vegetable oil spray

8 slices sandwich bread

4 teaspoons tarragon mustard

3 cups shredded Gruyere cheese or 1½ cups Gruyere and 1½ cups shredded Swiss cheese

4 slices ham, trimmed to fit on the bread with no overhang

1 sweet-tart apple, such as Fuji or Gala, cored and sliced in ⅛-inch wedges

Preheat the broiler. Spray a baking sheet lightly with cooking spray.

Place the bread on a work surface and spread 4 of the slices with 1 teaspoon mustard each. Top with a slice of ham and 4 or 5 slices of apple and sprinkle each with 2 tablespoons of the cheese.

Top with the remaining bread.

Place the sandwiches on the prepared baking sheet and sprinkle remaining cheese over the sandwiches, taking care to cover every bit of bread with the cheese. Broil for about 5 minutes or until the cheese is melted and forms a crust. Serve hot.

August 3

Croque-Madame Pommes

Another update for a classic sandwich. Hearty appetites might want two of these, but one open-faced sandwich with a salad will be perfect for a light lunch or supper.

Makes 4 open-faced sandwiches

Nonstick cooking spray

4 teaspoons all-purpose flour

Heaping ¼ teaspoon baking powder

⅛ teaspoon salt

3 tablespoons milk

2 eggs

½ cup grated Gruyere cheese or ¼ cup grated Gruyere and ¼ cup grated Swiss cheese

4 slices good-quality bread

4 teaspoons butter

½ large apple of your choice

Preheat the broiler. Spray a baking sheet lightly with the cooking spray.

Combine the flour, baking powder, salt, milk, and eggs and beat with a fork until well blended. Add the cheese and mix to combine.

Place the bread on a work surface and spread each with about 1 teaspoon butter, covering the entire surface. Place the slices, butter side up, on the prepared baking sheet.

Core the apple and cut it into ⅛-inch slices. Arrange the slices on the bread, overlapping them just slightly, to cover the bread. Spoon one-fourth of the egg mixture onto each slice of bread, covering all of the apples and trying not to drip the batter onto the baking sheet.

Broil for 4 to 6 minutes or until the batter puffs up and forms a golden crust.

Pancakes with Maple-Flavored Apples

Why pour on just maple syrup when you can top your pancakes with a fresh apple topping?
The Maple-Flavored Apples (see page 215) gives you the best of both.

Makes 12 pancakes

1 recipe Maple-Flavored Apples
   (see page 215)

1⅓ cups all-purpose flour

3 tablespoons brown sugar

1½ tablespoons baking powder

½ teaspoon salt

1¼ cups milk

¼ cup apple cider

2 eggs

1½ tablespoons unsalted butter,
   melted

1½ tablespoons vegetable oil

Prepare the Maple-Flavored Apples as directed on page 215. Keep warm.

Mix the flour, brown sugar, baking powder, and salt in a large bowl. Add the milk, cider, eggs, and melted butter and mix to form a batter. Let stand for a few minutes.

Heat the oil in a large griddle or skillet set over medium heat. With a ladle, scoop some batter onto the hot skillet, letting a steady stream of batter hit the surface in one spot. (Don't move the ladle while you pour.) Depending on the size of the pan, repeat to make 2 or 3 more pancakes.

Let the pancakes cook until the edges are golden and the surface bubbles. With a spatula, turn the pancakes and cook the other side. (The first side should be golden brown.) Cook until golden on the bottom and cooked through. With the spatula, transfer the pancakes to a platter and keep warm. Repeat with the remaining pancakes. Serve hot with Maple-Flavored Apples on top.

Maple-Flavored Apples

These apples are a perfect accompaniment for pancakes, waffles, or French toast, but you can also serve them as a side dish with pork or poultry.

Makes about 2 cups

2 large sweet-tart apples, such as Granny Smith

1 tablespoon unsalted butter

1 tablespoon vegetable oil

2 tablespoons pure maple syrup, plus more to taste if needed

Core and cut the apples into ⅛-inch wedges.

Heat the butter and oil in a frying pan set over medium heat until the butter is melted. Tilt to coat the pan. Add the apples and cook, stirring occasionally, for 1 minute. Turn the apples with tongs and cook for another minute, or until nicely softened.

Toss gently with the syrup to coat, and serve.

Rice Pudding with Apples and Pistachios

A classic dessert, rice pudding hits the spot. This version is made with Granny Smith apples and topped with toasted pistachios for crunch.

Makes 4 servings

4 cups milk

⅓ cup uncooked short grain rice

¼ cup light brown sugar

1 Granny Smith apple, cored and diced

1 teaspoon pure vanilla extract

2 tablespoons cornstarch

3 tablespoons heavy cream

½ cup chopped toasted pistachios

Whipped cream (optional)

In a 5-quart saucepan, bring the milk, rice, and sugar to a boil over high heat. Reduce heat to low and simmer for 30 minutes, uncovered, stirring frequently to prevent burning. Add the diced apples and cook for an additional 30 minutes, stirring occasionally.

In a small bowl, mix together the vanilla, cornstarch, and heavy cream. Add to the rice mixture and stir constantly until the mixture thickens. Remove from heat. Serve warm or cold, topped with chopped pistachios and whipped cream, if desired.

Savory Tart Filled with Sausage, Spinach, and Apples

This tasty treat works equally well for dinner, wrapped up for a picnic, or cut into small pieces as an hors d'oeuvre for a party.

Makes 1 (4- by 12-inch) tart

½ recipe Quick Puff Pastry (see Apple Apricot Bistro Tarts, page 26)

2 teaspoons to 2 tablespoons extra virgin olive oil

10 ounces baby spinach leaves

Salt, to taste

Freshly ground black pepper, to taste

8 ounces hot Italian sausage patties (or your favorite sausage)

1 small leek, white part only, washed very well, halved, and sliced thinly

1 large Granny Smith apple, peeled, cored, and diced

2 cloves garlic, minced

1 cup whole-milk ricotta

1 large roasted red pepper, skinned, seeded, and diced

2 tablespoons all-purpose flour

1 large egg

1 cup grated mozzarella cheese

1 cup finely grated Parmigiano-Reggiano cheese

1 large egg mixed with 1 tablespoon water or cream

Prepare and chill the dough as directed on page 26.

Preheat the oven to 400° F. Position the oven rack in the center of the oven. Put one baking sheet on top of another and line the top one with parchment paper. Roll out the chilled dough to a 12- by 12-inch square.

To make the filling, heat about 2 teaspoons of the oil in a large frying or sauté pan and cook the spinach over medium-high heat until just wilted. Season with salt and pepper to taste. Remove from the pan and set aside to cool.

Add 1 or 2 more teaspoons of oil to the pan, set it over medium-high heat, and add the sausage. (The amount of oil required will depend on how much fat is in the sausage.) Cook, stirring frequently to break up the sausage, until cooked through. Remove from the pan and set aside to cool.

Return the pan to the heat, add 2 more teaspoons oil if needed, and cook the leek, stirring occasionally, for about 2 minutes, or until translucent and softened. Add the apples and cook, stirring, until they begin to soften and turn golden. Add the garlic and cook, stirring, for 30 to 45 seconds, until fragrant. (Do not let the garlic brown.) Set aside to cool.

Combine the ricotta, red pepper, flour, egg, mozzarella, and Parmigiano in a bowl and mix to incorporate. Stir in all of the cooled vegetables, apple, and sausage.

Pile the filling in the center of the dough, making a mound about 3½ inches wide and leaving ½ inch at the top and bottom (the side closest to you and farthest from you). Fold in the uncovered ½-inch edges. Fold about 4 inches of dough from the right side over the filling to completely enclose it, pressing the edge down a little to seal it. Lift the filled, sealed mound and carefully roll it to the left, over onto the remaining section of unfilled dough. Pinch the seam to seal completely.

Gently lift the filled and sealed pastry onto a parchment-lined baking sheet. Brush lightly with egg wash. Bake for 25 to 30 minutes. Cool on a rack. Serve warm or at room temperature.

Apple and Peach Smoothie

When peaches are at their very sweetest, blend one with an apple for a luscious smoothie.

Makes about 2 servings

1 apple of your choice
1 very ripe peach, peeled, pitted, and quartered
1½ cups vanilla yogurt or low-fat vanilla yogurt
1 cup ice cubes
¼ cup granulated sugar,
   plus more to taste if needed

Peel and core the apple and cut it into rough chunks. Place them into a food processor or blender, add the peaches, yogurt, ice, and the sugar. Process until smooth and frothy. Taste and add sugar if necessary.

August 9

Snow Peas with Apples

Serve this dish over rice for a sweet, salty, spicy, and crunchy lunch.

Makes 4 servings

1 teaspoon olive oil

2 tablespoons minced fresh ginger

2 cloves garlic, minced

2 Gala or Fuji apples, cored and thinly sliced

4 cups snow peas, strings removed

1 tablespoon soy sauce, or to taste

⅓ cup chopped peanuts or cashews (optional)

Heat the olive oil in a large nonstick sauté pan set over high heat. Add the ginger and garlic and cook for 1 minute, stirring constantly.

Add the apples and sauté until the apples soften, about 3 to 4 minutes.

Add the snow peas and soy sauce and sauté for 2 to 3 minutes longer or until the water has evaporated and the peas are crisp tender. Season with salt and serve.

Pan-Seared Shrimp with Apple-Fennel Slaw

Succulent shrimp rest on a bed of tangy apple-fennel slaw.

Makes 4 servings

Dressing

1 clove garlic, minced

1 teaspoon honey

1 teaspoon Dijon mustard

1 tablespoon soy sauce

1 tablespoon mirin (available in Asian markets)

1 tablespoon orange juice

1 teaspoon toasted sesame oil (available in Asian markets)

2 teaspoons extra virgin olive oil

Apple-Fennel Slaw

1 Granny Smith apple, cored and julienned

1 fennel bulb, finely shredded

Juice of 1 orange

½ teaspoon sea salt

½ teaspoon freshly ground black pepper

Shrimp

12 jumbo shrimp, shelled and deveined

½ teaspoon sea salt

½ teaspoon freshly ground black pepper

1 tablespoon olive oil

To make the dressing, in a small bowl, whisk together the garlic, honey, Dijon, soy sauce, mirin, and orange juice. Slowly drizzle in the sesame oil and olive oil, whisking until the dressing is emulsified. Set aside.

To make the apple-fennel slaw, in a medium bowl, combine the apple, fennel, orange juice, salt and pepper. Toss to combine and set aside to marinate while you cook the shrimp.

Season the shrimp with the salt and pepper. Heat the olive oil in a large nonstick sauté pan set over high heat. Add the shrimp to the hot pan. Sear the shrimp on both sides for 1 to 2 minutes, until pink. Do not overcook.

Divide the apple-fennel slaw among 4 plates. Drizzle with the dressing and serve immediately.

Curried Pea and Apple Soup

Enjoy this delicious soup either hot or cold.

Makes 4 servings

1 teaspoon olive oil

1 sweet onion, diced

2 cloves garlic, minced

2 Honeycrisp apples, peeled, cored, and chopped

1 (14-ounce) bag frozen peas

2 tablespoons Thai green curry paste (available in Asian markets and some supermarkets)

4 cups vegetable or chicken broth

½ teaspoon sea salt

½ teaspoon freshly ground black pepper

2 to 3 dashes hot sauce (optional)

¼ cup fresh cilantro leaves, chopped

1 red chili pepper, seeded and minced

Heat the olive oil in a 5-quart Dutch oven set over medium-high heat. Add the onion and sauté until translucent, about 5 minutes. Add the garlic and stir an additional 30 seconds. Add the chopped apples and sauté 5 minutes longer, until they start to soften. Add the peas, curry, broth, salt, pepper, and hot sauce if desired. Bring to a boil over high heat, reduce heat to low, and simmer until apples are fork-tender, 5 to 10 minutes.

Transfer the soup to a blender or use an immersion blender and puree until smooth.

If serving cold, chill the soup in the refrigerator for several hours. If not, ladle into soup bowls and sprinkle with chopped cilantro and chili pepper.

Strawberry Apple Chiller

Serve this frothy summer drink at your next picnic or get-together.

Makes 2 cocktails

2 cups very ripe strawberries, washed and hulled

2 cups chunks Golden Delicious apple

4 ounces rum

2 ounces apple brandy

2 ounces triple sec

3 ounces fresh lime juice

2 ounces simple syrup

Freeze the strawberries and apples.

Blend the frozen fruit with the rum, brandy, triple sec, lime juice, and simple syrup in a blender or food processor until smooth and frothy. Divide between 2 tall glasses.

Graham Crackers with Almond Butter and Apple Slices

This simple snack can be ready to eat in a few minutes.

Makes 2 servings

2 tablespoons almond butter

2 graham crackers, broken into squares

½ apple of your choice, cored and thinly sliced

Spread ½ tablespoon almond butter on each graham cracker. Top with sliced apples and serve.

August 14

Apple and Kale Salad

While you can use any type of kale in this recipe, **Chef Eva Pesantez** suggests the red Russian variety. Its bright color makes this dish a visual treat.

Makes 4 to 6 servings (starter) or 2 servings (entrée)

¾ cup chopped pecans

1 bunch red Russian kale

3 tablespoons extra virgin olive oil

4 teaspoons good quality red wine vinegar

¾ teaspoon kosher salt

¼ teaspoon ground black pepper

2 cups loosely-packed julienned apple, such Stayman or Winsap

1 cup sharp white Cheddar, cut into ¼-inch cubes

Lightly toast the pecans in a 300° F degree oven for about 10 minutes until they become fragrant. Set aside to cool.

Wash and dry the kale, getting out as much water as you can. Holding the stem, gently "peel" off the leafy end. When all the kale is off, discard the stem. Stack the leaves and cut them into strips about ½-inch thick. Place in a bowl.

Whisk together the oil, vinegar, salt, and pepper and pour over the kale. Mix well and let it sit for about 5 minutes.

Add the apples, Cheddar, and toasted pecans to the kale and mix well.

NOTE: If your bunch of kale is really big, you might need to increase the amount of dressing.

"One of my very favorite things to do with apples is the simplest: applesauce. I take a variety of apples (my favorites are Honeycrisp, Pink Lady, Ida Red, Winesap, and Braeburn), cut them up with the peel, and toss them into a heavy stainless steel pot with a lid. I add about 1 to 1½ inches of water and, depending on my mood, sometimes a cinnamon stick. I cover the pot and let it cook over low heat for 15 to 20 minutes, until the apples have turned to mush. Then I pass them through a ricer or a mesh strainer. Leaving the skins on gives the sauce a beautiful rosy hue. Let it cool and then eat it plain or on latkes. I also use it to sweeten my Greek yogurt. Any way you eat it, you will love it!"

- Chef Eva Pesantez

Chef Eva Pesantez

CURRENTLY: Executive Chef, Brother
Jimmy's (multiple locations)

NOTABLE FOR: Selected to cook at Macy's
Culinary Council

FEATURED ON: FOX5, CW11, *Every Day
with Rachael Ray* Magazine

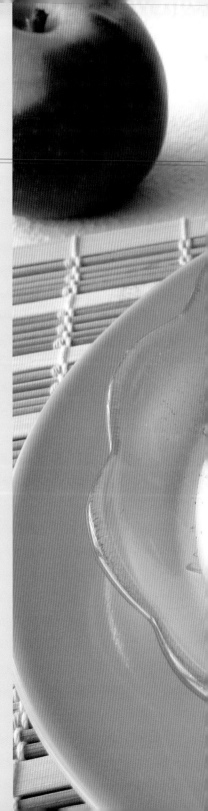

Apple Mojito Panna Cotta

This light, elegant, refreshing dessert hits the spot on a hot summer evening—but it will work any time.

Makes 4 servings

1½ teaspoons unflavored powdered gelatin

½ cup milk

1 sprig fresh mint leaves

3 tablespoons granulated sugar

Tiny pinch of salt

1¼ cups heavy cream

2 tablespoons apple brandy or cider

Zest of 1 small lime

1½ teaspoons fresh lime juice

1 large apple of your choice

¼ cup orange juice

2 tablespoons unsalted butter

Fresh mint sprigs for garnish

In a small saucepan off the heat, soak the gelatin in the milk for 10 minutes. Then heat the mixture over low heat until the gelatin dissolves and the temperature reaches 130° to 140° F on an instant-read or candy thermometer. Add the mint, sugar, and salt. Stir to dissolve. Remove from the heat. Let stand for 10 minutes.

Prepare a large bowl of ice water. After 10 minutes, remove the mint from the gelatin mixture, add the cream, brandy or cider, lime zest, and juice and whisk to combine. Strain. Chill by dipping the bottom of the pan into the ice bath, stirring until the mixture has reached 60° F on an instant read or candy thermometer. Pour into ramekins. Refrigerate until set, but jiggly.

Meanwhile, peel and core the apples. Cut into 1/8-inch wedges and dip into the orange juice to coat lightly. Melt the butter in a frying pan set over medium heat. Add the apples and cook, stirring, until softened.

Unmold the ramekins onto individual dessert plates. Garnish with the apples.

PBJ and Apple Tortilla

A fun variation on the classic PBJ sandwich.

Makes 1 serving

1 whole wheat tortilla

1½ tablespoons peanut butter

1½ tablespoons jelly of your choice, such as strawberry or grape

½ cup Fuji or Honeycrisp apple, cored and thinly sliced

Spread the tortilla with the peanut butter and jelly and top with the apple slices. Fold the bottom and top up and over the filling and then fold the right and left sides over the filling. Serve.

Apple Yogurt

Pair this with some Apple-Cinnamon Granola (see page 29) for a satisfying breakfast.

Makes 4 servings

3 cups apple of your choice, cored and diced

½ cup apple cider

2 cups nonfat vanilla Greek yogurt

2 teaspoons honey

1 teaspoon pure vanilla extract

½ teaspoon ground cinnamon

In a 2-quart saucepan set over high heat, cook the apples in the apple cider until soft, about 10 minutes; let cool.

Reserve 1 cup of the cooked apples. Put the rest in a blender with the yogurt, honey, vanilla, and cinnamon. Blend to combine.

Transfer the yogurt mixture to a bowl and stir in the reserved cooked apples. Serve immediately or refrigerate in a lidded container for up to 1 week.

Apple, Cheddar, and Ham Corn Muffins

Use the last of August's crop of fresh corn on the cob to make these mouth-watering muffins.

Makes 12 muffins

1⅔ cups all-purpose flour

¼ cup yellow cornmeal

1 teaspoon salt

1 tablespoon baking powder

1 cup diced Gala or Fuji apples

½ cup whole kernel corn

½ cup diced honey-glazed ham

1 jalapeno pepper, seeded and minced

1 cup shredded extra-sharp Cheddar cheese

6 tablespoons olive oil

4 large eggs, lightly beaten

½ cup water

Preheat the oven to 400° F. Line a muffin pan with baking cup liners; set aside.

In a large mixing bowl, combine the flour, cornmeal, salt, and baking powder. Add the diced apples, corn, diced ham, jalapeno pepper, and cheddar; stir to combine.

In a medium bowl, whisk together the olive oil, eggs, and water. Add the wet to the dry ingredients and stir until just combined; do not overmix.

Fill each baking cup with batter. Bake in the middle of the oven until golden brown and puffed, about 20 minutes. Let cool slightly on a wire rack before serving.

August 19

Spicy-Sweet Baked Apples with Sharp Cheddar

Both savory and sweet, this dessert gets its slight kick from cayenne pepper.

Makes 4 servings

Nonstick cooking spray	1 teaspoon ground cinnamon
3 Granny Smith apples	½ teaspoon cayenne pepper
1 tablespoon fresh lemon juice	1 tablespoon cornstarch
3 tablespoons honey	½ cup shredded extra-sharp Cheddar cheese
1 teaspoon sea salt	

Preheat the oven to 375° F. Spray an 8- x 8-inch baking dish with cooking spray and set aside.

Core and slice the apples and sprinkle them with the lemon juice to prevent browning. In a large bowl, combine the sliced apples, honey, salt, cinnamon, cayenne, and cornstarch. Spread the apples in the prepared pan and bake until they are crisp tender, about 20 minutes.

Turn the oven setting to broil. Top the cooked apples with shredded cheddar and broil until the cheese is melted and slightly browned. Serve immediately.

August 20

Apple Fruit Leather

Tuck these chewy roll-ups into a picnic basket, backpack, or lunch box for whenever you want a quick, wholesome snack.

Makes about 12 roll-ups

3 cups peeled and chopped apples of your choice
2 teaspoons fresh lemon juice
2 teaspoons apple juice, plus more if needed
2 teaspoons honey
¼ teaspoon ground cinnamon (optional)
¼ teaspoon pure vanilla extract (optional)

Preheat the oven to 165° F. Line a 13- x 5-inch baking sheet with parchment paper; set aside.

Combine the apples and lemon and apple juices in a medium saucepan set over medium heat. Cook, stirring frequently, until the fruit is softened, about 20 minutes. Cool and place the cooked apples, honey, and, if desired, the cinnamon and vanilla in a food processor and process until smooth. The mixture should be pourable, but thick enough to hold its shape. If the mixture is too thick, add more apple juice.

Pour the mixture onto the prepared baking sheet. Spread with a spatula so that the mixture is evenly distributed to a thickness of ⅛ inch.

Transfer the baking sheet to the oven and bake for 8 to 12 hours. The fruit leather is done when it is no longer tacky in the middle.

Remove from the oven and peel off of the baking sheet. Cut into strips and roll in parchment paper. Store in an airtight container.

Apple Tip:

For centuries, apple cider vingar has been used for both medicinal purposes and as a dietary supplement. Historical uses include:

Cleaning and polishing

Destroying weeds

Dressing salads

Making pickles

Grilled Scallops, Apple, and Scallion Skewers

Pop these on the grill the next time you'd like a tasty meal with little fuss.

Makes 6 servings

1 tablespoon apple cider vinegar

1 tablespoon fresh lime juice

½ teaspoon Dijon mustard

½ teaspoon sea salt, divided

½ teaspoon freshly ground black pepper, divided

3 tablespoons extra virgin olive oil, divided

1 Granny Smith apple

12 scallions, trimmed and cut in half crosswise

12 large scallops, cut in half horizontally

1 tablespoon sesame seeds, toasted

Preheat a grill to medium high. Soak the skewers in water for 30 minutes.

In a small bowl, whisk together the vinegar, lime juice, mustard, ¼ teaspoon salt, and ¼ teaspoon black pepper. Slowly drizzle in 2 tablespoons of olive oil, whisking to form an emulsion.

Core and cut the apple into 1-inch chunks. Add the apples and scallions to the dressing. Toss to coat.

In a medium bowl, season the scallops with the remaining oil, salt, and pepper.

Thread each skewer with 1 apple chunk, 1 piece of scallion, and 2 scallop halves. Arrange the skewers on the grill. Grill 1 minute per side or until lightly charred and the scallops are cooked through.

To serve, arrange on a platter, drizzle with the dressing, and sprinkle with the sesame seeds.

Apple-Quinoa-Spinach Stuffed Peppers

Quinoa, a grain-like seed, makes a wonderful, nutrient-packed stuffing for red bell peppers.

Makes 4 servings

1 cup quinoa, rinsed

2 cups vegetable or chicken broth

Nonstick cooking spray

4 red bell peppers, halved lengthwise through the stem, seeds and membranes removed

2 teaspoons olive oil

1 Granny Smith apple, cored and diced

1 cup sweet onion, diced

2 celery stalks, diced

2 cloves garlic, minced

2 cups baby spinach

¼ cup fresh basil leaves, chopped

2 cups fresh tomatoes, chopped

1 teaspoon sea salt

1 teaspoon freshly ground black pepper

¼ cup crumbled feta

Preheat the oven to 400° F.

In a 2-quart saucepan set over high heat, combine the quinoa and broth. Bring to a boil, reduce heat to low, cover, and simmer for 20 minutes.

Spray a 9- x 13-inch baking dish with cooking spray. Place the bell peppers cut side up in the baking dish; set aside.

Heat the olive oil in a large nonstick sauté pan set over medium-high heat. Add the apples, onions, and celery and sauté until lightly browned and softened, about 5 minutes. Add the garlic and spinach and stir until the spinach wilts. Add the basil, tomatoes, salt, and pepper. Cook, stirring occasionally, for 3 minutes. Fold the cooked quinoa into the spinach.

Fill the pepper halves with the quinoa mixture and sprinkle with crumbled feta. Bake until the peppers are tender, about 20 to 30 minutes.

That's Hot!

When you can't beat the heat, use it! While you can dry apples year-round in your oven, take advantage of the hot summer sun for an environmentally-friendly drying method.

Wait for ideal sun-drying weather conditions: low humidity and a temperature of about 100° F. Cut apples into ¼-inch thick slices and soak them in a mixture of lemon juice and salt. Line a cookie tray with cheesecloth. Set the apple slices on the tray, cover with additional cheesecloth to keep away pests, and leave in direct sunlight. Turn the slices once daily to ensure equal drying. If you're concerned about morning dew, bring the trays inside in the evening. The entire process should take about 4 days.

Some apples are bland in flavor when dried, so choose strong-flavored varieties, such as Galas, Fujis, and Granny Smiths. Ginger Gold is also a smart choice, producing dried apple slices with a complex and spicy flavor.

Escarole, Apple, and Walnut Salad with Ricotta Salata

Made from sheep's milk, ricotta salata is a fresh cheese that has been pressed, salted, and dried. It is especially delicious shaved or grated over green salads such as this one.

Makes 4 servings

Dressing

1 tablespoon apple cider vinegar
1 teaspoon Dijon mustard
1 teaspoon honey
½ teaspoon sea salt
½ teaspoon freshly ground black pepper
2 tablespoons walnut oil

1 head escarole, cored and roughly chopped
1 Honeycrisp apple, cored and sliced
½ cup chopped toasted walnuts
¼ cup chopped parsley leaves
¼ cup shaved ricotta salata

To make the dressing, whisk together the vinegar, mustard, honey, salt, and pepper in a large bowl. Drizzle in the oil, whisking continuously to form an emulsion.

Add the chopped escarole, apples, walnuts, and parsley. Toss to coat with the dressing. Top the salad with the ricotta salata. Divide the salad among 4 plates and serve immediately.

Apple Frangipane Tart

Apples and almonds make for a delicious partnership. Frangipane, a classic almond pastry confection, doubles as both crust and filling, for an utterly delectable tart.

Makes 1 (9-inch) tart

Frangipane Crust

1 egg yolk

1 teaspoon pure vanilla extract

¼ teaspoon almond extract

1¼ cup unbleached all-purpose flour

⅓ cup granulated sugar

¼ teaspoon salt

½ cup cold unsalted butter, cut into pieces

2 to 3 tablespoons ice cold water

Frangipane Filling

2 tablespoons unsalted butter

2 cups blanched almonds

⅔ cup granulated sugar

¼ teaspoon salt

3 eggs

1 teaspoon pure vanilla extract

½ teaspoon almond extract

2 tablespoons amaretto

Apples

4 small apples of your choice

⅓ cup apple jelly

First start the crust. Beat the egg yolk with the vanilla and almond extracts and set aside.

Combine the flour, sugar, and salt in a food processor fitted with a metal blade and pulse a few times to mix. Add the butter and process until well blended. Transfer to a bowl and add the egg mixture. Mix by hand to combine. Add the water and toss with a spatula or your fingers to combine. When the dough comes together, form it into a disk, wrap it in plastic, and refrigerate for at least 30 minutes or up to 1 day.

When you are ready to bake, roll the dough out on a lightly floured work surface to make about a 12-inch circle. Carefully fit it into a 9-inch tart pan without stretching it. Chill for 30 minutes.

When you are ready to bake, preheat the oven to 375° F. Position the oven rack in the lower third of the oven. Remove the dough-lined tart pan from the refrigerator. Place it on a sheet pan.

Pierce the bottom of the tart a few times with a fork. Line the dough with a piece of parchment or foil and fill with pie weights. Bake for 8 to 10 minutes, until the dough is firm to the touch. Remove the sheet pan from the oven and carefully remove the weights and parchment from the tart. Return the pan and tart shell to the oven to bake for another 3 to 5 minutes, until lightly golden. Allow the tart shell to cool while you prepare the filling. (Leave the oven temperature at 375° F.)

Melt the butter in a small pan and cook until it turns a nutty brown color. Set aside to cool. Combine the almonds, sugar, and salt in a food processor and process until very finely ground; do not let the nuts turn to paste.

Add the eggs, vanilla and almond extracts, and amaretto and pulse about 4 times, or until just combined. Scrape down the sides of the processor bowl as needed. Spread the filling on the cooled crust, evening it out with a wooden spoon or spatula.

Peel and core the apples and cut them into quarters. Use a sharp knife to cut slits into the outer (convex) side of the apple about ⅛ inch apart, leaving the apple wedge whole. Nestle the apples into the frangipane filling with their inner (concave) side down, positioning most of them around the circumference and placing a few in the center.

Bake for 10 minutes. Reduce the heat to 350° F and bake for another 20 to 25 minutes, or until a toothpick inserted into the filling comes out with a few moist crumbs. While the tart is baking, melt the apple jelly in a small pan set over medium heat. When the tart is done, remove it from the oven and brush the hot tart with the jelly. Let cool and serve at room temperature.

Spicy Apple Nuts

Addictively good, these nuts will quickly disappear so make extra.

Makes about 4 cups

⅓ cup apple chips, processed in a food processor until finely ground

⅓ cup dark brown sugar, packed

⅓ cup granulated sugar

1½ teaspoons sea salt

¼ teaspoon cayenne pepper

1 teaspoon ground cinnamon

1 egg white

1 tablespoon apple cider

1 cup walnuts

1 cup pecans

1 cup hazelnuts

1 cup peanuts

Preheat the oven to 300° F. Line a baking sheet with foil.

In a medium bowl, whisk together the processed apple chips, brown and white sugar, salt, cayenne, and cinnamon.

In a large bowl, beat the egg white and apple cider until frothy. Add the nuts and toss to coat evenly. Add the sugar mixture and toss again.

Transfer to the prepared baking sheet and bake for 15 minutes. Stir the nuts and bake for another 15 minutes. Break up any nuts that stick together and cool completely before storing in an airtight container.

Core Fact:

Apples contain a high amount of pectin, a type of plant fiber. Apple pectin binds to cholesterol and shuttles it out of the body, thereby reducing blood pressure, among other health benefits.

Apple Spice-Crusted Seared Tuna with Avocado

Try this spice combination with shrimp and scallops too.

Makes 4 servings

Spice Rub

¼ cup apple chips,
   processed in a
   food processor
   until finely
   ground

1 teaspoon black
   sesame seeds

½ teaspoon white
   sesame seeds

1 teaspoon sea salt

½ teaspoon garlic
   powder

½ teaspoon ground
   ginger

¼ teaspoon cayenne
   pepper

½ pound sushi-grade
   tuna steak, at
   room temperature

1 teaspoon sesame oil

1 ripe avocado

¼ cup fresh lime
   juice

½ cup chopped
   cilantro leaves

To make the spice rub, combine the processed apple chips, black and white sesame seeds, salt, garlic powder, ginger, and cayenne pepper in a small bowl.

Pour the spice mixture over the tuna, pressing the spices into both sides and crusting it evenly.

Heat the oil in a medium nonstick sauté pan set over high heat. Add the crusted tuna steak and sear 1 to 2 minutes per side, depending on the desired degree of doneness. Remove to a cutting board and let rest for 3 minutes. Slice the tuna steak against the grain.

Peel the avocado and cut into thin slices and drizzle with the lime juice to prevent discoloration. Arrange the avocado on 4 salad plates. Top with the sliced tuna and sprinkle with cilantro. Serve immediately.

Grilled Apple Salad with Herb Vinaigrette

Apples taste divine on the grill. The sugar in the fruit caramelizes them to a smoky sweetness.

Makes 6 servings

Vinaigrette

3 tablespoons apple cider vinegar

1 shallot, minced

1 clove garlic, minced

¼ teaspoon sea salt

½ teaspoon freshly ground black pepper

1 teaspoon lemon zest

½ teaspoon chopped fresh thyme

½ teaspoon chopped fresh rosemary

½ teaspoon chopped fresh oregano

½ teaspoon chopped fresh parsley

⅓ cup extra virgin olive oil

3 crisp sweet apples, such as Fuji or Crispin, cored and sliced

3 cups mixed salad greens

To make the dressing, combine the vinegar, shallot, garlic, salt, pepper, lemon zest, and herbs in a large bowl; whisk to combine. Drizzle in the olive oil, whisking to form an emulsion. Add the apple slices to the vinaigrette and toss to coat. Marinate at room temperature for 2 hours.

Preheat a grill.

Remove the apple slices from the vinaigrette, reserving the liquid. Place the apple slices on the grill and grill until softened and lightly browned, about 5 minutes. Turn the apples and grill for 5 more minutes.

Toss the salad greens with the remaining vinaigrette until well coated. Divide the dressed greens among 6 salad plates and top each with grilled apple slices. Serve immediately.

Prosciutto-Wrapped Apples and Figs

The salty ham combines with the sweetness of the apples and the figs to produce a sensational appetizer.

Makes 12 hors d'oeuvres

12 figs, stemmed and quartered

2 Honeycrisp or Crispin apples, cored and each cut into 12 slices

24 fresh basil leaves

12 slices prosciutto di Parma, cut in half lengthwise

½ teaspoon freshly ground pepper

Preheat the oven to 400° F.

Wrap each strip of prosciutto around 1 fig quarter, 1 apple slice, and 1 basil leaf. Place the wrapped fruits on a foil-lined baking sheet. Roast until the prosciutto is crispy, about 12 minutes. Serve immediately.

Apple and Almond Tart with Lemon Mascarpone Cream

A study in contrasts: creamy and crunchy, sweet and tart—
but delicious throughout. The combination of lemon mascarpone cream with apples
and almonds makes this tart unique.

Makes 8 (4-inch) tarts

Press-in Crust

2½ cups unbleached, all-purpose flour

1 cup unsalted butter, at room temperature

⅔ cup granulated sugar

¼ teaspoon salt

Filling

2 Granny Smith apples, peeled and cored

1 tablespoon sweet white wine or Calvados or apple juice

½ cup all-purpose flour

½ cup granulated sugar

Zest and juice of 1 small lemon

2 eggs

1 cup mascarpone, at room temperature

Topping

1½ cups sliced almonds

To make the dough, mix the flour, butter, sugar, and salt in a food processor or by hand to combine. Turn the mixture out into a large bowl or onto a work surface and knead the dough to bring it together. Flatten the dough to make a disk, wrap tightly in plastic wrap, and chill for at least 30 minutes or up to 24 hours.

When you are ready to bake, divide the dough into 8 pieces of equal size (about 3 ounces each). Press each piece into a 4-inch tart pan. Refrigerate for 30 minutes.

Preheat the oven to 375° F. Position an oven rack in the bottom third of the oven. Remove the dough-lined tart pans from the refrigerator. Place them on a sheet pan.

Pierce the bottom of each tart a few times with a fork. Line the dough in each pan with a piece of parchment or foil and fill with pie weights. Bake for 8 to 10 minutes, until the dough is firm to the touch. Remove the sheet pan from the oven and carefully remove the weights and parchment from each tart. Return the pan and tart shells to the oven to bake for another 3 to 5 minutes, until lightly golden. Allow the tart shells to cool while you prepare the filling. Reduce the oven temperature to 350° F.

Cut the apples into small dice and place them in a small bowl. Toss with the Calvados, wine, or juice. Let stand for 15 minutes. Drain, saving any remaining liquid to add to the mascarpone cream if desired.

In a separate bowl, whisk the flour, sugar, lemon zest and juice, eggs, mascarpone, and up to 2 tablespoons reserved soaking juice from the apples.

Divide the diced apples evenly into the cooled tart shells. Top with the mascarpone cream. Sprinkle the tarts evenly with the sliced almonds.

Bake at 350° F for 15 minutes, or until the custard is set but still soft and the almonds toasted. Cool on a rack.

Apple Butter Frozen Yogurt with Chocolate and Gingersnaps

A scrumptious frozen dessert studded with chunks of dark chocolate and crushed gingersnaps.

Makes 4 servings

1 pint vanilla frozen yogurt, softened

½ cup apple butter

4 ounces bittersweet chocolate, chopped

4 gingersnap cookies, crushed

Pour the softened yogurt into an ice cream machine. Freeze for 30 minutes. Add the apple butter, chocolate, and cookies. Freeze for 10 more minutes. Transfer the frozen yogurt to an airtight container and freeze an additional 30 minutes before serving.

Apple Cinnamon Bread Pudding

Made with cinnamon raisin bread, this bread pudding can whipped up in no time.

Makes 12 servings

Nonstick cooking spray

4 cups cubed stale cinnamon raisin bread

1 teaspoon ground cinnamon

1 Granny Smith apple, peeled, cored, and diced

2 cups milk

½ cup packed light brown sugar

3 tablespoons unsalted butter

¼ cup apple brandy

3 large eggs

1 teaspoon pure vanilla extract

½ cup chopped walnuts

Whipped cream

In a large bowl, combine the bread cubes, cinnamon, and diced apples.

In a medium 2-quart saucepan set over medium heat, combine the milk, brown sugar, butter, and brandy; cook until the butter is melted.

In a medium bowl, whisk together the eggs and vanilla. Whisk a little of the hot milk mixture into the eggs at a time, so as not to cook the eggs. Combine the milk and eggs with the bread and apples. Let the pudding soak for 30 minutes.

Meanwhile, preheat the oven to 350° F. Coat an 11- x 7-inch baking dish with nonstick cooking spray. Put a pot of water on the stove and bring to a simmer.

Gently stir the walnuts into the pudding. Pour into the prepared pan. Place the pan into a deep roasting pan and add enough simmering water to come ½ inch up the side.

Bake until a knife inserted in the center comes out clean, about 40 to 45 minutes. Serve with whipped cream on the side.

Mother's Day Heart Wreath

Surprise Mom with an apple-laden wreath that you make yourself. You can decorate this wreath any way you like. Pick a heart-shaped wreath to remind her who loves her. If you wish, you can use dried apple slices that you make yourself (see Dried Apples, page 323) or buy from the craft store.

Makes 1 wreath

Small silk leaves with wire stems

Large silk leaves with wire stems

1 heart-shaped grapevine wreath

Artificial apples, pears, crabapples, and other fruits from the craft store

Florist's wire

Attach the smaller leaves to the wreath at intervals of a few inches, working around the entire perimeter. Wrap the wire stems in and around the wreath so that none are sticking out.

Attach the larger leaves to the wreath in clusters and use florist's wire to attach the fruit to the clusters. You need not cover the whole wreath or make it symmetrical—unless you want to.

Attach the fruit to the leaf clusters with florist's wire.

September 1

Red Swiss Chard with Apples

Be sure to include some of the Swiss chard stems when making this side dish. They provide a distinct crunchiness.

Makes 4 servings

1 tablespoon olive oil

1 red onion, diced

2 cloves garlic, minced

1 Jonathan or Golden Delicious apple, peeled, cored, and diced

6 cups chopped red Swiss chard

2 tablespoons apple cider vinegar

½ teaspoon sea salt

1 teaspoon freshly ground black pepper

Heat the oil in a large nonstick sauté pan set over medium-high heat. Add the onions and sauté until soft, about 3 to 5 minutes. Add the garlic and cook, stirring constantly, until fragrant, about 30 seconds. Add the apples, tossing to coat in the oil, and cook for 1 minute longer.

Add the Swiss chard and stir to coat. Add the vinegar, salt, and pepper. Cover and cook for 10 minutes. Serve hot.

Potato Pancakes and Apples with Horseradish Crème Fraîche

Horseradish perks up these crispy pancakes served on top of crunchy apple slices.

Makes 12 hors d'oeuvres

Pancakes

- 1 (12-ounce) baking potato, peeled and grated
- 2 tablespoons horseradish
- 1 egg
- 1 tablespoon all-purpose flour
- ½ teaspoon sea salt
- ½ teaspoon freshly ground black pepper
- 2 tablespoons olive oil
- 1 Honeycrisp or Fuji apple
- 2 tablespoons fresh lemon juice

Dressing

- 2 tablespoons crème fraîche
- 1 teaspoon horseradish
- ¼ teaspoon sea salt
- ¼ teaspoon freshly ground black pepper
- 1 tablespoon chopped chives

Preheat the oven to 350° F. Line a baking sheet with foil and set aside.

To make the pancakes, combine the grated potato, horseradish, egg, flour, salt, and pepper in a large bowl.

Heat 1 tablespoon olive oil in a large nonstick sauté pan set over medium-high heat. Add 1 tablespoon of the potato mixture to the pan, flattening to form a 2-inch pancake. Repeat to make 6 pancakes. Fry the pancakes until golden brown on each side, about 2 minutes per side. Transfer the browned pancakes to the prepared baking sheet and cook in the oven for 5 minutes.

Core the apple and cut into 12 slices. Toss with the lemon juice to prevent the slices from browning. Set aside.

To make the dressing, in a small bowl, combine crème fraîche, horseradish, salt, pepper, and chives and mix well.

To serve, cut the pancakes in half. Arrange the apple slices on a platter, top each with a pancake half and a dollop of the dressing.

Wild Rice, Apple, and Pecan Salad

Native to North America, wild rice isn't a member of the rice family. It's actually a grain that comes from an aquatic grass. Paired with apples and pecans, it makes a sensational late summer meal.

Makes about 4 servings

1 cup uncooked wild rice

3 cups vegetable or chicken broth

¼ teaspoon salt

2 Granny Smith apples, cored and diced

½ cup diced red bell pepper

½ cup dried cherries

¼ cup chopped toasted pecans

¼ cup diced red onion

¼ cup chopped fresh parsley

2 cloves garlic, minced

Dressing

2 tablespoons apple cider vinegar

2 tablespoons extra virgin olive oil

½ teaspoon sea salt

½ teaspoon freshly ground black pepper

Combine the rice, broth, and salt in a 3-quart saucepan set over high heat. Bring to a boil, reduce heat to simmer, cover, and cook until the rice is tender, about 45 to 50 minutes.

Drain the rice and place in a large bowl. Add the diced apple, bell peppers, cherries, pecans, red onion, parsley and garlic; toss to combine.

To make the dressing, whisk together the vinegar, olive oil, salt, and pepper in a small bowl. Pour over the rice salad and toss to combine.

Serve warm or cover and refrigerate for 4 hours or until chilled.

Harvard Cooler

The perfect celebratory drink when you return to campus for a big game. But don't worry if you can't squeeze in a road trip. It's good when you watch the game on TV, too.

Makes 2 cocktails

4 ounces apple-flavored schnapps

2 ounces fresh lemon juice

2 cups ice cubes

Sparkling apple cider, very cold, for topping

Combine the schnapps and lemon juice in a shaker with 1 cup ice. Shake well and strain into 2 tall glasses, each filled with ½ cup ice. Top each with sparkling cider.

Fruit Salad with Basil-Lime Syrup

The bright taste of citrus and basil elevates this fruit salad from the ordinary to the sublime.

Makes about 6 servings

Syrup

½ cup sugar

½ cup water

½ cup Thai basil leaves

1 tablespoon lime zest

Fruit Salad

½ pineapple, peeled and cubed

1 mango, peeled and cubed

1 papaya, peeled and cubed

2 Gala apples, peeled, cored, and cubed

1 tablespoon chopped Thai basil leaves

Combine the sugar and water in a 2-quart saucepan over high heat and bring to a boil. Cook until the sugar dissolves, about 1 minute. Remove from the heat and stir in the basil and lime zest. Cool completely. Strain the mixture, discarding solids.

When ready to serve, combine the fruit and chopped basil in a large bowl. Drizzle with the syrup and toss to coat.

Snack-Time Apple Cake

A healthful after-school snack that the kids will love. Or serve it for breakfast; it's good anytime.

Makes 1 (8-inch) cake

¼ cup unsalted butter, at room temperature

¼ cup granulated sugar

¼ cup brown sugar

2 eggs

1¼ cups shredded apple of your choice

¼ cup rolled oats (old-fashioned or quick)

¼ cup apple juice or cider

½ cup whole-wheat flour

½ cup all-purpose flour

¼ teaspoon freshly grated nutmeg

¼ teaspoon salt

1 teaspoon ground cinnamon

Vanilla yogurt or the yogurt of your choice, for serving (optional)

Apple slices dipped in apple juice, for serving (optional)

Preheat the oven to 350° F. Position the oven rack in the center of the oven. Grease an 8-inch cake pan and line it with parchment paper.

Cream the butter with an electric mixer set a low speed until softened and light in color. Add the sugars and cream again until thoroughly incorporated. Beat in the eggs. With a wooden spoon, stir in the apple.

Pour the oats into a small bowl, add the cider, and soak for 10 minutes. Add to the apple mixture and stir to combine.

Whisk together the flours, nutmeg, salt, and cinnamon. Stir the flour mixture into the apple mixture until just combined. Scoop the batter into the prepared pan. Bake for 35 to 40 minutes, or until the cake springs back when gently pressed. Cool in the pan on a rack. Serve warm or at room temperature, topped with sweetened yogurt and apple slices if desired.

Core Facts:

A perfect choice for kids, Gala is a small, mildly sweet, crisp apple. What's more, its yellow-red skin is resistant to bruising.

First developed in New Zealand, Gala is the result of a cross between Golden Delicious and a Kidd's Orange Plant.

Young Galas are light in color—basically orange streaks over yellow. Mature Galas are a deep, dark red.

Caramel Apple Bread Casserole

Since the caramel sauce takes more than 1½ hours to prepare, you might want to make it ahead of time.

Makes 16 servings

Caramel Sauce

1 cup unsalted butter
1 pound dark brown sugar
¾ cup light corn syrup
1 (14-ounce) can sweetened condensed milk
½ teaspoon salt
1 teaspoon lemon juice
½ cup heavy cream
1 teaspoon pure vanilla extract

Casserole

6 cups peeled and diced apples of your choice
8 cups cubed French bread
8 eggs
1 cup heavy cream
½ cup milk
1 teaspoon ground cinnamon
1 teaspoon pure vanilla extract

To make the caramel sauce, combine the butter, sugar, corn syrup, condensed milk, salt, and lemon juice in the top of a double boiler. Cook over simmering water for 1 hour, stirring occasionally. Stir in the heavy cream and continue to cook for 30 minutes longer. Remove from the heat and stir in the vanilla.

Preheat the oven to 350° F.

To make the casserole, spread 1 cup of the caramel sauce in the bottom of a 9- x 13-inch baking dish. Top with the diced apples and bread.

In a medium bowl, whisk together the eggs, cream, milk, cinnamon, and vanilla. Pour over the bread mixture.

Bake the casserole uncovered until golden brown, about 40 to 45 minutes. To serve, spoon into serving dishes and serve with the rest of the warmed caramel sauce.

Apple Tip:

Buy your apples in bulk and recycle the crates. Wooden apple crates make wonderful baskets, shelves, nightstands, shadow boxes, planters, and even storage bins for bathrooms and home offices. Paint them, line them with burlap, turn them on their sides, mount wheels to their bases—and create something both cheap and chic for your home.

Poached Apples with Whipped Mascarpone and Almonds

Poached apples are an elegant dessert that will impress your guests, yet are quick and easy to prepare.

Makes 4 servings

3 cups apple juice or cider
1 vanilla bean, split, beans scraped
2 firm, tart-sweet apples, such as Northern Spy or Pink Lady, peeled, halved, and cored
¾ cup mascarpone cheese, at room temperature
1 teaspoon lemon zest
¼ cup slivered almonds

Combine the apple juice or cider and the vanilla bean pod plus scraped seeds in a 3-quart saucepan set over medium-high heat. Bring to a boil. Add the apples, reduce the heat to low, cover, and simmer until tender, about 10 minutes.

Use a slotted spoon to remove the apples and vanilla pod and set aside. Bring the liquid back to a boil over medium-high heat and cook uncovered, stirring occasionally, until reduced to a syrupy consistency, about 5 minutes.

In a medium bowl, whip the mascarpone and lemon zest with a handheld mixer until light and fluffy.

To serve, place each poached apple on a dessert plate and fill with the mascarpone. Drizzle with syrup and sprinkle with the almonds.

Caramel Apple Nachos

Nachos are traditionally made with melted cheese and salsa. Here tortilla chips are served with a sweet gooey mixture of apples, marshmallows, caramel sauce, and chocolate.

Makes 6 servings

2 cups unsalted tortilla chips
2 cups peeled and diced Granny Smith apples
1¼ cups mini marshmallows
1 cup semisweet chocolate chips
¼ cup caramel topping

Preheat the oven to 350º F. Line a baking sheet with foil.

Arrange the tortilla chips in a single layer on the prepared baking sheet. Top with the apples, marshmallows, and chocolate chips. Drizzle with the caramel sauce.

Transfer to the oven and bake until the marshmallows are golden brown and puffed, about 7 to 8 minutes. Serve piping hot.

Apple Tip:

Originating in Australia in 1868, the Granny Smith apple is named after Maria Ann Smith, who propagated the cultivar in 1868. As Granny Smiths mature, they transform from yellow to grass-green and their strong tart flavor mellows as they ripen.

Wild Mushroom and Apple Ragu

Serve over polenta for an easy, meat-free meal.

Makes about 6 servings

2 tablespoons extra virgin olive oil

1 large sweet onion, diced

3 cloves garlic, minced

1½ pounds mushroom mix, such as oyster, cremini, shiitake, and royal trumpet

1 teaspoon salt

1 teaspoon freshly ground black pepper

½ cup Marsala

1 apple of your choice, peeled, cored, and diced

1 cup vegetable broth

⅓ cup heavy cream

½ cup chopped basil leaves

Heat the oil in a large nonstick sauté pan set over medium-high heat. Add the onions and sauté until lightly browned and softened. Add the garlic and cook, stirring constantly, for 30 seconds or until fragrant.

Add in mushrooms and sauté, stirring occasionally, until the natural water released from the mushrooms has evaporated. Season with the salt and pepper.

Remove the pan from the heat and add the Marsala. Put the pan back on the burner and cook, stirring occasionally, for 3 to 5 minutes or until the wine has evaporated. Add the diced apple and broth and simmer until the sauce has reduced by half, about 30 minutes.

Remove from the heat, stir in the heavy cream and basil, and serve.

Braised Chicken and Apples

This dish is extra good when served over mashed potatoes or egg noodles.

Makes 6 servings

1 (5-pound) chicken, cut into 8 to 10 pieces

1 teaspoon salt

1 teaspoon freshly ground black pepper

2 tablespoons olive oil

2 tablespoons unsalted butter

2 Granny Smith apples, peeled, cored, and sliced

2 cups chopped celery

1 cup chopped onion

3 cloves garlic, minced

1 teaspoon sweet Hungarian paprika

1 teaspoon dried parsley

1 teaspoon dried thyme

½ cup dry white wine

1 cup chicken stock

2½ tablespoons all-purpose flour

⅓ cup sour cream

2 tablespoons chopped fresh basil

Season the chicken pieces with the salt and pepper.

Heat the oil and butter in a 5-quart braising pan set over medium-high heat. Add the chicken and sear on each side until brown and crispy. Remove the chicken to a plate and set aside.

Add the apples, celery, onion, and garlic; sauté until softened and slightly caramelized, about 5 minutes. Add the paprika, parsley, thyme, and wine and scrape up the browned bits on the bottom. Bring to a boil, reduce heat, and simmer uncovered for 3 minutes.

In a small bowl, whisk together the chicken stock and flour. Add the mixture to the braising pan, bring to a boil, and stir until the sauce thickens. Return the chicken to the pan, reduce the heat to low, cover, and simmer for 1 hour.

Remove the chicken and 1 cup of the vegetables to a serving platter.

Transfer the sauce to a blender, add the sour cream, salt, and pepper and puree until smooth. Pour the sauce over the chicken and garnish with the chopped basil.

Core Fact:

Low in calories and high in fiber, apples can be a dieter's best friend. One study showed that women who consumed a cup of dried apples daily over the course of one year lost weight and lowered their cholesterol levels.

September 12

Apple Frittata

A frittata—a baked omelet—is one of the most versatile dishes around and it's great for brunch, lunch, or Sunday supper for a crowd. Here it's filled with apples and other good things.

Makes 6 servings

3 tablespoons olive oil

2 cloves garlic, finely chopped

1 large onion, cut in ¼-inch pieces

1 red bell pepper, cut into bite-sized pieces

1 yellow bell pepper, cut into bite-sized pieces

4 ounces sliced white mushrooms

2 sweet-tart apples, such as Gala or Fuji, cored, peeled, and cut into ½-inch pieces

¾ cup green beans, cut into bite-sized pieces

12 large eggs

¼ cup milk

½ teaspoon salt

Few grinds black pepper

4 slices Genoa salami, cut into bite-sized pieces

½ cup grated Parmesan and Romano cheese

Preheat the oven to 350° F. Pour the oil into a 10- or 12-inch ovenproof skillet with a lid, and tilt the pan to coat the sides and bottom. Set over medium heat, add the onion and garlic, and cook, stirring, for 7 to 10 minutes, or until translucent and soft.

Add the peppers and cook, stirring, for about 3 minutes, or until softened. Add the mushrooms and cook, stirring, until their liquid is released and it evaporates. Add the apple and beans to the skillet and cook for about 2 minutes to soften. Remove from the heat.

Beat the eggs, milk, salt, and pepper in a large bowl until light yellow. Remove the skillet from the heat and pour the eggs over the contents. Add the salami and stir once or twice, just to incorporate. Sprinkle with the cheese.

Cover and bake on the center rack of the oven for 35 to 45 minutes, or until the egg is cooked through. Remove the cover for the last 10 or 15 minutes of cooking so that the cheese gets nice and brown. Serve from the skillet.

Applesauce Lemon Berry Baby Cakes

Delectable little baby cakes that aren't just for kids! If cherries are in season,
substitute them for the blueberries.

Makes 12 baby cakes

1 cup plus 2 tablespoons cake flour

1½ teaspoons baking powder

¼ teaspoon salt

¼ cup smooth, unsweetened applesauce

1 tablespoon apple juice concentrate (undiluted)

Zest of 1 small or ½ large lemon

1 egg

3 egg yolks

½ cup plus 2 tablespoons granulated sugar

¼ cup vegetable oil

3 egg whites

⅛ teaspoon cream of tartar

1½ cups chopped blueberries

Preheat the oven to 325° F and move the oven rack to the center position. Line 12 mini cake pans, custard cups, or 8-ounce ramekins with parchment or grease only the bottoms.

Sift the flour, baking powder, and salt into a bowl. Resift and set aside. In a small bowl, mix the applesauce, juice concentrate, and zest.

Combine the egg and the egg yolks in the bowl of a mixer fitted with the whisk attachment and beat on medium-high speed for 2 to 3 minutes, or until very light and thickened. Slowly add ½ cup sugar and continue beating for 3 to 4 minutes, or until very light and ribboned. Pour in the oil in a thin stream and beat 30 to 45 seconds.

With the mixer on low-medium speed, add one-third of the flour mixture, then half the applesauce mixture. Scrape down the sides and bottom of the bowl. Add one-third of the flour mixture, the rest of the applesauce, and the last of the flour. Scrape down the sides and bottom, making sure all the flour is incorporated. Do not over-beat or the batter will deflate.

In a separate, clean bowl with a clean whisk attachment, beat the egg whites until foamy. Add the cream of tartar and beat to soft peaks. Gradually pour in 2 tablespoons sugar and beat until stiff peaks form. Carefully fold the beaten whites into the batter. Scoop the batter into the prepared pans.

Sprinkle the berries over the cakes and bake for 21 to 25 minutes, until the tops of the cakes are dry and beginning to brown and the cake springs back if pressed gently. It shouldn't pull away from the sides of the pan until taken from the oven to cool. Cool in the pans for 2 or 3 minutes. Run a thin knife around the edges to loosen them; then carefully turn out and cool upright on a rack.

Apple Tip:

The Ginger Gold, a large, cone-shaped apple with cream-colored flesh, is slower to brown than other apple varietals. It grows early in the fall season and does not store well. The ideal Ginger Gold is firm, smooth, heavy, and solid.

Noodle Pudding with Apples and Cranberry Sauce

A delectable side dish for Rosh Hashanah or any festive fall get-together.

Makes 12 servings

8 ounces egg noodles

3 large eggs

1 cup cottage cheese

¼ cup light brown sugar, packed

1 cup low-fat sour cream

½ cup milk

1 Ginger Gold or Golden Delicious apple, peeled, cored, and diced

1 teaspoon salt

1 teaspoon freshly ground black pepper

1 teaspoon lemon zest

½ teaspoon pure vanilla extract

½ teaspoon ground cinnamon

¼ teaspoon freshly ground nutmeg

¼ cup apple juice concentrate, thawed (not diluted)

½ cup whole-berry cranberry sauce

Preheat the oven to 350° F. Grease an 8- x 8-inch baking dish and set aside. Cook the noodles according to package directions.

In a large bowl, whisk the eggs until frothy. Add the cottage cheese, light brown sugar, sour cream, and milk and stir to combine. Add the apples, salt, pepper, lemon zest, vanilla, cinnamon, nutmeg, and apple juice concentrate; mix well.

Add the cooked egg noodles and pour into the prepared baking dish. Spoon dollops of cranberry sauce around the noodle pudding.

Transfer the baking dish to the oven and bake until the top is golden brown and crispy, about 45 minutes. Serve hot or at room temperature.

Rosh Hashanah Apples and Honey

The Jewish New Year has many customs associated with it. One of the most popular is dipping crisp apple slices into honey in hopes for a sweet year.

Makes 4 servings

1 apple of your choice, cored and sliced

1 teaspoon fresh lemon juice

½ cup good quality honey

In a medium bowl, toss the apples with the lemon juice. Serve with honey on the side.

Roasted Chicken with Apples and Plums

Apples and plums are tasty accompaniments to a perfectly roasted chicken.

Makes 6 servings

1 (4-pound) roasting chicken, rinsed and patted dry

1 tablespoon olive oil

1 tablespoon sea salt

1 tablespoon freshly ground black pepper

1 lemon, halved

1 head garlic, halved

4 sprigs fresh rosemary, plus 1 tablespoon chopped

3 cups sliced plums

2 cups sliced Honeycrisp or Pink Lady apples

¼ cup honey

Preheat the oven to 450° F.

Rub the chicken with the olive oil and season inside and out with 3/4 tablespoon sea salt and ¾ tablespoon pepper. Stuff the lemons, garlic, and rosemary sprigs inside the chicken cavity. Tuck the wings under the breast and tie the legs together with kitchen twine. Place in a large roasting pan. Transfer to the oven and roast for 20 minutes.

While the chicken is roasting, combine the plums, apples, chopped rosemary, and the remaining salt and pepper in a large bowl.

Remove the chicken from the oven and arrange the apples and plums around the chicken. Transfer the chicken back to the oven and roast an additional 30 to 35 minutes, or until the plums and apples are tender and a thermometer inserted into the leg joint registers 165° F. Allow to rest for 15 minutes before carving.

Core Fact:

Cripps Pink, also known by its trademark name Pink Lady, is a crisp, tart apple. Grown primarily in Australia, South Africa, southern Europe, and the USA, this apple variety takes its time maturing. Sometimes leaves are removed from the tops of trees in order to maximize sunlight penetration and allow the apple's distinctive pink color to develop.

Apple Colada Smoothie

A cross between a non-alcoholic piña colada and a milkshake, with the bright note of apple.

Makes about 2 cups

1 apple of your choice
½ cup fresh or canned pineapple juice
½ cup cream of coconut
1 cup vanilla ice cream
1 cup ice cubes

Peel and core the apple and cut it into about eight pieces. Place them into a food processor or blender and add the pineapple juice, cream of coconut, ice cream, and ice. Process until smooth and frothy. Taste and add more sugar if necessary.

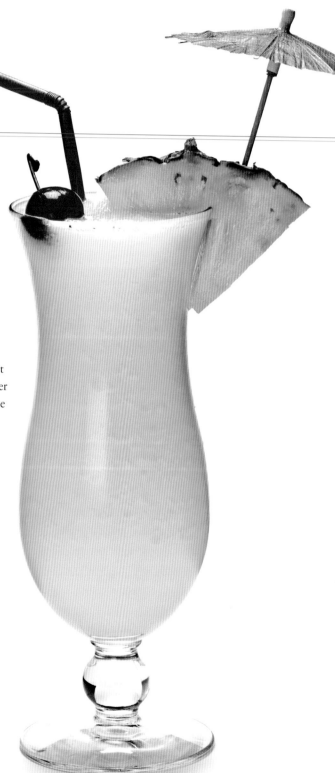

Brown Sugar–Glazed Apples

Serve this versatile dish with a savory pork roast or as dessert with a scoop of ice cream.

Makes 4 servings

2 tablespoons unsalted butter

4 medium Paula Red or Jonathan apples, peeled, cored, and sliced

½ cup light brown sugar, packed

½ teaspoon ground cinnamon

½ teaspoon sea salt

Melt the butter in a large sauté pan set over medium heat. Add the apples, brown sugar, cinnamon, and salt. Reduce the heat to low and cook, covered, for 10 minutes. Remove the cover, raise the heat to medium, and cook, stirring frequently, for 5 minutes longer or until the apples are tender and glazed. Serve either warm or cold.

Crisp Veal Sweetbreads with Apple Onion Marmalade and Apple Bourbon Gastrique

A gastrique is a French sweet and sour sauce. Here **Chef Mark Fischer** uses apples for the sweet and vinegar for the sour. The sauce is then drizzled over crispy sweetbreads topped with tangy marmalade, making the dish one not to be missed.

Makes 8 servings

Sweetbreads

2 pounds veal sweetbreads

1 onion, coarsely chopped

1 carrot, coarsely chopped

1 celery stalk, coarsely chopped

1 tablespoon dried thyme

1 tablespoon kosher salt

Place the sweetbreads and the remaining ingredients in a 4-quart saucepan; cover with cold water and bring to a boil. Reduce heat immediately and cook for 20 minutes at a gentle simmer. Drain, discarding all but the sweetbreads.

Press the sweetbreads between two pans, until cool. After the sweetbreads have cooled, gently peel away the connective membranes. (It will be impossible to completely remove it all, but do your best.) Separate the cleaned sweetbreads into 8 equal 3-ounce portions. Reserve. This can be done a day in advance.

Apple-Onion Marmalade

1 white onion, finely diced

1 tablespoon unsalted butter

1 tablespoon olive oil

½ cup granulated sugar

1 cup apple juice

½ cup apple cider vinegar

3 Honeycrisp Apples, peeled, cored, and diced into ¼-inch cubes

1 poblano pepper, diced brunoise-style*

1 tablespoon minced fresh thyme

Salt and freshly ground black pepper, to taste

Sauté the onions in the butter and oil until lightly caramelized and fragrant. Add the sugar, apple juice, and vinegar and reduce to a syrup. Add the apples and the chilies and stir to coat. Cook just until the apples are tender. Stir in the thyme, salt, and pepper and adjust the seasonings. Reserve.

*Brunoise is a knife-cutting technique in which the food is julienned and then turned slightly and diced again, producing ⅛-inch cubes.

Apple Bourbon Gastrique

2 cups apple cider

1 cup bourbon

3 cloves garlic, crushed

1 shallot, thinly sliced

½ cup brown sugar, packed

2 tablespoons fresh lemon juice

Kosher salt and freshly ground black pepper, to taste

Place all the ingredients in a non-reactive saucepan, bring to a simmer, and reduce the mixture to ½ cup. It should be smooth and syrupy when cool. Reserve.

For the Dish

1 cup Wondra flour

2 tablespoons unsalted butter

Kosher salt and freshly ground black pepper

Heat a large skillet set over medium-high heat. Preheat the oven to 350° F. Generously season the sweetbreads with the kosher salt and fresh ground pepper. Add the butter to the skillet and cook until frothy.

Dredge the sweetbreads in the flour and add to the skillet slowly. Be careful not to add too quickly or the temperature of the butter will drop. Cook on one side until crispy, flip, and cook on the other until crispy. Remove the sweetbreads to a tray and finish in the preheated oven for about 5 minutes, or until heated through.

While the sweetbreads are finishing in the oven, add the marmalade to the skillet, stirring, so that all the bits of food are incorporated and the apple mixture is warmed through.

Plate the sweetbreads individually. Top each portion with some warmed marmalade. Drizzle with the gastrique and serve.

Chef Mark Fischer

CURRENTLY: Owner of the Pullman in Glenwood Springs, Colorado; phat thai in Denver, Colorado, and Charm School Butchers in Carbondale, Colorado

NOTABLE FOR: An Esquire "Best New Restaurant" mention

Committed to: Supporting local farms and ranches and the Slow Food movement

Chicken Scaloppine with Apples

This riff on Jacques Pépin's classic veal dish will impress your guests and warm their bellies on a winter night.

Makes 6 servings

3 tablespoons butter

12 ounces cremini mushrooms, sliced

3 medium apples of your choice, peeled, cored, and diced

12 thin chicken cutlets

1 teaspoon salt

1 teaspoon freshly ground black pepper

¼ cup all-purpose flour

1 tablespoon olive oil

⅓ cup apple brandy, such as Calvados

½ cup chicken broth

½ cup heavy cream

Melt 2 tablespoons butter in a large sauté pan set over medium heat. Add the mushrooms and cook, stirring and shaking the pan for about 4 minutes, or until the mushrooms have released their liquid and are well browned. Add the apple and cook for 1 to 2 minutes, until just beginning to soften. Remove to a platter.

Season the chicken cutlets with ½ teaspoon salt and ½ teaspoon pepper. Coat the cutlets in the flour, shaking off the excess.

Heat the olive oil and the butter in a large nonstick sauté pan set over medium heat. Add the cutlets a few pieces at a time and sauté until lightly browned on both sides, about 3 minutes per side. Transfer to a platter, cover, and keep warm.

Add the apple brandy and chicken broth to the pan. Scrape up any of the browned bits on the bottom and cook over medium heat, stirring frequently, for 5 minutes.

Add the cream, bring to a boil, and then lower the heat to medium-low and simmer until the mixture has reduced by half and coats the back of a spoon, about 10 minutes. Season with the remainder of the salt and pepper. Pour the sauce over the chicken cutlets and serve immediately.

Apple Cupcakes with Apple Butter Frosting

Studded with chunks of apples, these delectable cupcakes showcase the bounty of fall's apple harvest.

Makes 12 cupcakes

1½ cups all-purpose flour

1¼ teaspoons baking powder

¼ teaspoon baking soda

½ teaspoon ground cinnamon

½ teaspoon ground ginger

½ cup unsalted butter, softened

¾ cup light brown sugar, packed

¼ cup granulated sugar

2 large eggs

1 teaspoon pure vanilla extract

½ cup sour cream

½ teaspoon lemon zest

2½ cups peeled diced Golden Delicious apples

Frosting

¼ cup unsalted butter, softened

2 teaspoons pure vanilla extract

½ teaspoon salt

3 cups confectioners' sugar

½ teaspoon ground cinnamon

¼ teaspoon freshly ground nutmeg

¼ cup apple butter

12 apple chips for garnish (optional)

Preheat the oven to 350° F. Line a muffin pan with baking cup liners; set aside.

In a medium-sized bowl, combine the flour, baking powder, baking soda, cinnamon, and ginger; mix well.

In a large bowl, beat the butter and both sugars with a handheld mixer until light and fluffy, about 3 minutes. Add the eggs, vanilla, sour cream, and zest. Mix until well incorporated.

Add the dry ingredients to the wet and beat on medium to combine. Fold in the apples.

Scoop the batter into the prepared muffin pan, filling almost all the way to the top.

Bake until a toothpick inserted in the middle cupcake comes out clean, about 25 minutes. Cool completely before frosting.

To make the frosting, combine all the ingredients in a medium bowl and whip until light and fluffy. Frost the cupcakes and top with an apple chip if desired.

Apple Cranberry Sauce

This is a quick and easy sauce, delicious with roast chicken or turkey.

Makes about 3 cups

1 pound Golden Delicious apples, peeled, cored, and chopped

¼ cup fresh orange juice

1 (16-ounce) can whole-berry cranberry sauce

1 teaspoon orange zest

½ teaspoon ground cinnamon

½ teaspoon sea salt

Combine the apples and the orange juice in a 3-quart saucepan set over medium-high heat. Bring to a boil, reduce heat, and simmer, covered, for 10 minutes or until the apples are just tender. Add the cranberry sauce, orange zest, cinnamon, and salt. Let cool to room temperature before serving.

Apple Dulce de Leche Crepes

Dulce de leche is a creamy caramel sauce made from milk and sugar. It is especially delicious when paired with apples.

Makes about 12 servings

1 cup all-purpose flour

¼ cup granulated sugar, plus 2 teaspoons

½ teaspoon salt

4 large eggs

1¼ cups milk

1 teaspoon lemon zest

Nonstick cooking spray

1¼ cups store-bought dulce de leche

1 Granny Smith apple, peeled, cored, and grated

Vanilla ice cream (optional)

In a medium bowl, whisk together the flour, 2 teaspoons sugar, and salt. Set aside.

In another medium bowl, whisk together the eggs, milk, and lemon zest. Stir the dry ingredients into the wet and mix until smooth. Cover and let rest at room temperature for 1 hour.

Spray a 7-inch crepe pan or nonstick sauté pan set over medium heat with cooking spray. Ladle 3 tablespoons of the batter into the pan, tilting to coat the bottom of the pan. Once the bottom begins to brown, about 30 seconds, flip and brown on the other side. Transfer the finished crepe to a plate. Re-spray the pan and continue making crepes with the remaining batter.

Preheat the oven to broil and line a baking sheet with foil.

In a medium bowl, combine the dulce de leche and grated apples.

Spread 1½ tablespoons of the apple mixture onto each crepe, ⅔ of the way from the top and bottom and then fold the left and right sides over by 1 inch and loosely roll up the crepe from bottom to top. Place the rolled crepes on the foil-lined baking sheet.

Sprinkle the rolled crepes with ¼ cup sugar and broil until caramelized, about 1 minute. Serve with vanilla ice cream if desired.

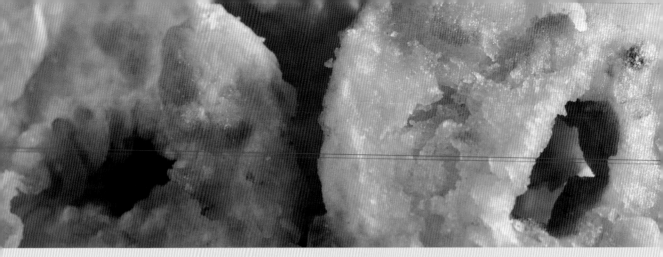

September 24

Crispy Apple Rings

Move over onion rings! In this recipe, apples take center stage, deep-fried to crispy perfection.

Makes about 8 servings

Batter

1 egg white

1 cup amber beer

1 cup all-purpose flour

1 teaspoon salt

½ cup fresh lemon juice

2 tablespoons light
brown sugar, packed

4 Granny Smith apples,
peeled, cored, and
sliced into ¼-inch-
thick rings

Vegetable oil, for frying

Confectioners' sugar, for
sprinkling

To make the batter, whisk the egg white in a large bowl until frothy. Whisk in the beer and then the flour and salt. Mix together until the batter is smooth and free of lumps. Let stand, covered, at room temperature for 1 hour.

To make the marinade, combine the lemon juice and brown sugar in a small bowl. Arrange the apple slices on a baking sheet in a single layer. Pour the lemon juice mixture over the apples, cover, and let stand at room temperature for 1 hour, turning apples halfway through. Remove the apples from the marinade and pat dry with paper towels.

In a 5-quart saucepan, add enough oil to reach a depth of 2 inches. Using a deep-fry thermometer, heat the oil to 375° F.

Dip each apple slice into the batter and let the excess batter drip off. Fry the apples in batches (do not overcrowd), turning them once, about 2 minutes per side. Transfer the fried apple rings to a plate lined with paper towels to drain. Sprinkle with confectioners' sugar and serve immediately.

Apple Tiramisu Parfaits

A stunning dessert, with layers of roasted apples and spongy ladyfingers mingling with whipped cream and a warm pumpkin caramel sauce.

Makes 12 servings

Roasted Apples

6 cups peeled diced Gala apples
2 tablespoons unsalted butter, melted
2 tablespoons fresh lemon juice
½ teaspoon ground cinnamon
½ teaspoon salt

Mascarpone Cream

½ cup heavy cream
½ cup confectioners' sugar
1 teaspoon ground cinnamon
1 teaspoon pure vanilla extract
8 ounces mascarpone cheese, softened
    at room temperature

Pumpkin Caramel Sauce

½ cup canned pumpkin
1½ cups store-bought caramel sauce

1 cup apple cider
½ cup Calvados
4 dozen ladyfingers, split
12 apple chips (optional)

Preheat the oven to 400° F. Line a baking sheet with foil and set aside.

To roast the apples, combine the diced apples, butter, lemon juice, cinnamon, and salt in a large bowl. Toss to coat the apples. Spread onto the prepared baking sheet. Transfer to the oven and roast until the apples are tender and caramelized, about 30 minutes, stirring halfway. Set aside to cool.

To make the mascarpone cream, whip the heavy cream with a hand held mixer on medium-high speed until it starts to stiffen. Add the powdered sugar, cinnamon, and vanilla and continue to whip until stiff peaks form. Fold in the softened mascarpone; set aside.

To make the caramel sauce, whisk together the pumpkin and caramel sauce in a medium bowl until smooth; set aside.

Combine the apple cider and Calvados in a shallow bowl. Dunk ladyfingers in mixture, remove to plate, and set aside.

To assemble, place a layer of ladyfingers in the bottom of each of 12 parfait glasses. Spoon a layer of mascarpone cream over the ladyfingers. Top with 2 tablespoons of the roasted apples and 1 tablespoon of the pumpkin caramel sauce. Repeat the layers and top each glass with any remaining cream and caramel. Garnish each dessert with an apple chip if desired.

Apple-Graham Cracker Trail Mix

Kids can make this easy mix themselves and take it with them anywhere.

Makes about 8 servings

1 cup dried apples, chopped

1 cup bite-sized graham-cracker pieces

1 cup yogurt-covered raisins

1 cup Apple-Cinnamon Granola (see page 29)

1 cup broken pretzel pieces

1 cup peanuts or nut of your choice

Mix all the ingredients together and store in an airtight container.

Apple Tip:

One of America's most popular apples, Red Delicious is a medium-sized, conical apple with a bright red skin. Its mild sweet flavor contains hints of melon.

Apple Oat Muffins

These muffins are wheat free, a plus for those who avoid or can't process gluten.

Makes 12 muffins

2 cups oat flour

2 teaspoons baking powder

¼ teaspoon baking soda

1½ teaspoons ground cinnamon

¼ teaspoon ground ginger

⅛ teaspoon cardamom

¼ cup light brown sugar, packed

¼ cup nonfat yogurt

½ cup apple cider

2 large eggs, lightly beaten

1 large egg white, lightly beaten

¼ cup olive oil

½ teaspoon pure vanilla extract

1 cup shredded peeled Red Delicious apple

½ cup chopped toasted walnuts

Preheat the oven to 350° F. Line a muffin pan with baking cup liners; set aside.

Combine the oat flour, baking powder, baking soda, cinnamon, ginger, cardamom, and sugar in a medium bowl.

In a large bowl, beat together the yogurt, cider, eggs, egg white, olive oil, and vanilla. Add the dry ingredients into the wet and stir until just combined. Fold in the shredded apples and walnuts.

Fill each muffin cup about ¾ full with batter. Bake until a toothpick inserted in the middle comes out clean, about 15 minutes. Cool before serving.

Applesauce Smoothie

You can make a tasty smoothie with fresh apples—or applesauce. If you use bottled applesauce, use the best quality you can find.

Makes about 2 servings

1 cup applesauce (see page 17 or use store-bought)

1½ cups vanilla yogurt or low-fat vanilla yogurt

1 cup ice cubes

2 tablespoons granulated sugar, or to taste

Combine the applesauce, yogurt, ice, and sugar in a food processor or blender. Process until smooth and frothy. Taste and add more sugar if necessary.

Green Apple Martini

The vivid green of this cocktail sets it apart from more traditional martinis.

Makes 2 cocktails

Ice cubes

2½ ounces vodka

2½ ounces sour-apple schnapps

2½ ounces lemonade

2½ ounces lemon-lime soda

2 thin green apple slices, for garnish

Fill a cocktail shaker with ice cubes. Add the vodka, schnapps, lemonade, and soda. Cover and shake well. Strain the drinks into chilled martini glasses and garnish each with an apple slice.

September 30

Sausage and Rice-Stuffed Baked Apples

A wonderful main dish for fall, serve these savory stuffed apples with a bitter green salad.

Makes 4 servings

4 baking apples, such as Gala or Winesap

8 ounces chicken-apple sausage, removed from casing

⅓ cup diced sweet onion

⅓ cup diced celery

⅓ cup diced carrot

3 cloves garlic, minced

½ cup cooked rice

¼ cup chicken stock

1 teaspoon fresh marjoram, chopped

½ teaspoon sea salt

½ teaspoon freshly ground black pepper

¾ cup apple cider

Preheat the oven to 375° F.

To prepare the apples, slice the top off each one. Use a melon baller to core the apples (discard core) then scoop out the flesh, leaving about a ½-inch-thick shell. Place the apples into a 8- x 8-inch baking dish. Dice the scooped-out flesh and set aside.

Heat the oil in a large sauté pan set over medium-high heat; add the chicken sausage, onion, celery, carrot, garlic, and diced apple. Sauté until the sausage is browned and cooked through, about 5 to 7 minutes. Remove from heat, stir in the rice, chicken stock, marjoram, salt, and pepper.

Pour the apple cider into the bottom of the dish. Fill each apple with the sausage mixture. Bake, uncovered, until the apples are tender, about 35 to 45 minutes. Serve with the cooking liquid drizzled on top.

Curried Apple Cauliflower Soup

Tangy Granny Smith apples add a touch of sweetness to this soup and blend in well with the spicy curry.

Makes 4 servings

1 tablespoon olive oil

1 sweet onion, diced

4 cloves garlic, minced

1 teaspoon curry powder

1 Granny Smith apple, peeled, cored, and chopped

4 cups cauliflower florets

2½ cups vegetable or chicken broth

½ teaspoon salt

½ teaspoon freshly ground black pepper

¼ cup Greek yogurt

1 tablespoon chopped chives, for garnish

Heat the olive oil in a 4-quart saucepan set over medium-high heat. Add the diced onions and sauté, stirring occasionally, until the onion is soft and lightly browned. Add the garlic and curry powder and stir until fragrant, about 30 seconds.

Add the chopped apple, cauliflower florets, broth, salt, and pepper. Bring to a boil, lower the heat to simmer, cover, and cook for 15 to 20 minutes or until the cauliflower is tender.

Transfer the soup to a blender or use an immersion blender and puree the soup until smooth. Add the yogurt and stir to combine. Reheat if necessary, then serve garnished with the chives.

Lamb Tagine with Apples, Prunes, and Apricots

A Berber dish that hails from North Africa, tagine is named after the conical earthenware pot in which it is traditionally cooked. If you don't have such a pot, a Dutch oven makes a fine substitute.

Makes 4 servings

2 tablespoons olive oil

1 pound boneless lamb leg, trimmed and cut into 1-inch pieces

1 teaspoon cayenne pepper

1 teaspoon sea salt

1 sweet onion, chopped

2 cinnamon sticks

2 cups chicken or lamb broth

1 cup apple cider

1 tablespoon unsalted butter

1 Granny Smith apple, peeled, cored, and sliced

2 tablespoons granulated sugar

12 dried prunes

12 dried apricots, halved

¼ cup chopped fresh cilantro, for garnish

¼ sliced almonds, toasted, for garnish

Heat the olive oil in a tagine or a 4-quart Dutch oven set over medium-high heat.

In a medium bowl, combine the lamb, cayenne, and salt; toss to coat.

Add the lamb to the tagine in batches (don't crowd the meat), and brown on all sides. Transfer the lamb to a plate and set aside.

Add the onion to the tagine and sauté until softened, about 5 minutes. Return the meat to the pan along with the cinnamon sticks, broth, and apple cider. Bring to a boil, lower the heat, and simmer, covered, for 1 hour.

Meanwhile, heat the butter in a sauté pan set over medium heat. Add the apple slices and sugar and sauté until lightly caramelized and softened, about 5 minutes. Add the prunes and apricots and sauté an additional 2 minutes.

Once the lamb has simmered for 1 hour and is tender, add the fruit mixture and simmer for an additional 10 minutes. Serve over fluffy couscous and garnish with the cilantro and toasted almonds.

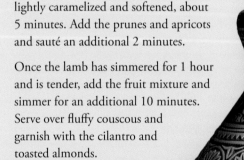

Couscous with Apple and Spices

Some people mistake couscous for an exotic grain, when it's actually tiny balls of pasta. In this dish, though, it's still wonderfully exotic: fragrant with fennel seed and packed with onion, apple, almonds, and raisins, it's a delicious experience.

Makes 4 to 6 servings

1 tablespoon olive oil

½ teaspoon fennel seeds

½ large onion, roughly chopped

1 apple of your choice

¼ cup sliced almonds

¼ cup raisins

¼ teaspoon ground cinnamon

2 or 3 grinds black pepper

3 cups vegetable or chicken broth

1¾ cup plain couscous

Heat the oil in a skillet set over medium-high heat. Add the fennel seeds and onion and cook, stirring occasionally, until the onions are soft and translucent but not browned and the fennel is fragrant. Lower the heat if necessary.

Meanwhile, peel and core the apple and cut it into ¼-inch chunks. Add it and the almonds, raisins, cinnamon, and black pepper to the onion and cook, stirring occasionally, until the apple is softened, about 5 minutes.

Add the broth and bring to a boil. Add the couscous and mix well to combine. Remove from the heat, cover, and let stand for 5 to 10 minutes, or until the couscous is tender and cooked through and all of the liquid is absorbed.

Apple-Cinnamon Buns

October 4 is Cinnamon Bun Day in Sweden. Celebrate by making a batch of these much-loved sticky treats.

Makes 16 buns

Dough

6½ tablespoons granulated sugar

1 teaspoon salt

5½ tablespoons unsalted butter

1 large egg

3½ cups bread flour, plus more for kneading

1 package rapid-rise yeast

1 cup plus 2 to 4 tablespoons whole milk

Filling

1½ tablespoons unsalted butter

3 Granny Smith apples, peeled and diced

⅓ cup granulated sugar

½ teaspoon cornstarch

1½ teaspoon ground cinnamon

1 teaspoon pure vanilla extract

Glaze

1 cup confectioners' sugar

3 tablespoons milk

To make the dough, combine the sugar, salt, and butter in the bowl of a stand mixer with a paddle attachment. Beat on medium-high speed for 1 minute. Add the egg and mix until incorporated. Add the flour, yeast, and milk and mix until the dough pulls away from the sides of the bowl. Turn the dough onto a lightly floured surface and knead until supple and smooth. Lightly oil a large bowl and transfer the dough to the bowl, turning to coat. Cover with plastic wrap and let rise at room temperature until doubled in size, about 2 hours.

To make the filling, melt the butter in a large skillet. Add the apples, sugar, cornstarch, and cinnamon and stir until the apples are coated with the sugar mixture. Cook, stirring frequently, until the apples are soft. Remove from heat and stir in the vanilla. Combine the sugar and cinnamon in a small bowl.

Punch down the dough. On a floured work surface, roll out the dough to a 12- x 14-inch rectangle. Sprinkle the cinnamon-sugar mixture evenly over the entire surface. Distribute the apple filling on the dough. Starting at a long side, roll the dough into a log, pinching the dough as you go. With the seam side down, cut the log crosswise into 16 slices. Transfer to the prepared baking sheet, placing the rolls 1½ inches apart. Cover lightly with plastic wrap and let rest for 75 minutes.

When ready to bake, preheat the oven to 350° F. Bake for 20 to 30 minutes, or until golden brown. Cool for 10 minutes. To make the glaze, stir together the sugar and milk until smooth. Drizzle over buns and serve.

Dried Fruit and Cereal Snack Mix

This kid-friendly snack will help keep hunger at bay until dinnertime.

Makes about 8 cups

2 cups dried apples, chopped

1 cup dried apricots, chopped

1 cup raisins

2 cups puffed corn cereal

1 cup mini marshmallows

1 cup coconut, toasted

Place all the ingredients in a large, resealable plastic storage bag. Shake until combined.

Apple and Cheddar Quesadillas

If you like your quesadillas spicier, use spicy brown mustard instead of the whole grain.

Makes 4 servings

4 (8-inch) whole wheat tortillas

4 tablespoons whole-grain mustard

1 cup sharp Cheddar cheese, shredded

4 slices deli ham or smoked turkey (optional)

¼ cup thinly sliced red onion (optional)

1 cup Fuji or Honeycrisp apple, cored and thinly sliced

Nonstick cooking spray

Lay tortillas on a flat working surface. Spread mustard on each. Top with the ham or turkey, onion, and apple slices. Finally, sprinkle with the cheese. Fold each tortilla in half.

Spray a large nonstick sauté pan with cooking spray and set it over medium-high heat. Lay 2 of the quesadillas in the skillet and cook 2 to 3 minutes per side or until the cheese is melted and the tortillas are golden brown. Repeat with the 2 remaining quesadillas. Cut each quesadilla in quarters and serve immediately.

Apple Stromboli

A stromboli is usually a savory baked sandwich—but this one is sweet, filled with apples, walnuts, cookie crumbs, brown sugar, and cinnamon. To make cookie crumbs, you can whiz the cookies in a food processor or put them into a sealable plastic bag, place the bag on a work surface, and pound them with the bottom of a pot.

Makes 1 (9-inch) loaf

½ recipe sweet yeast dough used in President's Day Apple Cherry Buns (see page 61)

⅓ cup cookie crumbs (from vanilla cookies or other plain cookies)

½ cup finely chopped walnuts

¼ cup light brown sugar

½ teaspoon ground cinnamon

⅓ cup raisins

¼ cup apple juice

1 tablespoon unsalted butter, softened

1 medium apple, peeled, cored, and cut in small dice

Zest and juice of ½ medium lemon

2 tablespoons granulated sugar

1 egg white mixed with 2 teaspoons water

Prepare the sweet yeast dough and let it rise for two hours, as directed on page 61. Line a baking sheet with parchment paper.

Meanwhile, mix the cookie crumbs, toasted nuts, brown sugar, and cinnamon in a small bowl. Set aside. Soak the raisins in the apple juice. Drain and pat dry

When the dough has risen, press the dough down and turn it out onto the counter. Flatten it slightly. Roll out the dough to make a 16- by 12-inch rectangle. Spread the dough with butter, leaving a 1-inch edge uncovered all around the perimeter. Sprinkle the buttered dough with the crumb mixture.

Toss the apple, lemon zest and juice, and sugar in a small bowl and sprinkle it over the crumb mixture. Fold the ends of the rectangle inward about 1½ inches on each side to cover the filling. Roll up the dough into a log. It will be about 9 inches long and 3 inches wide. Seal the seam by pinching it tightly.

Place the filled log on the prepared baking sheet, seam down. Press gently to flatten slightly. Cover lightly with greased plastic wrap. Let rise for 1 to 1½ hours, or until it increases in size by 50 to 70 percent.

When you are ready to bake, preheat the oven to 375° F. Position the oven rack in the center of the oven. Remove the plastic and brush the top of the stromboli with the egg wash. Bake for 25 to 30 minutes; if the stromboli seems to be browning too fast, then reduce the oven temperature to 350° F after 15 to 20 minutes. Cool the stromboli on a rack. Cool completely before slicing. Serve warm or at room temperature.

Cider French Toast with Apple Jelly

Adding apple cider gives French toast a sweet, fruity flavor. Serve with apple jelly for a multi-layered apple flavor.

Makes 4 slices

4 eggs

½ cup apple cider

½ teaspoon pure vanilla extract

½ teaspoon ground cinnamon

Nonstick cooking spray

2 teaspoons unsalted butter, plus more if needed

4 slices good-quality bread

Apple jelly to taste

Combine the eggs, cider, vanilla, and cinnamon in a bowl and beat with a fork until well blended.

Spray a skillet with cooking oil spray and set it over medium-high heat. Add the butter, let it melt, and tilt to coat the pan. Watch carefully to make sure the butter does not burn; reduce the heat or remove the pan from the burner for a minute if necessary.

Working with 1 or 2 slices at a time, submerge the bread into the egg mixture. Pierce a few times with a fork to allow the egg to soak into the bread. Place the bread into the skillet in a single layer, working in batches if necessary. Cook for about 2 minutes and turn with tongs. Cook an additional 1 to 3 minutes, or until the French toast is golden brown on the outside and cooked through and not mushy on the inside. Adjust the heat as necessary. Transfer to a platter and keep warm. Repeat with remaining bread and egg mixture.

Serve warm with apple jelly.

Apples Mostarda

Mostarda is an Italian condiment that resembles fruit chutney. Mustard gives it a bit of a kick. It is great served with boiled meat or thickly spread on toast.

Makes about 1½ cups

3 cups Granny Smith apples, peeled, cored, and diced

¼ cup fresh lemon juice

2 cups apple juice or cider

2 cups dry white wine

1 cup granulated sugar

2 tablespoons dried mustard

2 tablespoons mustard powder

Place the diced apples and lemon juice in a large bowl filled with cold water. Set aside.

In a 4-quart saucepan, combine the apple juice, white wine, and sugar and bring to a boil over high heat, stirring occasionally. Reduce the heat to medium-high and boil until the mixture has reduced to 1 cup, about 45 minutes to 1 hour.

Drain the apples and fold them into the hot syrup. Add the mustards and stir to combine. Cool and refrigerate in an airtight container for up to 3 weeks.

Apple and Gruyere Cheese Puffs

Cheesy and light, these bite-size puffs don't take long to prepare and are best eaten straight from the oven.

Makes about 30 cheese puffs

1 cup water

7 tablespoons salted butter, chopped

1 teaspoon salt

1 cup all-purpose flour

4 large eggs, at room temperature

½ cup diced Gruyere cheese

½ cup diced peeled Granny Smith apple

¼ teaspoon freshly ground black pepper

½ teaspoon chopped fresh thyme leaves

Preheat the oven to 425° F. Grease 2 baking sheets and set aside.

Combine the water, butter, and salt in a 4-quart saucepan set over medium-high heat and bring to a boil. Add the flour and stir vigorously with a wooden spoon until the mixture pulls away from the sides of the saucepan and forms a ball. Remove from the heat.

Add the eggs one at a time, incorporating each one before adding the next. The dough will be shiny when finished. Stir in the Gruyere, apples, pepper, and thyme.

Spoon the batter, about 2 inches apart, onto the prepared baking sheets; the puffs will expand so don't overcrowd.

Bake for 15 minutes or until crisp and golden. Serve immediately.

Where do most of the world's apples come from? The top ten countries currently at the pinnacle include (in order of production, from highest to lowest): China, United States, Turkey, Italy, India, Poland, France, Iran, Brazil, and Chile.

October 11

Apple, Walnut, and Gorgonzola Risotto

Splurge on a quality Gorgonzola when making this dish. You won't regret it.

Makes 8 servings

1 tablespoon olive oil

1 cup chopped sweet onion

2 cloves garlic, minced

1 cup Arborio rice

4 cups chicken broth, heated

1 cup crumbled Gorgonzola

1 cup diced Fuji or Honeycrisp apple

¼ teaspoon salt

½ teaspoon freshly ground black pepper

½ cup chopped toasted walnuts

2 tablespoons chopped fresh parsley

Heat the olive oil in a large nonstick sauté pan set over medium-high heat. Add the diced onion and sauté until lightly browned and softened, about 5 minutes. Add the garlic and cook until fragrant, about 30 seconds.

Add the rice and cook, stirring constantly, for 1 minute, coating the rice with the oil. Add 2 ladlefuls of hot broth, about 1 cup, and stirring constantly, cook over medium heat until the liquid is absorbed. Add another two ladles of broth and continue to stir until the liquid is absorbed. Repeat this procedure two more times until all the broth is absorbed and the rice is al dente and creamy. This process should take from 35 to 40 minutes.

Turn off the heat and stir in the Gorgonzola, diced apples, salt, and pepper. Cover and let stand for 5 minutes. Sprinkle with the walnuts and parsley and serve immediately.

Cranberry and Apple Cider Vinaigrette

Serve this salad dressing with a simple green salad of sliced apples, pears, and toasted walnuts.

Makes about 1¼ cups

1 cup fresh or frozen cranberries

¼ cup plus 2 tablespoons apple cider vinegar

¼ cup pure maple syrup

1½ tablespoons Dijon mustard

½ cup apple cider

2 tablespoons extra virgin olive oil

½ teaspoon sea salt

½ teaspoon freshly ground black pepper

Combine the cranberries, vinegar, and maple syrup in a 4-quart saucepan set over medium heat. Bring to a boil, reduce heat to low, and simmer uncovered until the cranberries begin to pop, about 10 minutes. Cool slightly.

Place the cranberry mixture and the rest of the ingredients in a blender and puree until smooth. Store in an airtight container in the refrigerator for up to 1 week.

Caramel Apple Crème Brûlée

Breaking into a hard caramel shell for a spoonful of rich custard is one of the delights of this classic dessert. This version is all the more delicious with apple slices at the bottom.

Makes 6 servings

2 tablespoons finely chopped walnuts

2 cups thinly sliced Granny Smith apples

2 cups water

6 tablespoons store-bought dulce de leche

¼ cup plus 2 tablespoons granulated sugar

¼ cup plus 2 tablespoons light brown sugar, packed

½ teaspoon ground cinnamon

Pinch of cardamom (optional)

½ teaspoon salt

2 cups heavy cream

5 large egg yolks

1 teaspoon pure vanilla extract

Preheat the oven to 350° F. Place the walnuts on a baking sheet and toast in the oven just until lightly brown and fragrant, 2 to 3 minutes (watch them carefully).

Place the sliced apples and water in a 4-quart saucepan set over high heat and bring to a boil. Reduce the heat and simmer until the apples are tender, about 10 to 12 minutes. Drain well. Arrange the apples in the bottoms of 6 ramekins or custard cups. Sprinkle toasted walnuts over apples and top with 1 tablespoon dulce de leche in each; place the ramekins in a deep-dish pan and set aside.

In a 4-quart saucepan over medium heat, whisk together ¼ cup granulated sugar, ¼ cup brown sugar, cinnamon, cardamom, salt, and heavy cream. Cook, stirring, over medium heat until bubbles form around the edges, about 5 to 7 minutes. Remove from heat.

In a medium bowl, whisk the egg yolks. Slowly add in a ladleful of the hot cream, whisking constantly. Add 1 more ladle of cream, stir to combine, and then pour the egg mixture into the remaining cream in the saucepan. Cook, stirring, for 3 to 5 minutes over medium-low heat. The mixture is ready when it coats the back of a wooden spoon. Remove from heat and stir in the vanilla.

Pour the custard into the prepared ramekins, filling them to the top. Transfer the pan with the filled ramekins to the oven and pour the boiling water into the bottom of the pan. Bake, uncovered, until the centers are just set, about 30 to 35 minutes. Remove the ramekins from the water bath and let cool for 20 minutes. Transfer back to the pan, cover, and refrigerate overnight.

When ready to serve, let the crème brûlée come to room temperature for 15 minutes. Combine 2 tablespoons of granulated sugar and 2 tablespoons brown sugar in a small bowl. Sprinkle the sugar evenly over the custards.

If using a kitchen torch, sprinkle the sugar evenly over the custards and heat the sugar with the torch until caramelized.

If using a broiler, preheat the oven to broil. Broil 8 inches from the heat until the sugar is caramelized, about 5 minutes.

October 14

Cider-Brined Duck Legs with Cherry and Apple Slaw

Cherries are a classic accompaniment to duck, but this recipe changes things up a bit by putting them into a luscious slaw made with apples and cabbage. The cider brine gives the duck a succulent flavor; you'll need to allow time for brining—a full day or overnight. You can make the Cherry and Apple Slaw (see page 285) while the duck is roasting; by that time you will have rendered duck fat that will give the slaw a flavor that can't be beat.

Makes 4 servings

4 (12-ounce) duck legs with thighs

4 cups water

4 cups apple cider or apple juice

2 tablespoons Calvados (optional)

¼ cup kosher salt

2 sprigs fresh thyme

Freshly ground black pepper to taste

1 recipe Cherry and Apple Slaw (see page 285)

Combine the water, cider or juice, Calvados, if using, salt, and thyme in a large pot that is big enough to hold all 4 duck legs. Cook over medium heat until the salt is dissolved. Cool to room temperature.

Place the duck legs into the cooled brine so that all are completely submerged. Refrigerate for 6 to 12 hours. Drain and discard the brine and thyme. Rinse and pat dry. Season with freshly ground black pepper

Preheat the oven to 375° F. Line a sheet pan or shallow roasting pan with foil. Over medium-high heat, heat a large skillet that is big enough to hold all the duck legs in one layer. Sear the duck legs for about 6 minutes per side, or until browned. Transfer the duck pieces to a rimmed sheet pan or into a shallow roasting pan. Pour off and reserve the duck fat. (You can use the reserved duck fat for the Cherry and Apple Slaw or another recipe.)

Roast the duck legs for 30 to 40 minutes, or until an instant-read thermometer inserted in to the thickest part of thigh reads 165° F. Set aside to keep warm, tenting loosely with foil until you are ready to serve. Serve hot on a bed of Cherry and Apple Slaw.

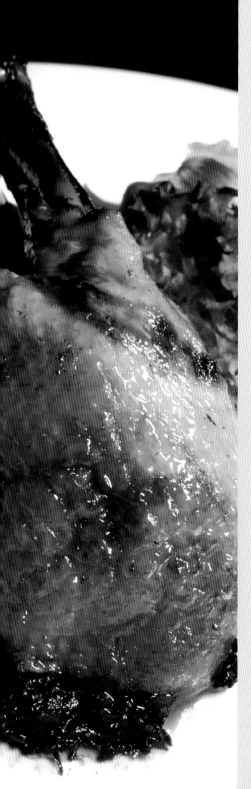

Cherry and Apple Slaw

This warm fruit slaw is fabulous with duck recipes such as Cider-Brined Duck (see page 284), but will go beautifully with pork or poultry also. It's a go-anywhere dish that would work for an elegant dinner party or a casual afternoon of tailgating.

Makes 4 servings

3 tablespoons duck fat (see page 284) or 1½ tablespoons vegetable oil and 1½ tablespoons unsalted butter

1 medium red onion, cut into ⅛-inch slices

6 cups thinly sliced red cabbage

1 large Granny Smith apple, peeled, cored, and grated

⅔ cup dried dark cherries

3 tablespoons dark cherry preserves

¼ cup apple cider

3 to 4 tablespoons balsamic vinegar, plus 1 or 2 teaspoons more if needed

½ teaspoon salt, plus more to taste if needed

⅛ teaspoon freshly grated black pepper, plus more to taste if needed

Set a skillet over medium heat. (If you are making the Cider-Brined Duck Legs, use the skillet in which you seared the duck.) Add 1 tablespoon duck fat or ½ tablespoon oil and ½ tablespoon butter. Add the onion and cook, stirring and shaking the pan frequently, for 6 to 8 minutes, or until nicely softened and starting to brown.

Add the remaining duck fat or oil and butter and the red cabbage. Cook, stirring to coat and mix, for about 1 minute, or until the cabbage starts to wilt. Add the apple, cherries, cherry preserves, cider, balsamic vinegar, salt, and pepper. Stir to mix well. Cover, reduce the heat, and simmer for 15 to 20 minutes, until cabbage is tender.

Remove the cover and cook over medium heat until any excess liquid evaporates. Taste and add salt, pepper, or vinegar as desired.

Fall Apple Salad of "Raked Leaves"

With this dish, **Chef Ryan Shelton** couples typical fall flavors—apple, squash, pomegranate, spices—with nature's own fall textures, that of crunchy, dry, fallen leaves in an edible context!

Makes 6 servings

Crunchy Leaf Garnish

2 medium apples of your choice

1 head Napa cabbage

¼ cups each gold and red beet juice (optional)*

2 ounces acorn powder (available at Korean markets)

1 teaspoon grapeseed oil

1 cup water

*Note: the gold and red beet juices intensify fall colors.

Salad

3 medium sweet apples, such as Honeycrisps, diced

1 large butternut squash, peeled, diced, and seeded

2 pomegranates, seeded

2 large shallots, peeled and diced

¼ cup sherry vinegar

½ cup olive oil

Curry Yogurt

½ cup plain Greek yogurt

1 tablespoon curry powder

1 teaspoon grapeseed oil

1 head red oak lettuce

To prepare the crunchy leaf garnish, begin by slicing the apples very thinly on a mandolin. Place the apple slices in a small saucepan, pour the gold beet juice over, if using, and add water just to cover. Bring the mixture to a very light simmer over medium heat and simmer for about 6 minutes. Remove from heat source and allow to cool to room temperature.

Separate 12 Napa cabbage leaves, reserving only the leafier top half. Place in a saucepan, cover with red beet juice, if using, and add water just to cover. Bring to a simmer over medium heat, remove from heat, and allow to cool.

On a silicon-lined baking sheet, lay out the apple slices and cabbage leaves, sprinkle lightly with salt, and dry out in the oven on its lowest setting until just crisp, possibly overnight. Carefully peel leaves off the mat and keep in a lidded container.

Place the acorn powder and grapeseed oil in a small saucepan and slowly whisk in 2 cups of water. Season with a pinch of salt. Bring the mixture to a simmer and whisk constantly until translucent. Pour the acorn mixture onto a silicon-lined baking sheet and spread to ⅛-inch thickness. Bake at 325° F until puffed and crispy. Break the wafer into leaf-sized pieces. Reserve in a lidded container.

For the salad, blanch the butternut squash in boiling salted water until very tender. Strain and allow to cool to room temperature before storing in the refrigerator.

To make the dressing, marinate the shallots in the sherry vinegar overnight. The next day, drain off most of the excess vinegar, reserving only the pickled shallots. Add the olive oil to the shallots and store in the refrigerator until needed.

For the curry yogurt, lightly toast the curry powder in grapeseed oil in a pan set over low heat until fragrant. Add the yogurt, stirring constantly until smooth. Pour out of the pan to cool and season with salt. Store in the refrigerator.

To finish: Toss the diced apples, pomegranates, and butternut squash in the shallot vinaigrette, season with salt, and mound in the center of 6 plates. Dot each mound with 3 to 4 dollops of the curry yogurt. Top with 3 leaves of red oak lettuce. Garnish the salad with the crispy leaves, stacking them so they resemble a pile of raked leaves. Serve and enjoy.

Chef Ryan Shelton

CURRENTLY: Bonny Doon Vineyard, Santa Cruz, California

TRAINING: Cooked in Michelin-starred kitchens of Baume and Chez TJ

FAMOUS FOR: His molecular gastronomy techniques

Sweet Potato–Apple Cider Soup with Caramelized Onions

On a crisp fall day take the time to make this warming soup.

Makes 8 servings

3 medium garnet sweet potatoes

2 tablespoons olive oil

2 cups thinly sliced sweet onion

½ cup apple brandy

1 cup apple cider

1 teaspoon sea salt

1 teaspoon freshly ground black pepper

½ teaspoon cayenne pepper

½ teaspoon ground cinnamon

4 cups chicken broth

Sour cream, for topping

Preheat the oven to 400° F.

Prick the potatoes with a fork and wrap each one in foil. Place them on a baking sheet and bake for 1 hour. Turn off the oven and let them sit in the oven for 30 minutes to finish cooking and cool slightly.

While the potatoes are roasting, start the onions. Heat the olive oil in a large nonstick sauté pan set over medium heat. Add the onions and sauté for 20 to 25 minutes, stirring frequently, until the onions are caramelized and very soft. Remove the pan from the heat and add the apple brandy. Return to the burner, raise the heat to medium-high, and boil for 30 seconds.

Reserve ¼ cup of the onions. Transfer the rest to the food processor bowl. Peel the cooked sweet potatoes and add the flesh to the bowl along with the apple cider, salt, pepper, cayenne, and cinnamon. Puree until silky and smooth.

Transfer the mixture to a 5-quart saucepan and whisk in the chicken broth. Bring the mixture to a boil, lower the heat, and simmer, uncovered, for 5 minutes.

To serve, ladle into 8 soup bowls and top with the reserved caramelized onions and sour cream.

Apple-Cranberry Cornbread

Light and moist, this cornbread is especially good when slathered with butter, honey, or preserves.

Makes 1 (9-inch) loaf

Nonstick cooking spray
½ cup all-purpose flour
1½ cups yellow cornmeal
¾ teaspoon salt
1 tablespoon baking powder
½ cup unsalted butter, melted
1¼ cups buttermilk
3 large eggs, at room temperature
1 cup cored, peeled, and diced Fuji apple
¼ cup dried cranberries, chopped

Preheat the oven to 400° F. Spray a 9- x 9-inch baking pan with cooking spray.

In a large bowl, sift the flour, cornmeal, salt, and baking powder; stir to combine.

In a medium bowl, whisk together the melted butter, buttermilk, eggs, apple, and cranberries. Add the wet ingredients to the dry and stir until just combined; do not over mix.

Pour the batter into the prepared pan and bake until the edges are golden brown and a knife inserted in the center comes out clean, about 18 to 20 minutes. Serve warm.

October 19

Apple Tea Mix

When placed in an attractive container, this tea mix makes an excellent hostess gift.

Makes 12 cups

1 cup dried apple, finely chopped
½ cup loose black tea
15 whole cloves
1 cinnamon stick

Combine the ingredients and store in an airtight container for up to 6 months. To brew, place 1 tablespoon of the tea mix in 1 cup hot water and steep for 2 minutes.

October 20

Apple Tapioca Pudding

A beguiling twist on classic tapioca pudding.

Makes about 2 dozen

Nonstick cooking spray
1½ cups boiling water
¼ cup instant tapioca
½ cup brown sugar
½ teaspoon ground cinnamon
¼ teaspoon salt
Zest of 1 lemon, chopped
1 cup dried apple, chopped

Preheat the oven to 375° F. Spray a baking dish with cooking spray.

Pour the boiling water into a bowl, add the tapioca, and let stand for about 15 minutes, or until it is clear and gel-like. Add the sugar, cinnamon, salt, and zest and stir to combine.

Scatter the dried apple in the prepared baking dish and pour the tapioca mixture over it. Bake for 20 minutes, or until the top is firm to the touch and the apples are softened and golden brown on top.

Apple Tip:

Get in the Halloween mood with shrunken apple heads! Dunk peeled whole apples in a mixture of lemon juice and salt (to prevent browning). With a sharp knife, carve eyes and a nose. Dry the apples at the lowest setting in the oven for 2 hours. Then set them outside to finish drying for 1 to 2 days.

Applesauce Carrot Pecan Muffins

Pecans add an extra dimension to this moist, luscious muffin.

Makes 12 muffins

1½ cups all-purpose flour

1½ teaspoons baking powder

½ teaspoon baking soda

1¼ teaspoons ground cinnamon

⅛ teaspoon ground cloves

½ teaspoon ground allspice

¼ teaspoon freshly grated nutmeg

¼ teaspoon salt

2 large eggs, beaten

1 cup light brown sugar, packed

½ cup vegetable oil

1 cup unsweetened applesauce

1 cup finely grated carrot

1 cup toasted pecans, chopped

2 tablespoons granulated sugar

Preheat the oven to 375° F. Line a 12-cup muffin tin with paper liners or grease well with unsalted butter.

Mix the flour, baking powder, baking soda, ¾ teaspoon cinnamon, the cloves, allspice, nutmeg, and salt in a large bowl.

In another bowl, combine the eggs, brown sugar, and oil and beat well blended. Add the applesauce, carrot, and pecans and mix just until well blended.

Scoop the batter into the muffin tin, filling each cup almost to the top. Mix the sugar and remaining ½ teaspoon cinnamon and sprinkle over the tops.

Bake for 17 to 20 minutes, until the muffins are lightly browned, the tops spring back when gently pressed, and a toothpick inserted into the center of a muffin comes out with just a few moist crumbs.

Grilled Cheese with Bacon and Apples

Banish the lunch doldrums with this different and tasty sandwich.
If you don't care for Cheddar, substitute another cheese.

Makes 2 sandwiches

Nonstick cooking spray

8 slices bacon

1 large apple of your choice,
   cored and cut into ⅛-inch wedges

3 tablespoons butter, softened

8 slices good-quality bread

½ cup shredded Cheddar cheese

Line a plate with paper towels and set aside. Spray a large frying pan with cooking spray.

Set the pan over medium-high heat, add the bacon, and cook for about 2 to 3 minutes. Tilt the pan to coat it with bacon fat.

Add the apples to the bacon and cook together, stirring occasionally, for 2 to 3 more minutes, or until the bacon is crisp and cooked through and the apples are slightly softened. Remove from the heat, transfer the bacon and apples to the prepared plate, and reserve the pan and its contents.

Place all 8 slices of bread on a work surface and spread one side of each with butter, coating the entire surface. Reserve any leftover butter. Turn 4 slices over so the butter faces down.

Sprinkle about 1 tablespoon of the cheese on each of the 4 unbuttered slices. Divide the bacon and apples evenly between them. Carefully sprinkle another tablespoon of the cheese on each. Cover with the remaining slices of bread, buttered side up.

Drain most of the bacon fat from the pan, leaving about 1 tablespoon in it. Put any remaining butter into the pan and, if necessary, spray again with cooking spray. Return the pan to the heat, reduce the heat to medium-low, and heat until the butter melts.

Carefully place the sandwiches into the pan in a single layer, working in batches if needed. Cook, occasionally pressing down on the sandwiches with a spatula, for 1 to 2 minutes, or until the cheese has begun to melt and the bread is golden. Be careful that it does not burn. When the cheese adheres to the bread, turn, and cook, pressing with a spatula, for 1 or 2 minutes, or until the bread is golden and the cheese has melted. Remove from the pan, slice, and serve.

October 23

Apple Danish

This easy treat combines tender, flaky pastry; sweet, fruity filling;
and creamy cheese for a brunch dish you'll want to eat all day long.

Makes 6 pastries

½ cup ricotta cheese

4 tablespoons granulated
   sugar

1 teaspoon lemon zest

1 egg

1 teaspoon pure vanilla extract

¼ teaspoon salt

1 large Golden Delicious
   apple

1 teaspoon fresh lemon juice

1 sheet frozen puff pastry,
   thawed

Preheat the oven to 425° F. Lightly grease a baking sheet; set aside.

In a medium bowl, whisk together the cheese, 2 tablespoons sugar, lemon zest, egg, vanilla, and salt; set aside.

Peel, core, and thinly slice the apple. Combine the slices with the lemon juice and 1 tablespoon sugar; set aside.

Cut the puff pastry sheet into 3 strips. Cut the strips widthwise to form 6 squares. Lay out the pastry squares on the prepared baking sheet. Divide the cheese mixture among the squares and then top with the apples, layering slices. Fold in 2 corners of each square so they meet in the middle of the pastry. Sprinkle with the remaining sugar.

Transfer the pan to the oven and bake until golden brown and puffed, about 20 minutes.

Chèvre en Crôute with Mixed Green and Apple Salad

Goat cheese rolled in flaky puff pastry and served atop a crisp apple green salad
makes a delightful first course or light lunch.

Makes 8 servings

2 tablespoons chopped fresh tarragon

2 tablespoons chopped fresh basil

1 (8-ounce) log of goat cheese

1 egg white

1 tablespoon cream

2 teaspoons water

1 sheet puff pastry, thawed

Salad

8 cups mixed greens

2 Honeycrisp apples, cored and
    thinly sliced

1 cup thinly sliced celery

¼ cup sliced toasted almonds

Vinaigrette

1 tablespoon fresh lemon juice

1 teaspoon honey

2 tablespoons apple cider vinegar

½ teaspoon sea salt

1 teaspoon freshly ground black pepper

2 tablespoons extra virgin olive oil

Preheat the oven to 400° F. Lightly grease a baking sheet and set aside.

Mix the herbs together on a plate. Roll the cheese in the herb mixture, pressing to adhere. Place the cheese back on the plate and freeze for 10 minutes.

Unfold the puff pastry sheet. Place the chilled goat cheese on the bottom third of the pastry and roll up, starting with the short side closest to you. Tuck in the ends and place the roll on the prepared baking sheet, seam down. To make egg wash, combine egg white and cream. Brush the top of the pastry with the egg wash.

Bake until the pastry is golden, about 15 to 20 minutes. Let stand for 5 minutes. Cut into 8 slices.

To make the salad, toss the mixed greens, apple slices, celery, and almonds in a large salad bowl. Whisk together the lemon juice, honey, vinegar, salt, and pepper. Gradually whisk in the oil to form an emulsion. Pour the dressing over the salad greens and toss to coat.

To serve, divide the salad among 8 small plates. Top each with a slice of the chèvre en crôute. Serve immediately.

Apple Pesto

This dish combines apples, basil, and walnuts to make a pesto your guests will be certain to dip into again and again.

Makes about 1 cup

3 cups packed fresh basil leaves

1 apple of your choice, peeled, cored, and roughly chopped

½ cup walnuts

1 tablespoon apple juice

2 teaspoons fresh lemon juice

¼ teaspoon salt

¼ cup walnut oil

In a food processor or blender, combine the basil leaves, apple, walnuts, apple juice, lemon juice, and salt. Pulse one or twice to combine. Then, with the motor running, slowly pour in the walnut oil. Process until the mixture is smooth. Transfer to a serving bowl and serve with apple slices and crackers.

Apple, Blue Cheese, and Walnut Dip

Serve this chunky dip with crudités or thick-cut potato chips.

Makes about 2½ cups

8 ounces cream cheese, softened

1 tablespoon apple cider vinegar

¼ cup diced sweet onion

1 clove garlic, minced

½ teaspoon sea salt

¼ teaspoon freshly ground black pepper

1 apple of your choice, peeled, cored, and diced

1 cup crumbled blue cheese

¼ cup chopped toasted walnuts

Using a handheld mixer, beat together the cream cheese, vinegar, onion, garlic, salt, and pepper until smooth. Stir in the diced apple, blue cheese, and walnuts. Transfer to a lidded container and chill for 2 hours to blend the flavors.

Mushroom and Apple Crostini

A tasty fall appetizer, these crostini are drizzled with a tangy herb vinaigrette. Any remaining dressing can be refrigerated in an airtight container and used with many kinds of green salads.

Makes 8 servings

3 tablespoons unsalted butter

1 cup diced sweet onion

2 cloves garlic, minced

4 cups assorted mushrooms, such as morels, shiitake, oyster, and crimini, sliced

1 Granny Smith apple, peeled, cored, and diced

2 teaspoons chopped fresh thyme

¼ teaspoon sea salt

½ teaspoon freshly ground black pepper

Herb Vinaigrette

¼ cup apple cider vinegar

1 tablespoon chopped fresh thyme

1 tablespoon chopped fresh tarragon

1 tablespoon chopped fresh parsley

2 tablespoons Dijon mustard

1 small shallot, minced

2 teaspoons honey

¼ teaspoon sea salt

½ teaspoon freshly ground black pepper

¼ cup extra virgin olive oil

24 thick (⅓ to ½ inch) baguette slices

Preheat the oven to 400° F. Grease a baking sheet and set aside.

Melt the butter in a large nonstick sauté pan set over medium-high heat. Add the onions and sauté until softened and lightly browned, about 5 minutes. Add the garlic and cook until fragrant, about 30 seconds. Add the mushrooms, apples, and thyme and sauté until browned and softened, about 8 minutes. Season with the salt and pepper.

To make the vinaigrette, whisk together the apple cider vinegar, chopped herbs, mustard, shallot, honey, salt, and pepper. Gradually whisk in the oil until an emulsion is formed.

Lay the baguette slices on the prepared baking sheet. Brush with the thyme vinaigrette. Bake until crisp, about 10 minutes. To serve, top each slice with the mushroom-apple mixture and drizzle more vinaigrette on top.

October 28

Apple-Ginger Punch

Ginger beer, a non-alcoholic fermented drink, tends to be spicier than most ginger ales. Combined with apple cider, it makes a bracing punch.

Makes 10 cups

4 cups apple cider, chilled
1 cup cranberry juice, chilled
1 cup orange juice, chilled

1 liter ginger beer, chilled
1 apple of your choice

Combine the apple cider, cranberry juice, and orange juice in a punch bowl. Slowly add the ginger beer. Core and slice the apple. Add to the punch and serve.

Grilled Apple-Cheddar Waffle Sandwich

Why let those leftovers from breakfast go to waste? Put together in a sandwich, they make a great lunch.

Makes 1 sandwich

1 tablespoon honey mustard

1 teaspoon pure maple syrup

½ teaspoon chopped fresh thyme or sage (optional)

2 waffles

¼ cup sharp Cheddar cheese, grated

¼ Golden Delicious apple, thinly sliced

Leftover breakfast ham or bacon (optional)

Leftover scrambled eggs (optional)

1 tablespoon canola oil

In a small bowl, whisk together the mustard, maple syrup, and thyme or sage, if desired.

Spread the mustard mixture on 1 waffle, sprinkle with the grated cheese, top with the apples slices and meat, if desired. Cover with the remaining waffle to make a sandwich.

Heat the oil in a medium nonstick skillet set over medium-high heat. Cook until the cheese melts and the waffles are toasted, about 5 to 6 minutes. Slice in half and serve piping hot.

Applesauce Meatballs

The introduction of applesauce makes these meatballs extremely moist. For optimal flavor, be sure to use turkey meat ground from the thigh.

Makes about 16 meatballs

1½ pounds ground turkey
½ cup finely chopped onion
1 large egg
½ cup unsweetened applesauce
1 cup bread crumbs
2 tablespoons chopped cilantro
1 teaspoon salt
½ teaspoon ground pepper
½ cup all-purpose flour
⅔ cup canola oil

In a large bowl, combine the turkey, onion, egg, applesauce, bread crumbs, cilantro, salt, and pepper and gently mix with your hands. Shape the mixture into 1½-inch balls. Lightly dredge the meatballs in the flour to coat.

Heat the canola oil in a heavy skillet set over medium-high heat. Fry the meatballs until they are brown on all sides, about 5 minutes. With a slotted spoon, transfer the meatballs to a serving platter and serve with your favorite sauce.

Caramel Apple Popcorn Balls

Planning a Halloween party? Be sure to include these classic treats. They look especially festive wrapped in orange cellophane and tied with black string.

Makes about 12 balls

2 tablespoons canola oil
1 cup popcorn kernels
4 cups dried apple, chopped
1 cup roughly chopped unsalted almonds

Caramel Sauce

2 cups apple juice
2 cups light brown sugar, packed
¼ cup light corn syrup
12 tablespoons unsalted butter, cut into pieces
2 teaspoons sea salt
¼ teaspoon ground cinnamon

Line 2 baking sheets with waxed paper.

Heat the oil in a 5-quart saucepan set over medium-high heat. Add the popcorn kernels, cover, and shake the pan until the popping stops. Pour the popcorn into a large bowl, discarding any unpopped kernels. Mix in the dried apple pieces and chopped almonds.

To make the caramel, place the apple juice, brown sugar, and corn syrup in a 3-quart saucepan set over medium-high heat. Stir with a wooden spoon to combine. Cook the caramel without stirring until a candy thermometer registers 280° F, about 30 minutes. The caramel should be a dark amber color. Remove from the heat and add the butter, stirring until melted. Add the salt and cinnamon. Return the pan to the burner and cook over medium-high heat until thickened, about 2 minutes.

Pour the sauce over the popcorn mixture and stir until evenly coated. Let cool for about 5 minutes. Grease your hands with oil or butter and shape handfuls of the mixture into balls. Place finished popcorn balls on the prepared baking sheets to set and cool.

November 1

Apple-Celery Root Slaw with Horseradish Dressing

Instead of the usual coleslaw, try this crunchy slaw. It goes especially well with thick-cut ham sandwiches.

Makes 6 servings

¾ cup mayonnaise

3 tablespoons horseradish

2 tablespoons fresh lemon juice

2 tablespoons Dijon mustard

1 tablespoon honey

1 teaspoon salt

½ teaspoon freshly ground black pepper

4 cups julienned celery root

2 cups julienned Granny Smith apple

¼ cup finely chopped chives

Whisk together the mayonnaise, horseradish, lemon juice, mustard, honey, salt, and pepper in a large bowl. Add in the celery root, apple, and chives. Toss to coat. This can be made 1 day ahead and chilled, covered, in the fridge until ready to serve.

Apple Cider-Glazed Apples and Turnips

Try this tasty side as an accompaniment to roast pork.

Makes 6 servings

1 tablespoon unsalted butter

1 tablespoon olive oil

⅔ cup apple cider

3 tablespoons light brown sugar

½ teaspoon salt

½ teaspoon freshly ground black pepper

½ teaspoon cayenne

3 cups purple turnips, peeled and sliced in ½- x 2½-inch pieces

1 cup Granny Smith apple, peeled, cored, and sliced in ½- x 2½-inch pieces

Preheat the oven to 400° F. Line a baking sheet with nonstick foil and set aside.

In a small 2-quart saucepan set over medium heat, combine the butter, olive oil, apple cider, brown sugar, salt, pepper, and cayenne. Cook for 2 minutes or until the sugar is dissolved and the butter is melted; set aside.

Arrange the turnips in a single layer on the prepared baking sheet and pour the apple cider-sugar mixture evenly over the top. Cover the dish with foil and bake for 20 minutes. Stir turnips and add the apple sticks. Continue to bake, uncovered, for 20 minutes longer or until turnips are tender and glazed and the liquid has evaporated.

Hot Buttered Rum with Apple Cider

A mellow brew for a chilly night. Bottoms up!

Makes 2 cocktails

⅔ cup boiling water

1 teaspoon granulated sugar, or to taste

4 ounces rum

4 ounces apple cider

1 tablespoon unsalted butter, or to taste

Divide the water between 2 mugs, add half the sugar to each, and stir to dissolve.

Add half the rum, cider, and butter to each. Let the butter melt a bit before serving.

Core Fact:

For healthy skin, munch on apples! Apples are a rich source of polyphenols, organic chemicals that help reduce oxidation—which causes our cells to age. Increase your apple intake for a fresher, younger complexion.

Apple Butter

Where's the butter? Despite its name, this velvety smooth spread contains not one gram of fat. So go ahead and slather it on muffins or thick slices of toast.

Makes about 6 cups

4 pounds Winesap or Granny Smith apples, peeled, cored, and quartered

1 cup apple cider vinegar

2 cups water

¼ cup Calvados (optional)

4 cups granulated sugar

1 teaspoon salt

2 teaspoons ground cinnamon

½ teaspoon ground cloves

½ teaspoon ground allspice

¼ teaspoon freshly grated nutmeg

1 tablespoon lemon zest

¼ cup fresh lemon juice

In a 5-quart saucepan set over medium-high heat, combine the apples, vinegar, and water and bring to a boil. Lower the heat, cover, and simmer for 20 to 30 minutes or until the apples are tender. Remove from heat.

In a heavy-duty blender or food processor, combine the apples and the liquid, sugar, salt, cinnamon, cloves, allspice, nutmeg, lemon zest, and lemon juice. Puree until smooth, about 1 minute.

Transfer the pureed apple mixture back to the saucepan and cook over medium-low heat, stirring constantly to prevent burning, for 1 to 2 hours or until thickened and most of the water has evaporated. Cool.

To store, transfer to airtight containers and store refrigerated for up to 2 weeks.

Apple Tip:

Typically found at farmers markets, Winesap is an heirloom apple that most likely dates back to the 18th century. While primarily used for cooking and baking, these tart apples can also be eaten out of hand. When adding a juicy Winesap to a recipe, you may need to add cornstarch or flour to absorb some of its moisture.

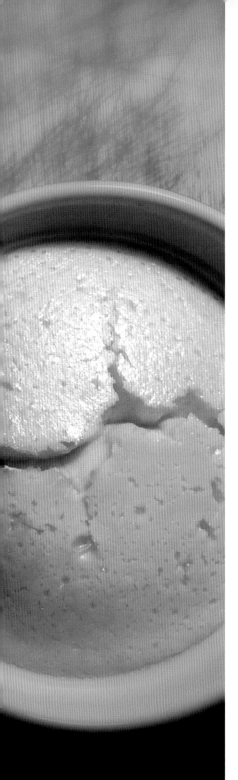

Little Apple Swirl Cheesecakes

Fresh apples and apple brandy give these personal cheesecakes
their apple-y personality.

Makes 5 (4-ounce) mini-cheesecakes

1 tablespoon butter

1 small Golden Delicious apple,
chopped

½ cup plus 2 teaspoons granulated
sugar

12 ounces cream cheese, at room
temperature

¹⁄₁₆ teaspoon salt

1 tablespoon apple brandy

2 tablespoons cream

2 teaspoons all-purpose flour

2 eggs

Preheat the oven to 325° F. Set a pot of water on the stove to simmer.

In a frying pan set over medium-high heat, melt the butter. Add the apple,
sprinkle with 2 teaspoons sugar, and cook, stirring often, for 2 minutes,
until the apple softens slightly. Set aside to cool.

Preheat the oven to 325° F.

With an electric mixer set at medium speed, beat the cream cheese until
smooth. Add ½ cup sugar, salt, brandy, cream, and flour. Beat in the eggs,
one at a time, just until well combined.

Divide the batter among the prepared ramekins. Drop a teaspoonful of
apple mixture into each ramekin and swirl with a knife.

Put a kettle of water on the stove and bring to a simmer. Place the
ramekins in a baking pan and pour enough simmering water into the pan
to come halfway up the sides of the ramekins. Place the pan into the oven
and bake for 26 to 30 minutes, or until the edges are firm but the very
center is still a bit jiggly but not liquid. Carefully remove the ramekins
from the hot water bath. Use heatproof silicone oven mitts (cloth mitts can
get wet and cause burns) and/or a strong spatula or silicone-coated tongs.

Apple-Pear Caramel Cake

Moist and delicious, this cake is well worth the effort.

Makes 1 Bundt cake

Caramelized Fruit

2 cups apple cider

1 cup granulated sugar

1 tablespoon unsalted butter

1 cup thinly sliced Granny Smith apples, peeled and cored

1 cup thinly sliced unripe Bartlett pears, peeled and cored

Cake

3 cups all-purpose flour

½ teaspoon baking soda

¼ teaspoon salt

½ cup unsalted butter, at room temperature

4 ounces cream cheese, at room temperature

4 ounces ricotta cheese

2 cups granulated sugar

1 tablespoon lemon zest

3 large eggs, at room temperature

2 tablespoons fresh lemon juice

1 cup buttermilk

Confectioners' sugar (optional)

To make the caramelized fruit, bring the apple cider to a boil over high heat in a 2-quart saucepan. Reduce the heat to medium and cook, stirring occasionally, until reduced to 1 cup, about 20 to 25 minutes. Stir in the sugar and cook over medium heat until the sugar dissolves and the mixture becomes thick with a deep caramel color, about 15 minutes. Remove from heat and cool for 1 minute. Stir in the butter, apples, and pears; mix well to combine. Return the pan to medium heat and cook, stirring constantly, 5 minutes or until the fruits have softened. Transfer the mixture to a bowl and cool.

To make the cake, preheat the oven to 325° F. Grease a Bundt pan with butter or cooking spray and set aside.

Sift together the flour, baking soda, and salt in a medium bowl; set aside.

With a handheld mixer on medium-high speed, beat the butter, cream cheese, ricotta cheese, sugar, and lemon zest in a large bowl until smooth and creamy, about 3 minutes. Beat in the eggs, one at a time. Beat in the lemon juice.

Add ⅓ of the flour mixture and incorporate. Add ½ of the buttermilk and incorporate. Repeat with ⅓ of the flour, the rest of the buttermilk, and end with the last of the flour. Beat just until the batter is smooth. Reserving ½ cup of the caramel liquid, fold in all of the cooled caramel apples.

Spread the batter into the prepared Bundt pan. Bake for 1 hour or until a skewer inserted in the middle comes out clean.

Remove the cake from the oven and cool for 5 minutes on a wire rack. Carefully invert the cake onto a serving platter and remove the pan. Drizzle the reserved caramel onto the cake. Let the cake cool and dust with the powdered sugar, if desired. Cut with a serrated knife and serve.

Sesame Apple Cookie

A perfect little energy booster! Sesame seeds and apples give these cookies a sweet, nutty flavor.

Makes 20 cookies

2 cups all-purpose flour

1 teaspoon baking powder

½ cup unsalted butter, at room temperature

¼ plus 2 tablespoons confectioners' sugar

1 egg yolk

¼ cup apple juice

½ cup finely chopped Dried Apples (see page 323) or use store-bought

1 cup sesame seeds

Preheat the oven to 350° F. Line a baking sheet with parchment paper.

Whisk the flour and baking powder in a bowl.

In a separate bowl, with an electric mixer set at low speed, beat the butter and sugar until light and smooth. Add the egg and apple juice and beat to combine. Add the flour mixture and beat to combine. With a wooden spoon, mix in the dried apple.

On a work surface, roll the dough into walnut-sized balls. Pour the sesame seeds into a shallow bowl and roll the balls in the seeds. Press the cookies flat on the prepared baking sheet. Bake on the prepared sheet for 9 to 12 minutes. Cool on a rack.

Baked Oatmeal with Maple Syrup

Makes 4 servings

1⅓ cups old-fashioned or quick rolled oats (not instant)

2 tablespoons golden raisins (optional)

2⅔ cups whole milk

1 teaspoon pure vanilla extract

½ cup pure maple syrup, plus more to taste if needed

1 whole egg and 2 egg yolks

1 large apple, peeled, cored, and chopped

2 tablespoons granulated sugar

1 tablespoon unsalted butter, melted

Cream or milk to taste, for serving (optional)

Preheat the oven to 325° F.

Place ⅓ cup oatmeal and 2 tablespoons golden raisins, if using, into each of 4 ovenproof (8-ounce) ramekins or serving bowls.

Whisk the milk, vanilla, maple syrup, egg, and yolks in a small bowl. Divide the mixture among the 4 ramekins. Stir each to combine.

Mix the apple, sugar, and melted butter in another small bowl and top each ramekin with a fourth of the diced apple mixture.

Bake for 23 to 30 minutes for a nice, creamy bowl of oatmeal, or longer if you prefer a firmer texture. Remove from the oven, stir the oatmeal, and let stand for 1 to 2 minutes. Serve hot with an extra drizzle of maple syrup and cream or milk, if desired.

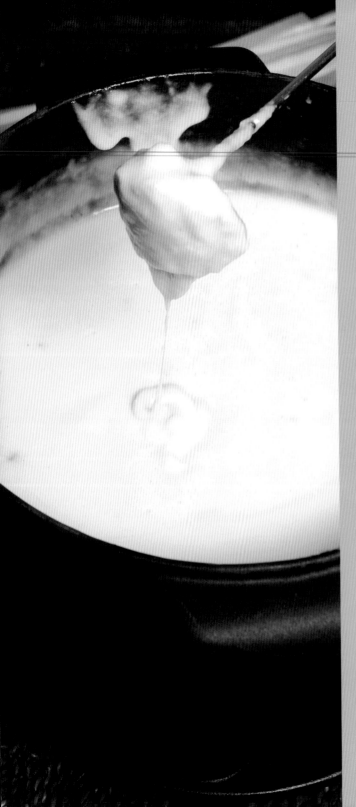

Cheese Fondue with Sliced Apples

Crisp fall apples cut the richness of the gooey cheese fondue, making a pleasing contrast.

Makes 6 servings

¾ pound Gruyere cheese, coarsely shredded
1 tablespoon cornstarch
1 clove garlic, halved
1 cup dry white wine
3 tablespoons lemon juice
¾ teaspoon sea salt
½ teaspoon freshly ground black pepper
3 apples of your choice, cored and sliced

In a large bowl, toss the shredded cheese with the cornstarch.

Rub the cut garlic clove halves around the inside of a fondue pot or 4-quart saucepan; discard garlic. Add the wine and 2 tablespoons lemon juice and bring to a boil over high heat. Lower the heat to medium and gradually add the cheese, whisking constantly until all the cheese is incorporated. Simmer the fondue over medium heat for 1 minute, stirring constantly. Remove from the heat and season with the salt and pepper; whisking to incorporate.

In a medium bowl combine the apples and remaining tablespoon of lemon juice. Serve the fondue with the apple slices on the side for dunking.

Cranberry-Apple Chutney

This spicy chutney is so good it might replace your favorite cranberry sauce come Thanksgiving.

Makes about 5 cups

½ cup apple juice

1¼ cups granulated sugar

1½ cups fresh or frozen cranberries

2 Granny Smith apples, peeled, cored, and diced

1 cup diced sweet onion

½ cup golden raisins

½ cup light brown sugar, packed

¼ cup apple cider vinegar

1 teaspoon ground cinnamon

¼ teaspoon salt

¼ teaspoon ground allspice

¼ teaspoon ground cloves

In a 4-quart saucepan set over high heat, combine the apple juice and sugar and bring to a boil. Reduce heat to medium-low and simmer, uncovered, for 3 minutes. Stir in the remaining ingredients. Return the mixture to a boil, reduce heat to low, and simmer, uncovered, stirring occasionally, for 20 to 25 minutes. Serve warm or cold.

November 11

Kale, Sausage, and Apple Soup

An intriguing mix of contrasting flavors.
In the end, they join together to create
a harmonious, satisfying dish.

Makes 4 to 6 servings

4½ tablespoons olive oil

4 to 5 links chicken sausage (about 12 to 16 ounces), sliced in ⅛-inch rounds

2 large apples of your choice

1 bunch kale, washed, trimmed (hard spines removed), and cut in chiffonade

1½ quarts chicken broth

3 cups broad egg noodles

Heat 2 tablespoons of the oil in a stockpot set over medium heat. Add the sausage in a single layer and cook, stirring occasionally, for 2 minutes. With tongs, turn the sausage and cook for 2 more minutes, or until golden. Transfer to a platter and keep warm.

Add 1½ tablespoons of the oil to the pot and cook the apples, stirring occasionally, for 5 to 7 minutes, or until soft and golden. Transfer to the platter with the sausages and keep warm.

Pour the remaining oil into the pot and add the kale. Cook, stirring occasionally, for 1 to 3 minutes, or until wilted and dark green in color. Return the sausage and apples to the pot. Add the stock and bring to a boil. Add the noodles and continue boiling for 8 to 10 minutes, or until the noodles are soft. Serve hot.

November 12

Wilted Greens Salad with Apple Dressing

The warm dressing wilts the greens and turns
this salad into something special.

Makes 6 servings

Apple Dressing

¼ cup apple juice

¼ cup apple cider

2 teaspoons honey

1 teaspoon Dijon mustard

½ teaspoon sea salt

½ teaspoon freshly ground black pepper

⅓ cup extra virgin olive oil

Salad

1 Honeycrisp apple, cored and chopped

¼ cup dried cranberries

¼ cup sliced toasted almonds

6 cups baby spinach

6 cups baby arugula

To make the dressing, combine the apple juice, apple cider, honey, mustard, salt, and pepper in a 2-quart saucepan set over medium heat. Bring to a boil, reduce heat, and simmer for 1 minute. Remove from heat, whisk in the olive oil, and set aside.

To make the salad, combine the chopped apple, cranberries, almonds, spinach, and arugula in a large salad bowl. Pour in enough dressing to coat the greens and toss. Serve immediately.

Apple Walnut Cupcakes with Cardamom Frosting

Cardamom has a spicy-sweet taste that pairs well with baked goods.

Makes 12 cupcakes

Cupcakes

¼ cup unsalted butter, at room temperature

3 tablespoons granulated sugar

¾ cup sweetened condensed milk

1 teaspoon lemon zest

1 cup all-purpose flour

1½ teaspoons baking powder

½ teaspoon baking soda

½ teaspoon salt

¼ cup milk

1 teaspoon pure vanilla extract

1 baking apple, peeled, cored, and diced

½ cup chopped walnuts

Frosting

¼ cup unsalted butter

¼ cup apple butter (see page 304), or use store-bought

¾ cup packed brown sugar

1 teaspoon pure vanilla extract

1 teaspoon ground cardamom

2 tablespoons milk

1 cup confectioners' sugar

Preheat the oven to 350° F. Line a muffin tin with paper liners or grease well with unsalted butter.

In a large bowl, beat the butter and sugar with a handheld mixer at medium-high speed until light and fluffy. Add the condensed milk and lemon zest; beat to incorporate.

In a small bowl, whisk together the flour, baking powder, baking soda, and salt. Add dry ingredients to wet and beat on medium to combine. Add the milk and vanilla to the batter and beat on medium-high speed until incorporated. Fold in the diced apple and walnuts. Scoop the batter into the prepared muffin tins, filling almost all the way to the top.

Bake until a toothpick inserted in the center one comes out clean, about 20 to 25 minutes. Remove from the oven and cool completely before frosting.

To make the frosting, melt the butter in a 2-quart saucepan set over medium heat. Add the apple butter and brown sugar and stir to combine. Bring to a boil and lower the heat to medium-low. Cook, stirring constantly, for 2 minutes. Add the vanilla, cardamom, and milk and stir to combine. Remove from heat and cool. Gradually beat in the confectioners' sugar. Allow to cool completely, then spread or pipe the frosting onto the cooled cupcakes.

Sweet Potato Casserole with Caramelized Apples

Instead of a sweet potato casserole overloaded with marshmallows, try this more grown-up version.

Makes 8 servings

4 large sweet potatoes

2 tablespoons salted butter, divided

2 tablespoons olive oil, divided

2 tablespoons heavy cream

½ cup applesauce

2 teaspoons grated fresh ginger

1 teaspoon lemon zest

1 teaspoon sea salt

1 teaspoon freshly ground black pepper

2 Honeycrisp or Fuji apples, peeled, cored, and sliced

3 tablespoons light brown sugar

Preheat the oven to 400° F. Grease a 4-quart baking dish and set aside.

Prick the potatoes with a fork and wrap each one in foil. Place them on a baking sheet and bake for 1 hour. Turn off the oven and let them sit in the oven for 30 minutes to finish cooking and cool slightly. Remove from oven and cool for 30 minutes.

Peel the potatoes, discarding the skins, and scoop the flesh into a large bowl. Add 1 tablespoon butter, 1 tablespoon olive oil, and the cream. Beat with a handheld mixer on medium-high until smooth, about 1 to 2 minutes. Mix in the applesauce, ginger, lemon zest, salt, and pepper. Transfer the mixture to the prepared baking dish; set aside.

In a medium bowl, combine the apples and brown sugar; toss to combine.

In a large nonstick sauté pan set over medium heat, melt 1 tablespoon butter with 1 tablespoon olive oil. Add the apples and sauté, stirring occasionally, until they are caramelized and golden brown, about 15 minutes. Top the sweet potato mixture with the apples. Bake for 10 to 15 minutes, or until warmed through. Serve hot.

Old-Fashioned Applesauce Cake

Moist and flavorful, this spiced cake will bring back memories of days gone by.

Makes 1 (8-inch) cake

½ cup shortening or ½ cup unsalted butter

⅔ cup brown sugar, packed

2 eggs

1 teaspoon pure vanilla extract

1 cup unsweetened applesauce

2 tablespoons molasses

1¾ cup all-purpose flour

1 teaspoon baking powder

½ teaspoon baking soda

¼ teaspoon salt

2 teaspoons ground cinnamon

½ teaspoon ground allspice

1 large apple, cored and cut into small dice

¾ cup chopped toasted walnuts

½ cup chopped pitted prunes or raisins

2 cups Dried Apples (see page 323) or store-bought dried apples, for garnish

Preheat the oven to 350° F. Position an oven rack in the center of the oven. Grease an 8-inch round (2-inch deep) cake pan.

With an electric mixer set at low speed, beat the shortening or butter with the brown sugar until creamy.

Add the eggs, one at a time, beating between additions to incorporate. Add the vanilla and beat to incorporate. In a separate bowl, beat together the applesauce and molasses.

Combine the flour, baking powder, baking soda, salt, cinnamon, and allspice. Add about one-third of the flour mixture to the butter mixture and beat for 20 to 30 seconds. Add half the applesauce mixture and beat for 20 to 30 seconds, to combine. Add another third of the flour mixture, then the remaining applesauce mixture, and then the remaining flour mixture, beating for 20 to 30 seconds between each addition.

With a wooden spoon, stir in the diced apple, walnuts, and prunes until thoroughly incorporated. Turn the batter into the prepared pan; it will be thick. Smooth the top with a spatula. Bake for 45 to 55 minutes, until golden and the cake springs back when gently pressed. A skewer inserted in the very center should come out with a few moist crumbs. Cool in the pan for 5 minutes; then carefully turn out onto a rack and cool completely.

If you are making the Dried Apples from scratch, follow the directions on page 17. Fold the dried apples in half and arrange on top of the cake.

November 16

Apple-Ginger Scones

These spicy scones have much less fat than traditional scones; the applesauce keeps them moist.
Serve them straight from the oven with plenty of butter.

Makes 8 scones

2 cups all-purpose flour

½ cup light brown sugar, packed

2 teaspoons baking powder

1 teaspoon grated lemon zest

½ teaspoon ground cinnamon

¼ teaspoon freshly grated nutmeg

¼ teaspoon ground ginger

¼ teaspoon salt

2 tablespoons unsalted butter, chilled

1 cup chopped dried apples

¼ cup chopped candied ginger

½ cup applesauce

¼ cup milk

1 large egg

1 tablespoon granulated sugar, for sprinkling

Preheat the oven to 375° F. Grease a baking sheet and set aside.

In a large bowl, whisk together the first 8 ingredients. Then dice the chilled butter and add to the flour mixture. With a pastry cutter or a fork or your fingers, blend the butter and the flour together until it resembles coarse crumbs. Stir in the dried apples and candied ginger.

In a small bowl, whisk together the applesauce, milk, and egg. Add the wet ingredients to the dry ingredients; stir until just incorporated. Do not over mix.

Turn the dough out onto a lightly floured surface and knead the dough about 10 times. Shape it into an 8-inch circle and cut into 8 wedges. Sprinkle with the sugar. Bake until a toothpick inserted in the middle comes out clean, about 15 minutes. Let rest a few minutes before separating the wedges. Serve warm.

November 17

The Kitchen Sink

True to its name, this cocktail's got everything but the kitchen sink. Cheers!

Makes 2 cocktails

2 ounces rye

1 ounce gin

2 ounces apple brandy

2 ounces apple schnapps

1 ounce fresh lemon juice

2 ounces fresh orange juice

1 cup crushed ice

Shake the rye, gin, brandy, schnapps, and lemon and orange juices in a shaker with 1 cup crushed ice. Strain into 2 cocktail glasses filled with ice cubes.

Apple Tip:

A good baking apple has flesh that won't break down in the oven. When selecting apples to bake, consider one of these 12 picks, whose flavors range from tart to sweet: Braeburn, Cortland, Gala, Golden Delicious, Granny Smith, Honeycrisp, Jonathan, Jonagold, Melrose, Northern Spy, Rome Beauty, and Winesap.

November 18

Granola-Stuffed Baked Apples

Is it for breakfast or dessert? You decide.

Makes 6 servings

Nonstick cooking spray

6 baking apples

1 tablespoon fresh lemon juice

½ cup golden raisins

½ cup granola

2 tablespoons light brown sugar

1 teaspoon ground cinnamon

¼ teaspoon salt

2 tablespoons unsalted butter, chilled

Preheat the oven to 350° F. Spray a 9- x 13-inch baking dish with cooking spray.

Core the apples and sprinkle the insides with lemon juice to prevent browning Place them in the prepared baking dish and set aside.

In a medium bowl, combine the raisins, granola, brown sugar, cinnamon, and salt. Spoon the mixture into the cored apples. Dice the chilled butter and scatter on top.

Bake until the apples are soft, about 45 minutes.

Goat Cheese, Bacon, and Apple Rose Tarts

An elegant hors d'oeuvre for the holidays. Goat cheese, bacon, and apple make for a luscious mouthful. They can be baked ahead of time and frozen; just reheat the frozen tarts at 300° F for 10 to 15 minutes, until warmed through.

Makes 24 mini-tarts

36 Dried Apples, plus more as needed (see page 323)

½ recipe Press-In Crust (see Apple and Almond Tart with Lemon Mascarpone Cream, page 236)

Filling

6 to 8 thin slices bacon, finely chopped

1 large shallot, minced

2 tablespoons minced fresh sage leaves

2 small Granny Smith apples, peeled, cored, and very finely diced

Freshly ground black pepper to taste

Salt to taste (optional)

2 teaspoons soft fresh goat cheese

Prepare the Dried Apples as directed on page 323. While they are baking, prepare and chill the Press-In crust as directed on page 236.

Divide the dough into 24 pieces of equal size and press each piece into two 12-cup mini-muffin tins. Refrigerate for 30 minutes or up to one day.

In a large frying pan set over medium-high heat, cook the bacon, stirring, until it begins to turn golden. Add the shallot and cook, stirring, until it begins to soften. Add the sage and cook, stirring, until crispy. Add the diced apples and cook, still stirring, until the edges begin to turn golden and the apples are soft but not mushy. Season with pepper. Taste and season with salt if necessary.

Fill each mini-shell with about 1 tablespoon of the filling. Top each with a little of the goat cheese, pressing down gently to cover the filling.

Place 2 dried apples on a work surface. Cut them in half. Roll a half partway and then place it on top of another half, slightly off-center. Roll the two together to make the "inner" rose petals. Place the rolled bundle on a third half, again slightly off center, and roll them to form a rose. Nestle it firmly into the goat cheese in one of the tarts. Repeat with the remaining dried apples and tarts.

Bake at 375° for 12 to 15 minutes, until the pastry is golden and the cheese just begins to color.

Dried Apples

These dried apples are easy to make, and can be used in so many ways: rolled to form the apple roses in the Goat Cheese, Bacon and Apple Rose Tarts (see page 322), as topping or filling in sweet and savory dishes, or alone as a snack. The recipe below directs you to cut the apples very thinly—$\frac{1}{16}$ inch thick— to fit easily and attractively into the tarts. For other recipes, you can cut them into $\frac{1}{8}$-inch rings. For recipes like the tarts, where a bit of color will make the finished produce more appealing, you can leave the skin on; otherwise, you can peel the apples if you prefer. Keep any leftovers in an airtight container.

Makes 2 to 2½ cups

8 to 10 large apples, washed and dried

Preheat the oven to 275° F. Line a baking sheet with parchment paper.

With a mandoline slicer or a very sharp knife, slice the apples to form rings that are $\frac{1}{16}$ inch thick. Place on the parchment and bake for 30 to 60 minutes, depending on how crisp you want the apples. (For folding and rolling, take them out of the oven sooner.) Watch these carefully to make sure they do not burn. Cool on the baking sheet.

Apple Sausage Coffeecake

Chef Michael Gilligan gives a fresh spin to the old tried-and-true coffeecake.
By adding sausages and apples to the mix, he creates a savory treat you won't be able to resist.

Makes 1 (9-inch) cake

Cake Batter

2½ cups all-purpose flour

¼ cup granulated sugar

2 teaspoons baking powder

2 teaspoons baking soda

1 teaspoon salt

2 cups buttermilk

2 cups sour cream

2 eggs

4 sausage patties

2 tart apples, peeled, cored and sliced ¼ inch thick

2 tablespoons brown sugar

1 teaspoon ground cinnamon

1 tablespoon unsalted butter

In a large bowl, sift together the flour, sugar, baking powder, baking soda, and salt. Make a well in the center and pour in the buttermilk, sour cream, and eggs; mix until smooth.

Preheat the oven to 450° F. In a large skillet, sauté the sausage patties until browned. Pour off any fat from the skillet, add the apple slices, and sprinkle with the brown sugar and cinnamon. Sauté until the apples just lose their crispness, about 1 to 2 minutes. Set aside.

Place the butter in a well-seasoned 9-inch iron skillet and heat in the preheated oven until bubbly and hot. Arrange the sausage patties in the pan and cover with the apples, distributing them evenly.

Pour the batter over the apples and bake until nicely browned, about 8 to 10 minutes. Cut into pie-shaped wedges and serve immediately.

Chef Michael Gilligan

CURRENTLY: Executive chef at Rusty Pelican, Miami, Florida

NOTABLE FOR: Cooking for Princess Diana and other members of the British Royal Family

WORKED AT: Robert De Niro's Tribeca Grill and Montrachet

Apple-Walnut Stuffing

Thanksgiving wouldn't be Thanksgiving without stuffing.
This version is crammed with sausage, apple, dried cherries, and plenty of walnuts.

Makes 10 servings

Nonstick cooking spray

6 cups cubed sourdough bread

1 pound fresh turkey sausage, removed from casing

1 cup sliced sweet onion

1 cup chopped celery

2 cloves garlic, minced

1½ teaspoons fennel seeds

1 teaspoon dried thyme

1 Golden Delicious apple, cored and diced

1 cup chopped walnuts

¾ cup dried cherries

1 teaspoon salt

1 teaspoon freshly ground black pepper

1 cup turkey or chicken stock

2 tablespoons unsalted butter, melted

Preheat the oven to 350° F. Spray a 9- x 13-inch baking dish with nonstick cooking spray.

On a large baking sheet, spread the cubed bread in a single layer and bake for 5 to 7 minutes, or until the bread is crisp and evenly toasted. Transfer the toasted bread to a large bowl and set aside.

In a large nonstick sauté pan set over medium heat, add the sausage and onions and sauté for 7 to 10 minutes, breaking up the sausage and stirring frequently, until browned. Add the celery, garlic, fennel seeds, and thyme; cook, stirring frequently, for 2 minutes.

Add the cooked sausage mixture to the toasted bread, along with the apple, walnuts, cherries, salt, and pepper and toss to combine. Stir in the stock and melted butter. Spoon the stuffing into the prepared baking dish and bake for 35 to 45 minutes, or until crisp and browned.

Core Fact:

The large, crisp Fuji apple, which was born in Japan, has a wonderfully sweet taste. Fujis pair beautifully with chicken, pork, prosciutto, shrimp, and walnuts, and are a delightful addition to cakes, gratins, pies, and tarts.

Brie Crostini with Apple-Currant Chutney

Red jalapeno jelly gives this spicy chutney its zing.

Makes 24 crostini

Chutney

1 Granny Smith apple, cored and roughly chopped

½ cup chopped sweet onion

1 tablespoon unsalted butter

1 teaspoon minced fresh ginger

1 clove garlic, minced

1 tablespoon apple cider vinegar

1 tablespoon honey

2 tablespoons Calvados or applejack

⅓ cup red jalapeno jelly

1 tablespoon dried currants

Crostini

Nonstick cooking spray

1 cup pumpkin seeds

1 (8-ounce) wheel Brie cheese, cut into 24 (¼-inch-thick) slices

24 (¼-inch-thick) slices baguette

Preheat the oven to 450° F. Spray a baking sheet with nonstick cooking spray and set aside.

To make the chutney, combine the apple and onion in a food processor and pulse until minced. Melt the butter in a 4-quart saucepan set over medium heat. Add the minced apple and onion and sauté, stirring occasionally, for 2 to 3 minutes, or until softened. Add the ginger and garlic and sauté for 1 minute, stirring occasionally. Add the vinegar, honey, Calvados, jelly, and currants and bring to a boil. Boil for 2 minutes. Set aside to cool.

Arrange the baguette slices on the prepared baking sheet and top each with a slice of Brie. Sprinkle the pumpkin seeds on top, covering the cheese. Bake until the Brie is softened and the nuts are toasted, about 4 to 5 minutes. Top each crostini with the cooled chutney and serve immediately.

Turkey Breast Roulade with Apple-Walnut Stuffing

Slice into this roasted turkey breast to reveal the moist stuffing inside.

Makes 12 servings

1 (3-pound) boneless turkey breast half
2 teaspoons sea salt
2 teaspoons freshly ground black pepper
1½ cups Apple-Walnut Stuffing (see page 326)
1 tablespoon olive oil

Preheat the oven to 350° F. Line a baking sheet with foil and place a roasting rack on top; set aside.

Remove the skin from the turkey breast. Turn the breast over and butterfly by cutting in half horizontally, leaving one side attached. Spread the meat flat and cover with waxed paper. Using a mallet, pound until the breast is ¾ inch thick. Season with 1 teaspoon salt and 1 teaspoon pepper.

Spread the stuffing evenly over the turkey, leaving a ½-inch border all around. Starting at a short end, roll up the breast, jelly-roll style. Tie the roll with cooking twine in three places to hold its shape. Brush the outside with olive oil and season with the remaining salt and pepper. Transfer the roulade to the prepared roasting rack.

Bake for 1 to 1½ hours, or until an instant-read thermometer inserted into the center of the breast reads 155° F. Transfer to a serving platter and tent loosely with foil. Set aside to rest for 10 minutes. Remove the twine and slice crosswise into 12 portions.

Hot Apple Cider

By November's end, there's often a nip in the air. Snuggle up by the fire with a steaming mug of hot apple cider.

Makes about 8 servings

4 cinnamon sticks
6 whole cloves
8 whole allspice berries
2 whole star anise
1 orange, sliced
2 tablespoons maple syrup
6 cups apple cider

Combine the cinnamon sticks, cloves, allspice, star anise, orange slices, maple syrup, and apple cider in a 5-quart saucepan set on high heat. Bring to a boil, reduce heat, and simmer for 30 minutes. Strain into mugs and serve.

Apple, Sausage, and Cheddar Strata

Strata is a great brunch dish. In this version, apples and sausage provide lively flavoring to the basic elements of bread, egg, cheese, and milk. Chicken sausage is a great solution for this dish because it is low in fat and won't make the strata greasy; frying it first gives it nice caramelization. You can use pork sausage if you like, but fry it first and drain before adding it to the strata.

Makes 6 to 8 servings

1 tablespoon butter, plus more for greasing

1 tablespoon vegetable oil

3 large apples, cored and cut into 1/8-inch wedges

3 chicken sausages, preferably apple-flavored, sliced in ⅛-inch rounds

12 slices Italian-style sandwich bread

1½ cups shredded Cheddar cheese

4 eggs

3 cups milk

¼ teaspoon salt

Heat butter and oil together in a frying pan over medium-high heat, add the apples and sausage rounds, and cook, stirring and turning occasionally, for about 10 minutes, or until both the apples and sausages are golden brown. Remove from the heat and let cool.

Butter a large baking dish. Place 4 slices of the bread into it in a single layer. (If all 4 slices don't fit, tear one slice in pieces and fit the pieces around the other 3 slices to fill any holes.) Mound half the apple-sausage mixture on the bread and top with ½ cup cheese, spreading it evenly over the entire surface. Repeat with 4 more slices of bread, the remaining apple-sausage mixture, and ½ cup cheese. Top with the last of the bread.

Mix the eggs, milk, and salt in a bowl. Pour the mixture over the casserole, sprinkle with the remaining cheese, cover, and refrigerate for 1½ hours or overnight.

When you are ready to bake, preheat the oven to 350° F. Bring the casserole to room temperature. Bake for 1 hour, or until the egg mixture has set to make a custard and a toothpick inserted into the center comes out clean.

Core Fact:

American folk hero Jonathan Chapman—otherwise known as Johnny Appleseed—dreamed of a world in which no one would go hungry. In 1792, at the age of 18, Appleseed set out from Massachusetts and headed west, carrying a leather sack filled with seeds collected free of charge from cider mills. Friendly towards all people and animals he met along his path, Appleseed planted nurseries in exchange for food and clothing.

Dark Chocolate and Almond Apple Crisp

Dark chocolate and chopped almonds put a new twist on an old favorite.

Makes 12 servings

Nonstick cooking spray

5 baking apples of your choice, peeled, cored, and thinly sliced

¼ cup granulated sugar

1 teaspoon ground cinnamon

½ teaspoon freshly grated nutmeg

¼ cup fresh orange juice

2 tablespoons apple brandy

Topping

1½ cups all-purpose flour

½ cup light brown sugar, packed

1 teaspoon ground cinnamon

½ teaspoon salt

¼ cup cold unsalted butter, diced

¼ cup chopped almonds

¼ cup dark chocolate chips

Preheat the oven to 325° F. Spray an 8- x 8-inch baking dish with cooking spray; set aside.

Combine the apples, sugar, cinnamon, nutmeg, orange juice, and apple brandy in a medium bowl. Toss to combine and set aside.

To make the topping, combine the flour, brown sugar, cinnamon, and salt in a medium bowl. Using a pastry blender or your hands, cut the butter into the flour until the mixture resembles coarse crumbs. Stir in the almonds and chocolate chips.

Spoon the apple mixture into the prepared baking dish and then top with the crumb mixture. Bake until the apples are soft and the topping crispy, about 1 hour.

Turkey-Apple Salad

The question of what to do with all that leftover turkey is answered with this recipe.

Makes 4 servings

2 cups diced cooked turkey

2 apples of your choice, cored and diced

2 tablespoons fresh lemon juice

1 cup sliced celery

¼ cup chopped celery leaves

¼ cup slivered toasted almonds

¼ cup dried cranberries

Dressing

¼ cup mayonnaise

2 tablespoons honey mustard

1 tablespoon balsamic vinegar

¼ teaspoon sea salt

½ teaspoon freshly ground black pepper

In a large bowl, combine the turkey, apples, and lemon juice; toss to coat. Add the celery, celery leaves, almonds, and cranberries; toss to combine.

To make the dressing, whisk together the mayonnaise, mustard, vinegar, salt, and pepper in a small bowl. Pour over the turkey mixture and toss to coat. Serve on top of salad greens or in toasted pita pockets.

Chicken Liver and Apple Pate

Apple brandy adds a depth of flavor to this heavenly spread, but if you prefer, you can substitute apple cider in its place.

Makes about 2½ cups

½ cup unsalted butter, divided

1½ cups diced Granny Smith apple

¼ cup diced shallots

2 cloves garlic, minced

¼ cup apple brandy

1 pound chicken livers, trimmed

1 teaspoon chopped fresh thyme

1 teaspoon sea salt

½ teaspoon freshly ground black pepper

¼ cup heavy cream

¼ cup dried cherries

Melt 1 tablespoon of the butter in a nonstick sauté pan set over medium heat. Add the apples and cook for 5 minutes, or until softened. Add the shallots and garlic and cook for 2 minutes. Remove the pan from the heat and add the apple brandy. Transfer the apple mixture to a food processor.

In the same sauté pan, melt 1 tablespoon of butter over medium-high heat. Add the chicken livers and cook, stirring occasionally, until browned on the outside but still pink in the center. Do not overcook. Cool for 5 minutes and add to the food processor, along with the remaining 6 tablespoons butter, thyme, salt, pepper, and heavy cream. Pulse 10 to 15 times or until well incorporated. Add the dried cherries and pulse until they are slightly chopped, about 5 more times.

Transfer the mixture to a glass airtight container and chill for at least 4 hours, or overnight. Serve with crackers, toast, or tart apple slices.

Baked Apple Pancake

Served straight from the oven, this pancake is
puffed up with apple goodness.

Serves 6

6 eggs

1½ cups milk

1 teaspoon pure vanilla extract

1 cup all-purpose flour

2 tablespoons granulated sugar

½ teaspoon salt

1 teaspoon ground cinnamon

¼ cup unsalted butter, at room temperature

4½ cups thinly sliced Granny Smith or Honeycrisp
apples, or a combination of the two

3 tablespoons light brown sugar, packed

Preheat the oven to 425° F. Grease a 9- x 13-inch
glass baking dish and set aside.

In a blender, combine the eggs, milk, and
vanilla; blend for 30 seconds on high. Add
the flour, sugar, salt, and cinnamon; blend
until smooth.

Heat the butter in a large nonstick skillet set
over medium heat. Add the apples and cook,
stirring, until they soften, about 5 minutes.
Transfer the apples to the prepared dish and
spread them out in a single layer. Pour the batter
over the apples, sprinkle with the brown sugar,
and bake until puffed and golden, about 20
minutes. Serve immediately.

Roasted Beet and Apple Salad

This unorthodox combination that makes a delicious, tangy-sweet salad. Separating the beets into two packets helps them cook evenly.

Makes about 2 dozen

4 to 6 small beets (9 to 10 ounces total), washed, but not peeled

2 medium Gala apples, peeled, cored, and cut into ½-in slices, then cut in half crosswise

1½ tablespoons apple cider vinegar

1 teaspoon melted apple jelly or honey

¼ cup olive oil

Salt, to taste

Freshly ground black pepper

Fresh thyme sprigs, for garnish (optional)

Preheat the oven to 400° F. Separate the beets into 2 groups, wrap them in 2 separate foil packets, and roast for 45 to 60 minutes, until tender and easily pierced with a knife. Cool in the foil.

About 10 minutes before the beets have finished cooking, place the apples on a small parchment- or foil-lined sheet pan and place them in the oven with the beets. Roast until golden at the edges and almost tender. (They will soften a bit more on standing.) If you aren't using Gala apples, watch them carefully, as some varieties will cook faster than others.

Meanwhile, make the dressing by whisking together the vinegar, jelly, oil, salt, and black pepper.

When the beets are cool, peel, remove the stems and root ends, and slice them the same size as the apples. Arrange the apples and beets on a plate. Drizzle with dressing. Garnish with thyme, if you desire.

Apple Bread

A streusel topping gives this sweet bread extra crunch.

Makes 1 (9-inch) loaf

½ cup unsalted butter, at room temperature

1 cup granulated sugar

2 large eggs, beaten

⅓ cup buttermilk

1 teaspoon pure vanilla extract

2 cups all-purpose flour

1 teaspoon baking soda

½ teaspoon salt

1 Fuji or Honeycrisp apple, cored, peeled, and diced

Topping

⅓ cup all-purpose flour

2 tablespoons granulated sugar

2 tablespoons light brown sugar

½ teaspoon ground cinnamon

3 tablespoons cold unsalted butter, diced

Preheat the oven to 350° F. Grease a 9- x 5-inch loaf pan and set aside.

In a large bowl, cream the butter and sugar using a handheld mixer on medium-high speed for 2 to 3 minutes, or until light and fluffy. Add the eggs, buttermilk, and vanilla, incorporating fully.

In a medium bowl, whisk together the flour, baking soda, and salt. Gradually add the dry ingredients to the wet ingredients, mixing on medium speed until fully incorporated, about 2 to 3 minutes. Fold in the apples. Pour the batter into the prepared loaf pan.

To make the topping, combine the flour, sugars, and cinnamon in a medium bowl. Cut in the butter until the mixture resembles coarse breadcrumbs. Sprinkle over the batter.

Bake for 55 to 60 minutes, or until a toothpick inserted in the middle comes out clean. Cool in the pan for 10 minutes before inverting onto a wire rack.

December 3

Raspberry Apple Chiller

This chiller makes use of frozen fruit for a drink that is both potent and refreshing.

Makes 2 cocktails

1 (12-ounce) package frozen unsweetened raspberries

2 cups Gala apple chunks, frozen

4 ounces rum

2 ounces apple brandy

2 ounces triple sec

3 ounces fresh lime juice

2 ounces Chambord

Combine the frozen fruit with the rum, brandy, triple sec, lime juice, and Chambord in a blender or food processor and blend until smooth and frothy. Divide between 2 tall glasses.

Almond Apple Chewies

These cookies will be the hit of the holiday season. If you want to be fancy, call them by their French name: Apple Almond Macarons.

Makes 16 cookies

1⅓ cups sliced or slivered blanched almonds, plus more as needed

⅔ cup granulated sugar

½ teaspoon almond extract

2 extra-large egg whites

⅔ cup very finely chopped Dried Apples (see page 323) or store-bought dried apples

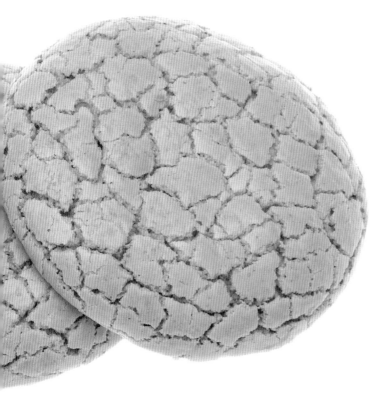

Preheat the oven to 325° F. Position the oven rack in the center of the oven. Line a baking sheet with parchment paper.

Combine the almonds and sugar in a food processor and process for 45 to 60 seconds, or until finely ground. Add the almond extract and egg white and pulse about 10 times, until the mixture comes together. You may need a few drops of water to do so; it should be the consistency of marzipan. If crumbly, add water by drops until it becomes a thick paste. Scrape the filling out of the processor onto a work surface and knead the apple into it.

Divide the dough into 16 pieces of equal size. Gently shape each cookie into a ball. If the dough sticks a little, dampen your hands to form the cookies; if it sticks a lot, it's too wet. Grind up some more almonds and work them into the dough, a little at a time, until it is the right consistency for forming the cookies. Place balls about 1½ inches apart on a parchment-lined baking sheet. Press lightly to flatten slightly.

Bake for 12 to 15 minutes, or until golden and firm to the touch. Let cool for 1 minute and then remove with a spatula to cool completely on a rack.

Cheesy Apple-Onion Muffins

Enjoy these savory muffins fresh from the oven along with a bowl of piping hot soup.

Makes 12 muffins

4 tablespoons unsalted butter

1 cup grated apple of your choice

1 cup chopped green onions

2 teaspoons chopped fresh thyme

2 teaspoons chopped fresh sage

1 teaspoon salt

1 teaspoon freshly ground black pepper

2 cups all-purpose flour

1 teaspoon baking powder

1 cup grated Gruyere cheese

1¼ cup milk

1 large egg

Preheat the oven to 375° F. Line a 12-cup muffin tin with paper liners or grease well.

Heat the butter in a large nonstick sauté pan set over medium heat. Add the apple and onions and sauté for 3 to 5 minutes, or until softened and lightly browned. Add the thyme, sage, salt, and pepper, and stir to combine. Set aside to cool.

In a large bowl, combine the flour, baking powder, and cheese; set aside.

In a medium bowl, whisk together the milk and egg and stir in the apple-onion mixture. Add the wet ingredients to the flour mixture and stir with a wooden spoon until just combined; do not overmix. Pour into the prepared muffin tins.

Bake for 12 to 15 minutes, or until the tops are golden brown and a toothpick inserted into the middle comes out clean.

Apple Walnut Crisp

Oats, walnuts, and pine nuts give this crisp a rich, nutty flavor that is irresistible.

Makes 4 servings

¼ cup cold unsalted butter, plus more for greasing

Nonstick cooking oil spray

¼ cup old-fashioned rolled oats

¼ cup pine nuts

¼ cup walnuts

½ cup granulated sugar

¼ cup all-purpose flour

¼ teaspoon ground cinnamon

¼ teaspoon salt

6 Gala apples

1 teaspoon cornstarch

Whipped cream, for serving (optional)

Preheat the oven to 350° F. Butter a glass or ceramic baking dish. Spray a baking sheet with cooking oil spray.

Spread the oats and nuts out over the baking sheet and sprinkle with 2 tablespoons sugar. Mix to coat and then even out the surface with a spatula. Bake for about 10 minutes, or until golden. Remove from the oven and let cool.

Increase the oven temperature to 375° F. Mix the flour, ¼ cup sugar, the cinnamon, and salt in a bowl. Cut in the chilled butter and mix with your fingertips until coarse crumbs form.

Core, peel, and cut the apples into ⅛-inch wedges. In a separate bowl, mix them with the remaining 2 tablespoons sugar and the cornstarch. Pour the apples into the prepared baking dish and even out the surface.

Mix the oat mixture into the flour mixture, sprinkle over the apples, and even the surface with a spatula. Bake for 50 to 55 minutes, or until the crumbs have baked into a golden brown crust. Serve warm with whipped cream, desired.

Apple-Stuffed Artichokes

Stuffed with a medley of apples, bread crumbs, and Pecorino Romano cheese, these artichokes make a tasty side dish.

Makes 2 artichokes

¼ cup grated Pecorino Romano cheese

⅓ cup Italian-seasoned bread crumbs

½ Granny Smith apple, peeled and diced

1 clove garlic, minced

½ teaspoon sea salt

½ teaspoon freshly ground black pepper

2 globe artichokes

2 teaspoons extra virgin olive oil

Bring a 5-quart saucepan filled halfway with water and fitted with a steamer to a boil; lower heat to simmer.

Combine the grated cheese, bread crumbs, diced apple, garlic, salt, and pepper on a plate. Set aside.

To prepare the artichokes, remove the top ⅓ of the artichoke with a serrated knife, trimming any remaining leaf tips with kitchen shears. Separate the center leaves and pull out the purple and yellow leaves and scoop out the chokes with a melon baller. Spoon the bread crumb mixture into this cavity as well as between the outer leaves.

Place the stuffed artichokes into the steamer, cover, and steam until the outer leaves can be easily pulled off, about 45 minutes to 1 hour. Serve hot or at room temperature.

Puff Pastry Snails with Apple, Pecan, and Cocoa Filling

These are "snails" that everyone will love: flaky on the outside and sweet, nutty, and chocolate-y on the inside.

Makes 18 pastries

½ recipe Quick Puff Pastry (see Apple Apricot Bistro Tarts, page 26)

Filling

6 tablespoons toasted pecans, finely ground

2 tablespoons unsweetened cocoa powder

¼ cup light brown sugar, packed

1 to 2 teaspoons ground cinnamon

1 small apple, such as Golden Delicious, Granny Smith, or Jonathan, peeled, cored, and very finely chopped

Glaze (optional)

2 tablespoons apple jelly

Prepare the Quick Puff Pastry as directed on page 26 and chill if necessary.

Preheat the oven to 400° F. Position the oven rack in the center of the oven. Line a baking sheet with parchment paper. Place the lined baking sheet into another baking sheet to prevent scorching.

Make the filling by combining the pecans, cocoa, brown sugar, and cinnamon and mixing lightly. Put the apple in a separate bowl.

Roll the dough out to an 18- by 19-inch rectangle, about 1/8 inch thick. Spread the filling mixture evenly over the dough, and sprinkle the chopped apple over it.

Starting at a long end, roll the dough up, not too tightly, to form a log about 9 inches long and 2¼ inches in diameter. Cut the log in ½-inch slices to yield 18 pastries.

Place them on the doubled, parchment-lined baking sheet, reshaping into circles, if needed. Bake for 14 to 17 minutes, until crisp and golden. While the pastries are baking, melt the apple jelly, if using. With a pastry brush, glaze the baked snails with it. Serve warm or at room temperature.

Apple Tip:

Jonathan is a medium-sized apple with a sharp, sweet taste. This versatile variety can be enjoyed raw or cooked and performs well in both sweet and savory recipes.

Apple and Cranberry Crumble

For his crumble topping, **Chef Dave Martin** uses Golden Grahams cereal, preferring its flavor and texture to that of rolled oats. You can use the versatile topping with your favorite crumble and streusel cakes too.

Makes about 12 (8-ounce) crumbles

Crumble Topping

2½ cups Golden Grahams cereal

2 cups chopped pecans

2 cups all-purpose flour

2 teaspoons ground cinnamon

1 teaspoon freshly grated nutmeg

8 ounces unsalted butter, cut into small pieces

1 cup brown sugar, packed

Apple-Cranberry Filling

⅔ cup unsalted butter

1½ cups granulated sugar

1 tablespoon ground cinnamon

1 tablespoon freshly grated nutmeg

1½ teaspoons kosher salt

12 green apples, cored, unpeeled, and finely diced

3 cups fresh cranberries

To make the topping, break the cereal into small pieces or briefly pulse in a food processor. Combine the cereal pieces and the remaining ingredients in a bowl, and, with your hands, blend them together until the mixture resembles coarse crumbs. Cover and refrigerate until ready to use.

When you are ready to make the apple-cranberry filling, preheat the oven to 400° F and grease 12 (8-ounce) ramekins.

Melt the butter in a saucepan; add the sugar, cinnamon, nutmeg, and salt and stir to combine. Add the apples and cranberries and, stirring, cook over medium heat until apple caramelize and begin to soften, about 10 minutes.

Scoop the apple mixture into the prepared ramekins. Top liberally with the crumble mixture and bake for about 8 to 10 minutes, or until browned and bubbly. Serve with your favorite gelato, ice cream, or whipped cream.

Chef Dave Martin

CURRENTLY: Consultant for various restaurants and food trucks; cookbook author

NOTABLE FOR: Being a chef-testant on the first season of Bravo's *Top Chef*

BRANDING: Flavor Quest Brand, Martin's line of premium sauces and rubs

December 10

Apple Pear Pie

A rich and satisfying pie made from the fruits of the year's harvest.

Makes 1 (9-inch) pie

1 recipe Pate Brisée (Flaky Pastry Dough;
   see Apple Dumplings, page 12)
¼ cup plus ⅔ cup light brown sugar
3 tablespoons all-purpose flour
⅛ teaspoon salt

2 eggs
1 cup sour cream
1 teaspoon pure vanilla extract
3 large apples of your choice
2 ripe but firm pears

Prepare the dough as directed on page 12. Divide the dough into two pieces, using slightly more than half for one disk (which will be the bottom crust). Chill as directed.

When you are ready to bake, preheat the oven to 400° F. Position the rack in the lower third of the oven. Roll out half the dough to a thickness of ⅛ inch, rolling it around the rolling pin. Place the rolling pin on a 9-inch pie pan and unroll the dough over it. Line the pie pan with the dough, leaving a 1-inch overhang all around. Refrigerate until you are ready to fill and bake the pie.

Sprinkle a work surface with ¼ cup brown sugar and roll the remaining dough out on it. Refrigerate the lined pie pan and the dough for the top crust while preparing the filling.

Combine ⅔ cup brown sugar, flour, salt, eggs, sour cream, and vanilla and whisk to combine well.

Peel and core the apples and pears and cut them into ⅛-inch slices. Pile the fruit into the chilled bottom crust. Carefully pour the sour cream mixture over the fruit. Place the top crust, brown sugar side up, over the fruit. Seal the edges by folding under. Crimp the edges. Cut two or three small slits in the top crust for steam vents. Bake for 10 minutes. Reduce the heat to 350° F and bake for another 30 to 40 minutes, or until the crust is a deep golden color. Cool the pie on a rack. Serve warm or cold.

Apple-Pimento Cheese Spread

Also known as cherry peppers, pimentos have a mild and sweet flavor that pair well with apples. Serve this addictive cheese spread with crackers or crisp apple wedges.

Makes about 2½ cups

4 ounces cream cheese, softened

2 cups grated sharp Cheddar cheese

1 Honeycrisp apple, cored and grated

¼ cup mayonnaise

3 tablespoons pimentos, chopped

2 tablespoons fresh lemon juice

½ teaspoon Worcestershire sauce

¼ teaspoon garlic powder

¼ teaspoon kosher salt

¼ teaspoon freshly ground black pepper

Using an electric mixer, beat the cream cheese until smooth. Add the remaining ingredients and mix until combined. Refrigerate at least 1 hour or overnight to allow the flavors to meld.

Red Lentil, Coconut, and Apple Soup

Garam masala, an aromatic blend of ground spices used in Indian cuisine, gives this soup its distinctive flavor.

Makes 8 cups

2 cups dried red lentils

1 tablespoon olive oil

1 cup chopped onion

1 (1-inch) piece fresh ginger, peeled and roughly chopped

1 tablespoon garam masala

1 Granny Smith apple, cored and roughly chopped

1 large carrot, peeled and roughly chopped

1 (14-ounce) can coconut milk

4 cups chicken broth

Sea salt, to taste

Freshly ground black pepper, to taste

Fresh chopped cilantro, for garnish

In a 5-quart saucepan set over high heat, combine the lentils with enough water to cover them. Bring to a boil, reduce heat, and simmer for 30 minutes. Drain and set aside.

Heat the oil in large nonstick skillet set over medium-high heat. Add the onion and sauté until softened and translucent. Add the ginger and garam masala and sauté until fragrant, about 1 minute. Add the apple and carrot and sauté for 5 minutes.

Return the lentils to the saucepan and add the apple-carrot mixture, coconut milk, and chicken broth. Bring to a boil, reduce heat, and simmer, uncovered, for 20 minutes, or until apples and carrots are tender. Transfer soup to a blender and puree until smooth. Season with salt and pepper.

Ladle soup into bowls and garnish with cilantro.

December 13

Prosciutto-Wrapped Gruyere and Apples on Rosemary Skewers

Although you can substitute toothpicks, the rosemary sprigs add an extra touch of sophistication.

Makes 16 appetizers

8 slices prosciutto, cut in half widthwise

1 small apple of your choice, peeled, cored, and cut into 16 slices

2 ounces Gruyere cheese, cut into 2-inch sticks

16 rosemary sprigs, for skewers

Preheat a griddle or a large nonstick sauté pan set over medium heat.

Arrange the prosciutto slices on a clean, dry work surface. Place an apple wedge and a piece of cheese in the center of each slice. Roll the prosciutto around the filling and secure with a rosemary sprig.

Sear on the preheated griddle pan until the prosciutto is golden and crispy and the cheese is melted, about 2 to 3 minutes on each side. Serve immediately.

Sweet Potato and Apple Latkes with Applesauce and Sour Cream

For a new twist on the traditional potato pancake, or latke,
try this version made with sweet potatoes and apples.

Makes 18 latkes

2 pounds garnet sweet
   potatoes, peeled

1 pound Honeycrisp or Fuji
   apples, peeled

1 small sweet onion, peeled

4 large eggs, lightly beaten

¾ cup plus 2 tablespoons
   matzo meal

¼ teaspoon ground
   cinnamon

1 tablespoon kosher salt

1 teaspoon freshly ground
   black pepper

½ cup vegetable oil

Sour cream, for serving

Applesauce, for serving

Preheat the oven to 300° F. Line a baking sheet with paper towels and set aside.

Using the coarse grater disk on a box grater or a food processor, shred the sweet potatoes, apples, and onion. Squeeze dry with paper towels. Toss together in a large bowl.

Add the beaten eggs, matzo meal, cinnamon, salt, and pepper. Mix well and let stand for 10 minutes.

Heat 2 tablespoons oil in a large nonstick sauté pan set over medium heat. Scoop ⅓ cup latke mixture from bowl and shape into a patty. Repeat until you have 4 or 5 patties. Slide patties into the oil. Do not overcrowd the pan. Cook until the edges are crispy and golden brown, about 3 to 4 minutes. Turn and cook until other side is golden brown, about 2 to 3 minutes. Drain on paper towels, transfer to baking sheet, and keep warm in the oven.

Add more oil to the pan and repeat until all of the batter is used. Serve hot with sour cream and applesauce.

Apple Tip:

Juicy Honeycrisp, the result of cross-pollination between Honeygold and Macoun, is mostly sweet with just a touch of tartness. Eat it out of hand or in salads. It's also an excellent saucing and baking apple.

Apple Doughnut Fritters

Make these fritters for Hanukkah, or any time you crave a sugary fried treat.

Makes 2 dozen fritters

Cinnamon Sugar

½ cup granulated sugar

1 teaspoon ground cinnamon

Fritters

4 cups vegetable oil

1 cup all-purpose flour

¼ cup granulated sugar

1 teaspoon baking powder

½ teaspoon ground cinnamon

½ teaspoon kosher salt

⅓ cup milk

1 large egg

1 teaspoon lemon zest

1 tablespoon fresh lemon juice

1 teaspoon pure vanilla extract

1½ cups diced Granny Smith apples

To make the fritters, heat the vegetable oil into a deep fryer or a 5-quart saucepan set over medium heat until the oil registers 360° F. Line a baking sheet with paper towels and set aside. Make the cinnamon sugar: mix the cinnamon and sugar together in a small bowl.

In a large bowl, sift together the flour, sugar, baking powder, cinnamon, and salt. In a medium bowl, whisk together the milk, egg, lemon zest, lemon juice, and vanilla. Make a well in the center of the dry ingredients and add the wet ingredients. Stir just to combine; fold in the apples.

Using a 1-inch cookie scoop, drop about 4 to 5 scoops of batter into the hot oil. Be sure not to overcrowd. The fritters will float to the top and puff to about double their size. Deep fry until golden brown on one side, about 2 minutes. Using a slotted spoon, flip the fritter and cook for 1 more minute. Remove with a slotted spoon and transfer to the prepared baking sheet. Repeat with the remaining dough.

Roll the hot fritters in the cinnamon-sugar mixture and serve immediately.

Apple Tip:

Impress dinner guests by setting out an apple honey bowl. With a sharp knife, slice off the top of an apple. Scoop out the flesh, leaving about ½ inch of the outer skin. Fill the apple with honey and then return its "lid."

Chocolate Apple Cupcakes

These adorable little "apples" are tasty, too.

Makes 12 cupcakes

Cupcakes

½ cup unsalted butter, cut up

2 ounces semisweet chocolate, finely chopped

½ cup cocoa, sifted

½ cup unsweetened applesauce

¾ cup granulated sugar

2 tablespoons brown sugar

⅓ cup plain Greek yogurt or sour cream

1 cup all-purpose flour

¾ teaspoon baking powder

½ teaspoon baking soda

¼ teaspoon salt

Icing

1⅓ cups unsalted butter, at room temperature

1 teaspoon pure vanilla extract

1½ cups confectioners' sugar, sifted

A few drops red food coloring

A few drops of cream or water

Garnish

Green fondant

½ cup red sprinkles

Thin pretzel sticks, broken into stem-sized pieces

Preheat the oven to 350° F. Position the oven rack in the center position. Line a 12-cup muffin tin with paper cupcake liners.

Put the butter and chocolate in a microwave-safe container. Melt on low power for 20 to 30 seconds. Remove from the oven, add the cocoa, and whisk until the mixture is smooth. Let cool to room temperature.

Whisk in the applesauce, sugars, and yogurt or sour cream. In a separate bowl, sift the flour, baking powder, baking soda, and salt. Mix the chocolate mixture into the flour mixture, stirring for about 30 seconds, or until well combined.

Scoop the batter into the prepared tin. Bake for 18 for 20 minutes, or until the top springs back when pressed lightly. Cool for 1 minute in the pan and then remove the cupcakes to cool completely on a rack.

While the cupcakes are baking, make the icing. With an electric mixer set at low speed, beat the butter and vanilla until smooth. Add the confectioners' sugar and beat until smooth and light-colored. Add the food coloring and, if needed to reach spreading consistency, a few drops of cream or water, and mix until thoroughly incorporated. Pour the sprinkles into a shallow bowl. Shape the fondant into 24 small leaf shapes and score lightly to make "veins."

When the cupcakes have cooled, frost the tops. Dip the tops into the sprinkles to coat completely. Place two leaves on each cupcake and insert a small piece of pretzel stick into the center of each as a stem.

December 17

Prosciutto and Apple Croissant Sandwich

Buttery croissants and sweet honey contrast nicely with salty prosciutto, tart apples, and peppery arugula.

Makes 2 sandwiches

2 croissants

2 tablespoons honey

2 tablespoons honey mustard

4 slices prosciutto

4 thin slices mozzarella cheese

½ Granny Smith apple, thinly sliced

Freshly ground black pepper, to taste

1 cup baby arugula

Preheat the oven to 425° F. Line a baking sheet with foil.

Split the croissants and place cut side up on the prepared baking sheet. Toast in the oven for 5 to 7 minutes, or until lightly golden and crispy.

Mix together the honey and mustard and spread on the croissants. Layer one side of each sandwich with 2 slices prosciutto, 2 slices mozzarella, and apple slices. Season with pepper, top with the arugula, and close each sandwich. Serve immediately.

December 18

Roasted Chicken with Apple Cider Sauce

A new go-to recipe for your repertoire—
so simple to make, with such basic ingredients,
but such a deep, rich flavor, you'll want to lick the plate.

Makes 4 to 6 servings

2 apples of your choice,
   cored and cut into
   8 slices

1 sweet onion, cut into
   8 slices

12 cloves garlic, peeled

2 teaspoons chopped
   fresh thyme

2 teaspoons sea salt,
   divided

2 teaspoons freshly
   ground black pepper,
   divided

1 (4-pound) chicken,
   cut into 8 pieces

1 tablespoon white wine
   vinegar

2 tablespoons honey

½ cup apple cider

Preheat the oven to 375° F. Position an oven rack at the top of the oven.

In a large bowl, combine the apples, onions, garlic, thyme, 1 teaspoon salt, and 1 teaspoon pepper; toss to coat. Transfer to a large roasting pan; set aside.

In a large bowl, combine the remaining salt and pepper, vinegar, and honey; add the chicken pieces and toss to coat. Arrange the chicken pieces on top of the apples and onions in the roasting pan. Pour the cider over the chicken.

Roast for 45 minutes to 1 hour, or until an instant-read thermometer inserted in a thigh or leg registers 165° F.

Loosely cover the chicken in foil and let rest for 10 minutes. Carefully puree the apple-onion mixture in a food processor or a blender until smooth.

Arrange the chicken on a platter, pour the sauce over the pieces, and serve.

Apple Potpourri

'Tis the season for a spice-scented home! Make your own apple potpourri in time for the holidays. Core and thinly slice 2 apples and lay them on nonstick cookie sheets that have been sprayed with cooking oil. Sprinkle the slices with cinnamon and bake at 150° F for 30 minutes. While the apple slices are baking, combine cinnamon sticks that have been broken into thirds with a few pinches of ground allspice and 2 to 3 drops of cinnamon oil. In a large lidded container, mix together the cooled, dried apple slices, pinecones, and other natural accents with the cinnamon sticks. Allow the mixture to develop in the covered container for a week or two, gently shaking it daily. Display your apple potpourri in small bowls around your home.

Holiday Wassail

This classic English Christmas drink originated as part of an ancient ceremony performed to ensure a good harvest of cider apples in the coming year. The word "wassail" is derived from a Middle English toast to good health. In earlier times, the warm brew was served with actual toast for dunking. These days, the toasts are with words only.

Makes 6 cocktails

2 cups apple cider
1 apple of your choice, peeled, cored, and grated
Peel of ½ orange, cut into strips or spirals, pith removed
7 small cinnamon sticks
1/16 teaspoon freshly grated nutmeg
1 cup hard cider
1 cup Calvados
Apple slices dipped into apple cider (optional)

Combine the cider, apple, orange peel, 1 cinnamon stick, and nutmeg in a saucepan. Bring to a simmer and simmer for 5 minutes. Strain into 6 goblets or mugs and divide the hard cider and Calvados between them. Garnish with apple slices, if using, and the remaining cinnamon sticks.

Apple-Stuffed Acorn Squash

Serve as an elegant side dish or as a complete vegetarian meal.

Makes 4 servings

2 acorn squash

Olive oil spray

1 teaspoon olive oil

1 cup diced sweet onion

1½ cups diced Granny Smith apples

3 cloves garlic, minced

1 teaspoon dried thyme

½ cup cubed challah bread

2 tablespoons dried cherries

1 teaspoon sea salt

1 teaspoon freshly ground black pepper

¾ cup chicken or vegetable broth

Maple syrup, warmed (optional)

Preheat the oven to 350° F. Line a baking sheet with foil and set aside.

Halve the acorn squash lengthwise and scoop out the seeds. Spray all four halves with olive oil spray and place face down on the prepared baking sheet. Bake for 40 minutes, or until tender.

To make the filling, heat the olive oil in a large nonstick sauté pan set over medium heat. Add the onion and apple and sauté for 5 minutes, stirring frequently. Add the garlic, thyme, challah bread, cherries, salt, and pepper; sauté for 3 to 5 minutes, or until golden and the vegetables are soft. Add the broth and set aside.

Stuff the squash with the apple stuffing, return to the oven, and bake for another 30 minutes. Serve with warm maple syrup, if desired.

Roasted Apple-Berry Sauce

Roasting gives this sauce an added dimension. Serve with sweet or savory dishes. It goes equally well with ice cream or a spicy pork tenderloin.

Makes about 4 cups

2 Granny Smith, Fuji, or Gala apples, peeled, cored, and roughly chopped

1 (16-ounce) bag frozen mixed berries, thawed

2 tablespoons honey, plus more if needed

1 tablespoon fresh lemon juice, plus more if needed

1 teaspoon lemon zest

Preheat the oven to 375° F. Line a baking sheet with foil.

Spread the chopped apples on the baking sheet and bake for 20 to 25 minutes, or until soft. In the last 5 minutes, add the berries to the baking sheet.

Let mixture cool slightly before transferring to a blender. Add the honey, lemon juice, and lemon zest and puree until smooth. Taste, and if you prefer a sweeter sauce, add more honey. If you prefer it tarter, add more lemon juice.

Moroccan Carrot and Apple Salad

While usually citrus fruits are usually found in Moroccan salads, this version uses crisp apples.

Makes 4 servings

2 apples of your choice

2½ teaspoons fresh lemon juice

1 cup grated carrot

½ cup chopped raisins

½ cup chopped flat-leaf parsley

2 tablespoons chopped mint

1 tablespoon extra virgin olive oil

½ teaspoon ground cumin

½ teaspoon sea salt

½ teaspoon freshly ground black pepper

Dice the apples and toss with the lemon juice to prevent browning. Combine all the ingredients in a large bowl and toss to coat. Cover and refrigerate for 1 hour to allow flavors to blend.

Chicken Salad with Apples and Pomegranate

With its bright red pomegranate arils, this festive salad is a light and refreshing change of pace among so many heavy holiday meals.

Makes 2 servings

Chicken

1 (6-ounce) boned chicken breast, skin on
Salt, to taste
Freshly ground black pepper, to taste
1 teaspoon olive oil

Dressing

2 tablespoons pomegranate juice
1 tablespoon Dijon mustard
1 teaspoon honey
2 tablespoons extra virgin olive oil

Salad

2 cups chopped curly endive
1 Honeycrisp apple, cored and diced
½ cup chopped toasted hazelnuts
2 tablespoons chopped chives
¼ cup pomegranate arils

Preheat the oven to 375° F. Wrap a brick or cast iron skillet in aluminum foil and set aside.

Season the chicken with salt and pepper. Heat the oil in a medium skillet set over high heat. Add the chicken skin side down. Place the brick or cast iron skillet on top of the chicken breast and transfer the skillet to the oven. Cook for 10 to 12 minutes, or until an instant-read thermometer inserted in the middle registers 165° F. Remove from the oven, remove the brick, and let stand, tented with aluminum foil, for 5 minutes.

To make the dressing, whisk together the pomegranate juice, mustard, honey, and oil, creating an emulsion.

Slice the chicken breast into about 8 pieces.

When ready to serve, toss the curly endive, apple, hazelnuts, and chives with the dressing. Divide the salad between two plates, top with the sliced chicken, and sprinkle with pomegranate arils. Serve immediately.

Roasted Pork Loin with Apple Cider-Mustard Sauce

A tender, succulent roast bursting with flavor.

Makes 6 servings

1 sprig fresh rosemary
1 clove garlic, peeled
2 teaspoons salt
2 teaspoons freshly ground black pepper
2 tablespoons olive oil
1 (2-pound) boneless pork loin
1½ cups sliced onion
2 baking apples, such as Rome or Cortland, peeled, cored, and sliced
2 carrots, sliced
2 celery stalks, sliced
2 tablespoons apple cider vinegar
2 tablespoons whole-grain mustard
1 cup apple cider
3 tablespoons unsalted butter

Combine the rosemary, garlic, salt, pepper, and 1 tablespoon olive oil in a food processor and process to a paste. Place pork loin in the roasting pan. Brush the paste on all sides of the pork loin.

Toss the onions, apples, carrots, and celery with the remaining olive oil and spread around the pork loin. Roast for 25 to 30 minutes, or until an instant-read thermometer registers 150° to 160° F.

Transfer the pork to a plate, tent with foil, and let stand for 10 minutes while you make the sauce. Remove the vegetables to a platter and pour the pan drippings into a saucepan set over high heat. Whisk in the vinegar, mustard, and apple cider and cook, stirring frequently, until reduced by half, about 5 minutes. Remove from the heat and whisk in the butter.

Slice the pork roast, arrange over the roasted vegetables, and drizzle some of the sauce over the meat. Serve the remaining sauce on the side.

Fruitcake-Stuffed Baked Apples

If you are inundated with fruitcake during the holiday season, this is a delicious way to use some of it up.

Makes 8 baked apples

8 baking apples, such as Winesap or Jonathan

1 cup chopped fruitcake

½ cup strawberry preserves

½ cup granulated sugar

½ teaspoon freshly grated nutmeg

1 cup dry red wine

1 teaspoon pure vanilla extract

Whipped cream, for topping (optional)

Preheat the oven to 350° F. Grease a 9- x 13-inch baking dish.

Core the apples, discarding the core and the seeds. Scoop out and reserve the flesh, leaving a ½-inch-thick shell. Place the cored apples in the prepared dish and set aside.

Chop the apple flesh and combine with the fruitcake and the preserves. Spoon the mixture into each apple.

In a medium bowl, whisk together the sugar, nutmeg, wine, and vanilla. Pour over the apples.

Bake, uncovered, until the apples are tender, about 45 minutes. Cool slightly and top with whipped cream, if desired.

Stuffed French Toast with Sautéed Apples

These French toast sandwiches with their sweet cream cheese filling will satisfy the heartiest of appetites.

Makes 4 servings

Topping

1 tablespoon butter

2 Granny Smith apples, peeled, cored, and thinly sliced

¼ cup light brown sugar, packed

¼ cup apple cider

¼ cup chopped toasted walnuts

½ teaspoon cinnamon

Filling

½ cup cream cheese

2 tablespoons pure maple syrup

French Toast

8 slices challah bread

2 large eggs

½ cup milk

1 teaspoon pure vanilla extract

1 teaspoon ground cinnamon

1 tablespoon unsalted butter

To make the topping, melt the butter in a large nonstick sauté pan set over medium heat. Add the apples and cook, stirring occasionally, for 2 to 3 minutes. Add the brown sugar, apple cider, walnuts, and cinnamon and cook, stirring occasionally, for an additional 4 to 5 minutes. Set aside.

To make the filling, mix together the cream cheese and maple syrup. Spread the filling on 4 slices of the challah bread and then top with the remaining 4 slices to make sandwiches.

To make the French toast, whisk together the eggs, milk, vanilla, and cinnamon in a shallow bowl. Dip each sandwich in the egg mixture, coating both sides.

Melt the remaining tablespoon of butter in a large nonstick sauté pan set over medium heat. Add the sandwiches and cook for 3 to 4 minutes on each side, or until golden brown.

Serve the French toast hot, topped with the apples.

Apple and Pear Souffles

Puffy and golden, these soufflés will dazzle your guests.

Makes 6 servings

2 large Granny Smith apples, peeled, cored, and diced

3 ripe pears, peeled, cored, and diced

½ cup granulated sugar, divided

1 tablespoon apple brandy

1 teaspoon pure vanilla extract

¼ teaspoon ground ginger

2 tablespoons water

1 tablespoon unsalted butter, at room temperature

1 tablespoon confectioners' sugar

8 egg whites, at room temperature

⅛ teaspoon cream of tartar

Combine the apples, pears, ¼ cup sugar, apple brandy, vanilla, ginger, and water in a 4-quart saucepan set over medium heat. Bring to a simmer, reduce heat to low, cover, and cook for 20 minutes. Uncover the pan and continue to cook for an additional 30 to 40 minutes, stirring often, until the fruit is completely soft. Transfer to a blender and puree until smooth. Let cool completely.

Preheat the oven to 425° F. Prepare 6 ramekins by coating each one with butter and sprinkling with confectioners' sugar.

In a large clean bowl, beat the egg whites with a hand mixer on high speed until light and foamy, about 1 minute. Add the cream of tartar and continue to beat on high for 30 seconds longer. Slowly stream in the remaining ¼ cup sugar until it is fully incorporated and stiff peaks form; do not overbeat.

Fold the egg whites into the apple-pear mixture. Spoon into the prepared ramekins, filling them all the way to the top. Place the filled ramekins on a baking sheet and transfer to the oven. Bake for 10 minutes, until puffed and golden. Serve immediately.

Apple Tip:

When removing the skin from apples, don't discard the peelings. Apple peelings can be used to make apple syrup, apple butter, apple tea, apple pectin, potpourri, and more.

December 28

Applesauce Yogurt Parfaits

During the busy holiday season, it's easy to forget about breakfast. Quick to put together, these parfaits will bring everyone to the table.

Makes 4 servings

1 cup applesauce (see page 17 or use store-bought)

¼ teaspoon ground cinnamon

½ cup apple granola (see page 29 or use store-bought)

2 tablespoons dried cranberries

1⅓ cups vanilla yogurt

In a small bowl, combine the applesauce and cinnamon; stir to combine.

Spoon 1 tablespoon of granola into each of 4 parfait glasses. Layer each with ⅓ cup yogurt, ¼ cup of applesauce, and ½ tablespoon cranberries. Sprinkle remaining granola on top of each and serve.

December 29

Cherry Appletini

Toast the holidays with this fruity cocktail.

Makes 1 cocktail

Ice
1 ounce apple schnapps
2 ounces vodka
1 tablespoon maraschino cherry juice
1 maraschino cherry, for garnish

Fill a shaker with ice. Add the schnapps and vodka. Shake for about 20 seconds. Pour into a chilled martini glass, spoon in the cherry juice, and garnish with a cherry.

Make a Wish

If you're hosting a dinner party, why not decorate your table with apple leaf wishes for the New Year? Cut the "leaves" from light-colored, heavy paper, one per guest. Punch a hole in each leaf and cut a small piece of twine for tying it to an apple stem. Give guests markers, leaves, twine, and apples, and have each write a New Year's wish on his or her leaf, fasten it to the apple, and set it on the table for all to share.

December 30

Roasted Duck Breast with Sweet Potato–Apple Puree

For an intimate dinner, set the table for two, light the candles, and serve this elegant dish on your best china.

Makes 2 servings

2 (8-ounce) duck breasts

1 teaspoon sea salt, divided

1 teaspoon freshly ground black pepper, divided

2 Golden Delicious apples, peeled, cored, and chopped

1 large sweet potato, peeled and roughly chopped

½ cup diced onion

3 cloves garlic, peeled

1 tablespoon chopped fresh thyme

½ cup apple juice

3 tablespoons unsalted butter

Preheat the oven to 400° F. Line a rimmed baking sheet with foil and set aside.

Score the duck breasts with a sharp knife all so that the fat will render evenly and become crispy. Season the duck with ½ teaspoon salt and ½ teaspoon pepper.

Heat a dry skillet over a medium-high heat. Place the duck breasts skin side down in the skillet and cook until the skin is golden and crispy. Transfer to the prepared baking sheet and roast, skin side up, for about 10 minutes. Transfer to a plate, tent with foil, and let stand for 10 minutes.

Meanwhile, combine the chopped apples, sweet potatoes, onion, garlic cloves, remaining salt and pepper, thyme, apple juice, and butter in a 4-quart saucepan set over medium-high heat. Bring to a boil, reduce heat to medium, cover, and simmer for 12 to 15 minutes, or until the apples are soft. Transfer the mixture to a blender or food processor and puree until smooth.

Slice the duck breast and serve over the sweet potato-apple puree.

Roasted Rack of Lamb with Apples and French Lentils

Peppery French lentils hold their shape better than other varieties, making them the ideal kind to use when preparing this stunning dish.

Makes 4 servings

1 (1½-pound) rack of lamb, trimmed with meat cut away at the tips

2 teaspoons salt, divided

2 teaspoons freshly ground black pepper, divided

2 tablespoons dry bread crumbs

2 tablespoons plus 1 teaspoon extra virgin olive oil, divided

3 teaspoons Dijon mustard, divided

2 shallots, minced

1½ cups cooked French lentils

1 Granny Smith apple, cored and diced

½ cup diced carrot

4 cups baby spinach

1 cup dried cranberries

1 teaspoon chopped fresh thyme

¾ cup chicken broth

1 tablespoon apple brandy (optional)

Preheat the oven to 450° F. Season the lamb rack with 1 teaspoon salt and 1 teaspoon pepper and set aside.

In a small bowl, mix together the bread crumbs, 1 teaspoon olive oil, ½ teaspoon salt, and ½ teaspoon pepper; set aside.

In a large nonstick ovenproof skillet, heat 1 tablespoon olive oil over high heat. Once the oil is hot, add the lamb, meat side down, and sear for 2 minutes, or until golden brown and crispy. Turn the lamb over and spread 2 teaspoons mustard over the meat. Sprinkle with bread crumbs. Roast the lamb until an instant-read thermometer inserted in the middle registers 140° F for medium rare, 160° F for medium, or 170° F for well done. Transfer to a plate, tent with foil, and let stand for 10 minutes.

While the meat is cooking, heat the remaining 1 tablespoon olive oil in a large nonstick sauté pan set over medium-high heat. Add the shallots and cook, stirring constantly, for 2 minutes, or until softened and lightly browned. Add the remaining 1 teaspoon mustard, cooked lentils, apple, carrot, spinach, cranberries, thyme, remaining salt and pepper, and apple brandy, if using. Cook, until the spinach is wilted and the liquid has slightly reduced, about 4 minutes.

Cut the lamb into chops and serve over the lentil-apple mixture.

Index

Desserts

Salt-Topped Cardamom Apple Oatmeal Cookies, 208

Sesame Apple Cookie, 310

Snack-Time Apple Cake, 245

Spicy-Sweet Baked Apples with Sharp Cheddar, 228

Stewed Dried Apples, 70

Upside-Down Apple Cake, 109

Main Courses

Alpermagronen, 22

Apple and Maple Syrup Turkey Burgers, 144

Applesauce Meatballs, 300

Apple-Spice Crusted Seared Tuna with Avocado, 234

Black Trumpet Mushroom Pudding with Roasted Apple Puree and Cured Venison, 76-77

Braised Chicken and Apples, 250

Brisket with Apples, 111

Chicken Scallopine with Apples, 262

Cider-Brined Duck Legs with Cherry and Apple Slaw, 284

Crisp Veal Sweetbreads with Apple Onion Marmalade and Apple Bourbon Gastrique, 260-261

Fennel, Apple, and Pancetta Pizza, 142

Fish Roasted in Parchment with Apples, 193

Grilled Kielbasa with Apple Sauerkraut, 135

Herbed Crab Cakes with Apple Horseradish Sauce, 152

Lamb Tagine with Apples, Prunes, and Apricots, 272

Liver with Apples and Onions, 122

Penne with Shrimp, Spinach, and Apple-Brandy Cream Sauce, 35

Pork and Apple Meatballs with Balsamic Glaze, 160

Pork Chops Smothered with Mushrooms and Apples, 166

Roasted Chicken with Apple Cider Sauce, 363

Roasted Chicken with Apples and Plums, 256

Roasted Duck Breast with Sweet Potato-Apple Puree, 377

Roasted Pork Loin with Apple Cider-Mustard Sauce, 368-369

Roasted Rack of Lamb with Apples and French Lentils, 378

Salmon with Sauce Beurre Pommes, 28

Sausage and Rice-Stuffed Baked Apples, 270

Sauteed Chicken with Savory Cider Gravy, 74

Soft Tacos with Chicken and Apples, 178

Thai-Style Chicken Curry with Apples, 56

Turkey Breast Roulade with Apple-Walnut Stuffing, 328

Turkey Burgers with Apple 156

Turkey Enchiladas with Apples, 116

White Pizza with Apple Slices, 183

Salads

Apple Ambrosia, 89

Apple-Beet Salad, 172

Apple-Celery Root Slaw with Horseradish Dressing, 302

Apple, Fig, and Feta Salad, 169

Apple and Kale Salad, 222

Apple and Mango Fruit Salad, 165

Arugula with Apples and Parmesan, 10

Baby Spinach Salad with Strawberries, Green Apples, and Pecans, 150

Cherry and Apple Slaw, 285

Chèvre en Croute with Mixed Green and Apple Salad, 295

Chicken Salad with Apples and Pomegranate, 368

Chickpea and Apple Salad, 96

Corn and Apple Salad, 179

Crispy Pork Belly Salad with Apple and Thai Herbs, 18-19

Curried Chicken Salad with Apples and Dried Fruit, 105

Curried Chicken Salad with Apples, Grapes, and Almonds, 55

Endive, Apple, and Walnut Salad, 90

Escarole, Apple, and Walnut Salad with Ricotta Salata, 231

Fall Apple Salad of "Raked Leaves", 286-287

Fennel, Apple, and Carrot Slaw, 133

Fresh Fruit Salad with Walnuts, Pecans, and Coconut, 192

Fruit Salad with Basil-Lime Syrup, 244

Green Papaya and Apple Salad, 57

Grilled Apple Salad with Herb Vinaigrette, 235

Grilled Salmon, Apple, and Spinach Salad, 185

Grilled Steak Salad with Apples, Blue Cheese, and Pecans, 196

Lentil, Feta, and Apple Salad, 199

Moroccan Carrot and Apple Salad, 367

Pan-Seared Shrimp with Apple-Fennel Slaw, 219

Pinova Apple and Mixed Baby Green Salad with Queso Fresco Cheese, 211

Raw Kale, Apple, Cranberry, and Feta Salad with Apple Cider Vinaigrette, 86

Red Cabbage and Apple Slaw with Ginger Dressing, 38

Roasted Beet, Apple, and Fennel Salad, 182

Roasted Beet and Apple Salad, 339

Smoked Trout and Apple Salad, 207

Spicy Apple Cabbage Slaw, 186

Spinach, Apple, and Blue Cheese Salad with Honey-Glazed Pecans, 104

Stacked Heart Fruit Salad, 50

Turkey-Apple Salad, 333

Waldorf Salad, 113

Warm Red Potato, Apple, and Corn Salad with Bacon, 96

Wild Rice, Apple, and Pecan Salad, 242

Wilted Greens Salad with Apple Dressing, 314

About the Authors

Melissa Petitto is a registered dietician and personal chef with an A-list clientele that includes Lucy Liu, Gwyneth Paltrow, and Christy Turlington. After studying at Johnson & Wales University—where she received the top honor of Apprentice Cuisinier—Petitto worked in the test kitchen at *Cooking Light* magazine. This is her first book.

Karen Berman is a writer and editor who specializes in food and lifestyle topics. She is the author of *Friday Night Bites, Easy-Peasy Recipes: Snacks and Treats to Make and Eat*, and several other books. She has contributed to the *New York Times* and writes for a variety of online and print publications.

Photo Credits

Thinkstock: endpapers, back cover, front cover, 1, 7, 9, 10, 11, 13, 14, 16, 17, 21, 23, 24, 25, 27, 28, 29, 30, 31, 33, 34, 35, 36, 38, 40, 41, 44, 46, 48, 50, 51, 54, 55, 57, 59, 60, 66, 68, 69, 70, 72, 73, 74, 75, 78, 79, 80, 84, 85, 88, 91, 94, 97, 98, 100, 101, 103, 106-107, 108, 110, 112, 118, 120, 122, 123, 124, 125, 126, 127, 129, 130, 133, 134, 135, 137, 138, 139, 140, 141, 143, 148, 149, 151, 152, 153, 156, 158, 159, 161, 165, 171, 172, 173, 174, 178, 179, 182, 183, 184, 189, 191, 192, 194, 196, 200, 201, 204, 205, 210, 212, 214, 217, 218, 220, 221, 224, 225, 226, 234, 236, 238, 239, 240, 241, 242, 244, 245, 246, 247, 249, 250, 253, 254, 255, 256, 257, 258, 262, 263, 264, 266, 269, 271, 272, 276, 278, 283, 284-285, 290, 294, 296, 298, 304, 305, 308, 310, 311, 312, 315, 317, 318, 320, 321, 322-323, 326, 327, 334-335, 338, 341, 342, 343, 348, 353, 354, 357, 361, 364, 372, 376

Kirsten Hall: 3, 20, 86, 92, 95, 132, 154, 176, 180, 197, 199, 209, 243, 259, 275, 299, 301, 375

Aaron Wright: 43

Tim Palin: 52

Brooke Newsome: 53, 270

Nicola O'Byrne: 71, 306-307

Erin Gleeson: 77

Melissa Petitto: 82, 119, 231, 261, 273, 281, 289, 330-331, 332-333, 336-337, 344-345, 346, 355, 356, 359, 365, 366, 367, 369, 370-371, 378

Jose Garcia: 115

Julia Hanan: 117

Monica Romero: 147

Jonathan Gordon: 163

Sarah Christensen Fu: 168

Ana Davila: 203

Paul Gelsobello: 223

Jennifer Olsen: 261

Peter Giles: 287

Michael Soekawa 291

Megan Herak: 292

Anne Sheldon-Duplaix: 302

Sarah Fabiny 313

Michael Pissari: 325

Michelle Demuth-Bibb: 351

Nicolas Maitret: 362